Give me, Heaven's Mate

BY JOANNE WILLIAMS

Tate Publishing. LLC

"Give Me Heaven's Mate" by Joanne Williams

Copyright © 2005 by Joanne Williams. All rights reserved.
Published in the United States of America
by Tate Publishing, LLC
127 East Trade Center Terrace
Mustang, OK 73064
(888) 361–9473

Book design copyright © 2005 by Tate Publishing, LLC. All rights reserved.

No part of this publication may be reproduced, stored in a retrieval system or transmitted in any way by any means, electronic, mechanical, photocopy, recording or otherwise without the prior permission of the author except as provided by USA copyright law. Scripture quotations marked "NKJV" are taken from *The New King James Version* / Thomas Nelson Publishers, Nashville: Thomas Nelson Publishers. Copyright © 1982. Used by permission. All rights reserved.

Scripture quotations marked "KJV" are taken from the *Holy Bible, King James Version,* Cambridge, 1769.

Scripture quotations marked "NIV" are taken from the *Holy Bible, New International Version ®*, Copyright © 1973, 1978, 1984 by International Bible Society. Used by permission of Zondervan Publishing House. All rights reserved.

Scripture quotations marked "TAB" are taken from *The Amplified Bible, Old Testament,* Copyright © 1965, 1987 by the Zondervan Corporation and *The Amplified New Testament,* Copyright © 1958, 1987 by The Lockman Foundation. Used by permission. All rights reserved.

ISBN: **1-5988603-9-9**

Marriage Is A Covenant Commitment

Marriage is a covenant commitment–a vow made to God and the partner not only to love, but also to be faithful and to endure in this lifelong exclusive relationship. God never intended for man to be alone. The very bone from which woman was created came from man. Woman was taken out of man, and then presented to man in order to complete him.

"Now the Lord God said, It's not good (sufficient, satisfactory) for the Man to be alone, I'll make him a helper, a companion (suitable, adapted, complementary) (Gen. 2:18 Message)

The Holy Spirit has been an awesome teacher, guide and helper in instructing me on God's plan for marriage, revealing that His perfect will for joining (KJV" cleave") each person to one another is to make one unit (Gen.2:24 KJV). The scriptural principles for joining refers to a strong, enduring bond, making one unit, bound together by unconditional commitment, love and acceptance-resulting in a combined unit much stronger than either individual had separately (Eccl.4: 9–12 KJV).

This publication is designed to provide accurate and authoritative information in regard to the subject matter covered. It is sold with the understanding that the publisher is not engaged in rendering marriage counseling, consultation or other professional services. If you require legal advice or other expert assistance, you should see the services of a competent professional.

Contents

PREFACE 11

ACKNOWLEDGEMENTS
    ROXIE WILLIAMS 14
    GLORIA HALL 15
    JUNE THORNTON 16
    JOE JACKSON 16
    CLYDE JENKINS 17
    KIM AND KIMBERELY CALLAWAY 17

FOREWORDS
    BISHOP FRANK J. WILLIAMS 19
    WIFE 21
    HUSBAND 23
    BELIEVERS TESTIMONIAL 25

HEAVEN'S MATE ENTRANCE 31

INTRODUCTION 39

MARRIAGE STILL TAKES THREE 43

MARRIAGE COVENANT 45

PART ONE:
PERSONAL ENCOUNTER: SALVATION 47

PART TWO:
LOVE IS A DECISION 51

PART THREE:
CHOICES IN CHRISTIAN LIFESTYLES: 61

PART FOUR:
SINGLE AND ENJOYING IT 71

PART FIVE:
HAPPINESS IS A CHOICE 82

PART SIX:
SINGLES BELIEVING GOD FOR THEIR MATE 92

PART SEVEN:
SINGLES PREVAILING IN PRAYER 95

PART EIGHT:
SPIRITUAL INCOMPATIBILITY 103

PART NINE:
MARRIAGE DELAYS/LATENESS/HINDRANCES 111

PART TEN:
GOD'S PLAN FOR MARRIAGE 114

PART ELEVEN:
MARRIAGE: GOD'S DESIGN FOR THE FAMILY 148

PART TWELVE:
MARRIAGE RELATIONSHIPS 152

PART THIRTEEN:
MARRIAGE TO AN UNBELIEVER 156

PART FOURTEEN:
HEAVEN'S MATE 163

PART FIFTEEN:
HEAVEN'S LOVE MATCHES 200

PART SIXTEEN:
SATANIC/DEMONICALLY INFLUENCED MATCHES 230

PART SEVENTEEN:
SATANIC/DEMONICALLY INFLUENCED HINDRANCES 252

PART EIGHTEEN:
WAITING FOR HEAVEN'S MATE 263

PART NINETEEN:
FINANCE AND MARRIAGE 276

PART TWENTY:
DESTROYING CYCLES OF DEFEAT 279

PART TWENTY-ONE:
BELIEVING AND RECEIVING YOUR MATE 289

PART TWENTY-TWO:
PRAYER AND SUPPLICATION 297

PART TWENTY-THREE:
ROMANCE/ INTIMATE RELATIONSHIP 319

PART TWENTY-FOUR:
INTERCESSORY PRAYER FOR MARRIAGE AND THE FAMILY 331

Part Twenty-five:
Marriage And Romance 341

Part Twenty-six:
Spiritual Compatibility 345

Part Twenty-seven:
Christ Centered Families 354

Part Twenty-eight:
Marriage Relationship And Finance 363

Part Twenty-nine:
Receiving God's Best 372

Part Thirty:
Heaven's Mate Exit 380

Singles Believeing God For A Mate

Selecting Your Mate

Seek ye out of the book of the Lord,
and read: no one of these shall fail,
none shall want her mate: for my
mouth it hath commanded and his
Spirit hath it gathered them
(Isaiah 34:16).

Mate Selection Process

God Knows

Who your mate is?
Where your mate is?
When you will meet your mate?
What time you will meet your mate?
When you will marry?
His purpose for uniting you both together
(Gen. 24:15–16; Esther 2:7–16; Ruth 4:9–13; Matt 1:20)

Waiting On Your God's Chosen Mate

Spiritual Qualities To Look For

Man or Woman in whom the spirit of God dwells

Salvation experience with Jesus

Personal walk with God

Striving to walk in guidelines with God's word

Member of a Bible/Word Teaching Church

Committed to following the principle and guidelines of God's word

(Col. 3:12–17; 1 Cor. 13:4, 7; 2 Cor. 1:3; Ps. 51)

Preface

Twenty one years ago, I waited for *God's best . . . His choice, selection, and Heaven's Mate* for my life. I allowed Him to do my matchmaking as I waited for His perfect timing to bring us together. We met, saw each other three times, wrote letters and talked telephonically for six months before his proposal and marriage.

Our marriage is the epitome of *"a marriage made in heaven"* because it was completely *"Heaven's Love Match."* Ministerial leaders, believers, mothers, relatives and friends each made known their choices and selections, but God's perfect will was, has and is being fulfilled through our lives. Absolute amazement, astonishment, and apprehension gripped the hearts and minds of both families, friends, and associates. The manifestation of His Word to fellow believers in the body of Christ confirmed the awesome wonder of God at work in the lives of His elect, proving twenty one years later that *"He never makes a mistake."* Heaven's mates are called, ordained, and sealed in the will and purpose of God before they were conceived in their mother's womb. From the beginning of our lives together, Frank and I committed ourselves to do God's will, and to fulfill His will in our lives at all cost. In our marriage and ministry, there have been many challenges, struggles, great tests and trials: but *"our love for God and each other"* has been one of the most powerful forces in the world. I thank God for the ordained paths that drew us together, because He is wise; His goodness that sustained our marriage, proves He never makes a mistake; and most importantly, He is sovereign.

Heaven's mates, who know and appreciate "Heaven's love matches," have learned that there is no wisdom on earth that exceeds the matchless wisdom of God. Heavenly blissfulness and showers of blessings await those who make the decision to seek, wait, follow, and obey God's choices for their lives. Looking back over our lives, we can say *"Heaven's Love Match"* and choice of mate was perfect. It is glorious and beautiful for the Lord to shine His countenance upon you, to experience the results and manifestation of the *"Word of God at work in your life,"* and to walk with Him, declaring "I am my beloved's and my beloved is mine."

Acknowledgements

Legacies are left and made everyday. As the ninety-six years old mother of fourteen, seven living, fifty-four grandchildren, sixty great-grandchildren and forty great-great grandchildren,- "My God has not only given me good health and strength, a good mind and memory, but He has given me joy, and shined His face with great blessings and honor upon me and the Williams family."

The "meeting of you and my son"- seeing each other three times, and married within six months was a shocker, surprise, and a spiritual wonder unto me, having lived, seen, and heard so much during my lifetime.

It was such a wonder, that after five months of you both writing and sometimes talking to each other on the telephone, "I had to meet this woman who had 'won' the heart of my son." Honoring my request, my son invited you down to meet me. In our first meeting, with all my mother's instinct and faith, I prayed unto God to "help my son make the right choice." Unknownly to you, during your visit, "the great set up" was in place. Pastors had their choices, sisters had their choices, nieces had their choices, nephews had their choices, and even I had my choice- but God! But God had His choice, and whom God bless no man curse. The purpose and will of the Lord came to pass, revealing that you were blessed among women and highly favored of God. This was proven the same day, - surprisingly to the family, with my son proposing, asking you "to marry him."

The wonder and astonishment on "how you both met" caused great skepticism in the entire family, causing you to experience great rejections, suspicions, and misconceptions. Your life has proven that you not only love, are committed, and dedicated unto God, but you are virtuous, prayerful, God fearing, and a woman who have learned the "power of prayer- praying through unto the breakthrough" and how to go through the hard places in the good and the bad times. For that, I thank God for your life and testimony. My son needed a woman with the sticking power God has taught, trained, and given unto you."

In hearing about the book, "Give Me Heaven's Mate," my first question was "Why write a book like that"- enjoy your husband, your lives together, ministry and each other. Now, I know that my Father gave "You both a story" that had to be told, to "help and encourage someone else. "Last summer, after twenty years of marriage and living with you both for over thirty days, your life showed me something in the fifty years my husband Henry and I were married, we never did. "You fasted, prayed together, studied, and supported each other daily." We did not learn to do that, yet God blessed, was gracious, and gave us over fifty years of togetherness in our marriage. Every married couple should establish an altar of prayer in their home. There is power in prayer. Prayer is the key to keep all that God has given, empowering us to go through the good and hard places together.

As your mother-in-law, after twenty-one years of watching, observing, listening and spending precious times with you Joanne, my daughter-in law, and the special care and love God has used you to share and give unto me, and especially unto my last son, Frank, the spiritual leader, and overseer of the Williams family; - Son- "you got the right wife"- Heaven's Mate.

Twenty-one years of trials, tests, persecutions, sufferings, determination to follow and obey God, to love each other, be, and especially do what God has called you to do; "enjoy your marriage, enjoy each other, the ministry and the special long awaited blessing my Father will release unto you in time to come."

God has blessed our family with a legacy of long and blessed marriages- some fifty, forty- and thirty and twenty-five years. He taught me to teach, train, and live a godly life before my children, providing the example for many virgins, virtuous women, and sons who love and are committed unto their wives. Son, as spiritual leader and overseer of the Williams family and the church branches over which you are the bishop and overseer, God led you and your wife to write the book "Give Me Heaven's Mate" to be a living testimony. It is an example of what the power and glory of God can do in the lives of those who trust him. Reflecting, that as He led "Isaac and Rebekah over two thousands years ago, that in meeting," Rebekah lifted up her eyes, and when she saw Isaac, she lighted off the camel." Rebekah knew at that time, she had the right mate, she knew God had given her "Heaven's Mate." "Son- you got the right mate"- Heaven's Mate.

Roxie Williams
Mother-In-Law
Williams Family

True Friends are for a "life time", a precious gift from God; as the scripture teaches, "a friend loveth at all time." You and I were God's gifts to each other at a much needed time in both our lives. Your inheritance of a family of six sisters and two brothers at a young age, and the sacrifice you made to assume the leadership of your siblings was a wonder and awe unto me. To see and hear you have committed your life to fulfill God's purpose in your life, and work with your husband Frank in the ministry was my confirmation that God had a purpose for entrusting you with such an awesome responsibility at an early age. Your years of testing, trials and experiences equipped you to share your life's experience and the power of God's leading in your life, in the Body Of Christ. "Give Me Heaven's Mate" for you is an absolute; for your commitment to love – as you have shown for God, your husband, family and to me is evidence of the love of a friend who loves forever. Again, your life is an awesome testimony of the love of God, manifesting that "you and Frank were meant to be together – "Heavens Mate".

Gloria Hall
Special Friend/ Confidant
Houston, Texas

"Give Me Heaven's Mate.... is not only for singles, married couples, and families, but, "The divine clinch needed to unveil God's rainbow of hope, faith, purpose, destiny, and focus, speaking not only unto singles, but unto "all who are believing him for a mate". He is still saying return unto me, "get a grip" on your life, values, focus on what you are doing, "stop the comprise", stop casting your pearls among swine. "I am here to lead you and to fulfill my divine destiny for your mate". Wait! Wait On Me! I will release your Heaven's Mate as you commit yourself unto prayer and waiting on me. This book is a faith lift and next level victorious living for singles, married couples, teens and families. It will provide direction, purpose, destiny and a firm grip on the need for character and integrity for all who are waiting on the mate God has chosen. It is a spiritual oasis for singles, married couples, teens and families in the twenty first century who are seeking, looking and waiting for their mate. I am looking forward to infiltrating and overflowing the airways with such "an oasis of hope" for many who are waiting, hoping and has their fleece saturated with prayers, fasting and supplications for their mate.

June Thornton
Publicist- Marketing Manager Specialist
North American Network
Bethesda, MD

The church altars, intercessory prayer groups, counselors, mentors and prayer requests are over-flowing with much prayers and supplication for this "Give Me Heaven's Mate" book. Many singles have made their selection, their choice, their decision on who they want to marry and then asks- Lord Bless! Prosper! Put your blessings upon our marriage- The error in their choice is, they forgot they never asked His purpose and will for the mate He had chosen or given them. This book is a necessity in the Body of Christ for many who are tilting to fantasies and cyber searches in selecting their mate. "Twenty-first century singles and married couples must know that marriage still takes three".

Elder Joe Jackson
Pastor, Bible Way Church
Gospel Artist- "Live In Praise"
Washington, D.C.

"Give Me Heaven's Mate"..... They said it couldn't be true; but I know and have seen the evidence that "my Father's work is real." Working with you and your husband for over fifteen years, and visiting your home and church has validated the evidence that God has enabled my eyes to behold. In visiting your home, the presence of the Lord greeted me; I felt and enjoyed the sweet spirit of the love Of God, your love for each other, and the peace, and joy of the Lord. Not Knowing at the time about the forth coming book, "Give Me Heaven's Mate", I spoke through a word of knowledge that you both would be used by the Lord to minister to singles, married couples and families locally and internationally. Your life and ministry has impacted the Body of Christ, ministering the Word of God through teaching, preaching, counseling, literature, impartation and the Word of God. Singles, married couples, teens and families are waiting for release of the revelations of the Word God has deposited within you to help position them to fulfill their destiny in the twenty first century. This word will be released through the both of you to minister to the Body of Christ, bringing great healing to many, both locally and globally, with great deliverance, and spiritual growth in their marriages, relationships, families and lives.

Pastor Clyde Jenkins
Pastor, Mt. Moriah Christian Center
Clinton, MD

Often times we grab a book because of its title, not really knowing its substance. As I began to read this book, it stirred the very core of my being with many of its unfailing truths. It's my belief that a book of such magnitude should be in the hands of men and women everywhere. Marriage is a gift from God that without the proper guidance of the Word of God, prayer, and determination to follow and obey His principles- failure is destined. "Give Me Heaven's Mate" book is the twenty first century version of "hitting the nail on the head," with compelling truths and revelations for todays generation. As an Author and Publisher, I am aware of the prayers, knowledge of God's Word, experience and spiritual revelations it took to complete such a divinely assigned awesome task. My wife Kimberly and I take great pleasure in acknowledging the impact reading this book and it's contents has had upon us, and believe the lives of singles, marriages, teens and families will be greatly enriched and enhanced upon reading this book. May this book richly bless the partakers of its fulfilling substance, believing that knowledge is power, and that the spirit of wisdom and revelation knowledge is imparted to all those who are open and receptive to its contents.

Kim & Kimberley Calloway
CEO'S
Poets/ Publishers
Kim's Originals
Temple Hills, MD

Foreword

By Bishop Frank J. Williams

Give Me Heaven's Mate is the twenty first century's "faith in God's word", take it to the next level; extreme spiritual makeover for singles believing God for their mate, relationships, marriages, and families believing God for healthy and happy marriages. Singles desiring a Christ centered, balanced, healthy, and happy marriage in the twenty first century must acknowledge, walk in the wisdom, knowledge and revelation of God's Word believing that "Marriage Still Takes Three."

Give Me Heaven's Mate is the "extreme spiritual makeover" for singles desiring to move from the status of singleness to married, vision to reality, destiny to purpose, defeat to victory, and failure to success in believing God for their mate.

The temptations of single life, the world's statistics, fear, doubt and unbelief have devastated many singles today. Making the transition in lifestyle from single to married should be ordained by the Lord, allowing Him to lead you from destiny to purpose. Extreme spiritual makeover is the divine process of surrendering and allowing Him to make many spiritual tilts, shifts, changes, adjustments, and realignments in your walk with Him, empowering you to fulfill His destiny in your life. His spiritual extreme makeover can be defined as a spiritual transformation through the renewing of your mind and growing up into the fullness of Him in all things. It means submission unto Him, to the extent of; what I think, what I feel, and what I desire, to obey His word, walking in His will, and fulfilling His destiny and purpose in my life, to include marriage. The word for "transformed" here is the Greek word "metamorphoo," which simply means, "to change into another form. Surrendering and welcoming change is preparation to the pathway for receiving the God- kind of mate.

In this book, singles, divorcees and everyone "believing God for a mate" must come to the "Reality"- Lord, what I am doing is not working; Lord, make me over, make me over again. I submit unto your extreme spiritual makeover. I am ready to receive and walk in your destiny and purpose for my life. In this Give Me Heaven's Mate book for singles and everyone believing God for their mate- Joanne Williams, provides scriptural and personal illustrations with examples that walks singles through the process of divine journey from singleness to marriage. Examples are given of Heaven's mates, satanically assigned mates, presumptuous faith mates, and singles desperate for a mate, through wisdom, knowledge and revelation of God's Word. Singles are walked through the journey of re-examining their walk with God, christian values, submission unto His will, spiritual priorities and the desire to sincerely fulfill their divine destiny on earth.

The devastation and impact of singles making wrong choices, wrong decisions and the effects of satan's counterfeits upon the lives of their partners, children, family and in the church have caused many to miss God's perfect will and purpose for their lives. The impact and effect of marriages resulting from spiritually incompatibility have increased the Christian divorce rates, available singles, and teen pregnancies in our families and world today. Give Me Heaven's Mate is a singles, married couples, christian family reading and marriage guideline that will not only impact, but bring clarity, direction and purpose with considerable meaning, joy and happiness in the lives of all who will adhere to the principles and guidelines written in this book.

Bishop Frank J. Williams
Jubilee Christian Center

Foreword

HEAVEN'S LOVE MATCH
(WIFE)

To My Beloved Wife Joanne,

Joanne, my alabaster flask of precious oil flows in our relationship daily. You are like the woman spoken of in Matthews 26:6–7, who had an alabaster flask of very costly fragrant oil and poured it on the head of Jesus. You have been used by God to break your alabaster box on me, and the body of Christ. Your oil flows like the waters of Niagara Falls that never stop flowing.

Joanne, you are the example of the Proverbs 18:22 wife, which says "He who finds a wife, finds a good thing, and obtaineth favor of the Lord." I have found a good wife, because I was led by and trusted in *"Heaven's Love Match,"* the match of our Heavenly Father. He matched us together by love and faith through His Word, and sealed us by His Holy Spirit. A good wife is understood to be one pleasing unto God, thus helpful to her husband, and a joy to all. Joanne, you are all of these and much more. You are a virtuous wife and your worth is far above rubies and priceless. My heart safely trusts in you.

Joanne, your name means "Yahweh's Gift," and a precious gift you have been unto me, your family and the body of Christ. You have made a self-sacrificing decision to follow Jesus Christ, unselfishly giving of your love, time, and energies. You have surrendered your destiny entrusted gifts, talents, and substance for the furtherance of the gospel and His called and chosen in the ministry.

In the scriptures, Joanna was described as wealthy, but humble. Heaven's riches, your passion for the Heavenly Mansion, would be yours as you have committed yourself unto Him. It has been a joy to behold and a marvel to experience daily as we continue following and obeying Him. It has been a joyous challenge to fulfill with you as a help mate. During our marriage, our love and devotion to God and each other has proven our Heavenly Father has given us His unsearchable riches and joy. As your husband, you have exemplified a woman in whom

God and I can trust, and the manifestation that He has indeed given me, "Heaven's Mate."

The blessings of God rest upon you as you continue to pray and fulfill His destiny for your life. Continue to seek His face with all wisdom, knowledge and revelation of His will for your life. My Heaven's Mate, I wish above all things that you may prosper in every way and (that your body) may keep well, even as (I know) your soul keeps well and prospers (3 John).

I thank God for my beloved "Heaven's Mate."

Husband/ Friend/ Lover,
Frank Joseph Williams

Foreword

HEAVEN'S LOVE MATCH
(HUSBAND)

To My Beloved Husband Frank,

My Heavenly Father has proven, as He spoke unto me twenty one years ago, "Blesseth are thou among women, for He has chosen and made our marriage as one *"Made in Heaven."* His divine call, will, and purpose in our lives is unveiling purpose and destiny foreordained from the foundation of the world. Your strong commitment to God, His people and me is manifested day-by-day as you strive to fulfill and complete His will in your life.

When God united us, and we said yes to our marriage, we said yes to fulfill His calling in our lives. Your consecration, devotion, and dedication to God and to me have been one of the mainstays in our marriage and ministry.

I give glory and honor unto God that He has placed us together as Partners in our marriage and ministry. He has kept us these years, enabling us to stay strong in pursuing Him and fulfilling His call upon our lives, even in hard times. Indeed, God has used your life as a testimony to bring honor and glory unto Him in our marriage, fulfilling His destiny in life, and completing your divine assignment. Our many lean years and hard times during the years proved that the price is not greater than God's grace, enabling us to remain faithful to the vision God has entrusted unto us.

Blessed and happy is the wife who recognizes her place in supporting her husband's call, and who faithfully serves God alongside her husband both in the good times and the bad.

God has led us step-by-step as we have striven to obey Him in small things and large things.

He led us to start from the "ground up," preparing us to fulfill His will on the earth, and enabling us to serve Him together in the ministry.

I enthusiastically, lovingly, and graciously give honor to whom honor is due. With love and gratitude, I honor and pay tribute to my beloved husband Frank.

Heaven's Love Match has completely been manifested in our lives. Heaven's choices, selections and love matches are awesome, wonderful, and a beautiful manifestation of the magnificent work of God. Your love, patience, understanding, and long suffering with me has paid great dividends in my life, our marriage and to the Body of Christ. I prayerfully, humbly and enthusiastically look forward to God's unveilings in our lives and ministries together in the days to come.

Wife/ Friend/ Lover,
Joanne Williams

Foreword

HEAVENLY FLOW POURED UPON US ALL
(BELIEVER'S TESTIMONIAL)

To Heaven's Mate, beloved husband and wife, I don't know where to start. There is so much that my spirit wants to say, however time won't permit. I have already informed Him if He wants me to reveal some of this now, I would be willing. He informed me "Yes," leading me to obey His will, not mine.

This week the souls of my husband and I have been blessed. Our cups have been poured into and are spilling over. Someone may ask the question "How?" I'm glad that you asked.

Our eyes were filled with tears as our hearts rejoiced in delivering this message. We couldn't wait to pour into someone else what has been poured into us.

My mouth doesn't taste the same. The vision of my spiritual eyes has been moved to the next level already. My ears have been washed again by the blood of Jesus, that I may hear His voice with confidence and assurance. Glory be to God of the highest!

My husband, friends, and I went to eat after Saturday night's service, my cup overflowing. God gave me the opportunity to witness and experience, the manifestation of His overflow. We rejoiced in the Word of God. I danced in the Holy Spirit. My husband, the eldest, and the quietest said, "We must leave." I said, *"Hold up - We were loud for satan, now it's time that we get radical for Jesus, hallelujah!"*

God allowed us to open the eyes and prick the ears of the customers that came in. They were at the right place at the right time to behold the glory of God. A friend of my husband, came in and embraced him in front of all the customers; blacks, Europeans and Hispanics. Fire it up, Holy Ghost! The heavenly flow was pouring.

My husband and I have met you on a few occasions, and enjoyed the ministry of the Word, but we experienced the Ministry of God's Word under an open Heaven in demonstration of His spirit and power.

Oh! My God! But this time! I have gotten the opportunity to really meet a "Proverb 31 Woman:"

A woman of obedience, quality, and of virtue who won't stand for anything and everything. She stands for truth and wants God's best for her life

- A woman of excellence
- A woman that the "Jesus" in me loves the "Jesus" in her
- The power of a praying woman
- A woman who knows her ministry in herself and her husband
- A woman who gives herself over to Jesus and to her husband, to her minister
- A woman of agape love
- A woman of God and most of all character

I have never met many of God's leading ladies, or First Ladies of today. Oh, but my soul rejoices when I think about communing and fellowshipping with the one and the only First Lady Pastor Joanne Williams. She is a mighty woman of God and a soul winner for Jesus. I love you with the love of Christ, our Heavenly Father.

In my witness in the restaurant, I informed my family that I would ask Bishop and his First Lady to take charge of being my husband's and my spiritual father and mother in the body of Christ. My husband said, "OK, that's good news, if your answer is yes."

In the name of Jesus,
We vow that we will ask each of you to mentor us in the gospel

- We promise we won't stand for anything, and accept everything
- We will build on our marriage so it will be a solid foundation, like yours, in Christ Jesus
- We will pray specifically for each of you daily
- I will continue to be a woman of excellence and Christ-like; My husband, a man after God's own heart
- We ask that you both would pray daily that we would be just as rich as you both are in the Word of God.

Glory be to God for your mission. It has been well with our souls. God will reward you continuously. Truly, Bishop and Pastor Joanne, God has allowed you both to leave a legacy in the state of Louisiana.

Tanya M. Johnson-Minister
Baton Rouge, Louisiana

About Heaven's Mate Marriage
JOANNE & FRANK WILLIAMS

Frank and Joanne Williams have been married over twenty-one years. Frank is currently Bishop of Jubilee Christian Center, fulfilling divine destiny in multiple locations with church branches in Houston, Texas and Petersfeild, South Carolina. The Book "Give Me Heaven's Mate" and companions will be used by churches, ministries, Christian schools, corporate offices, universities, singles, married couples, teens and families in the United States and internationally. It will provide divine principles, instructions, teachings, counseling, insights, and revelations to restore and strengthen the Body of Christ to return and follow God's original plan for marriage and the family. The plan remains the same- "marriage still takes three." This book will enlighten and encourage singles believing God for their mate to follow God's design and plan for seeking, waiting, revealing, meeting, and receiving the mate He has chosen. "Marriage still takes three." He is the missing person; presence, and covering in many marriages today. His covering and presence *is not only absent but unsolicited.* We cannot expect the blessings of God upon our marriage when we do not seek, ask, or consult Him- leaving Him out of His plan and purpose, the creator of all things- the essential presence for the union of marriage.

Heaven Mate's Entrance

SINGLES BELIEVING GOD FOR THEIR MATE

PREPARATION TO RECEIVE HEAVEN'S MATE

ARE YOU READY TO RECEIVE AND BE BLESSED WITH HEAVEN'S MATE?

Self Reflections

- Do you Desire Heaven's Mate?
- Are you ready for Heaven's Mate?
- Do you believe God Knows what is best for you?
- Do you believe God's destiny/ purpose is best for you?
- Are you willing to wait upon God's best for you?
- Does God want the very best for you?
- Are you willing to trust God with your destiny?
- Can you trust the knowledge and wisdom of God to lead you into your destiny?
- Do you agree God's timing is best?
- Are you tired of living a compromising life?
- Have you completed your Divine Preparation to receive Heaven's Mate?
- Are you willing to submit to God's Preparation for Heaven's Mate?
- Can you be trusted with Heaven's mate?
- Do you believe God's Matches Are Matchless!
- Do you believe in God?
- Do you believe the Word Of God?

Singles Believing God For A Mate
Selecting Your Mate

> Seek ye out of the book of the Lord,
> and read: no one of these shall fail,
> none shall want her mate: for my
> mouth it hath commanded and his
> Spirit hath it gathered them
> (Isaiah 34:16).

Mate Selection Process
God Knows

- Who your mate is?
- Where your mate is?
- When you will meet your mate?
- What time you will meet your mate?
- When you will marry?
- His purpose for uniting you both together
  (Gen. 24:15–16; Esther 2:7–16; Ruth 4:9–13; Matt 1:20)

Spiritual Qualities To Observe

- Man or Woman in whom the spirit of God dwells
- Salvation experience with Jesus
- Personal walk with God
- Striving to walk in guidelines with God's word
- Member of a Bible/Word Teaching Church
- Committed to following the principle and guidelines of God's word
  (Col. 3:12–17; 1 Cor. 13:4, 7; 2 Cor. 1:3; Ps. 51)

Fulfilling Divine Destiny And Purpose During The Mate Selection Process

In Him we also were made [God's]heritage (portion) and we obtained an inheritance; for we had been foreordained (chosen and appointed beforehand) in accordance with His purpose, Who works out everything in agreement with the counsel and design of His [own] will (Eph. 1:11).

Divine Purpose In Manifestation

Discernment In Manifestation

Divine Choices
Divine Selections
Divine Confessions
Divine Motions
Divine Priorities
Divine Attitudes

Marriage To Heaven's Mate

Divinely Destined Marriages
Divinely Purposed Marriages
Divinely Mandated Marriages
Divinely Predestined Marriages
Divinely Ordained Marriages
Divinely Decreed Marriages

Divinely Chosen Marriages For The Glory And Honor Of God
Confidence And Assurance In Your Divine Choices

Divine Choices

The steps of a [good] man are directed and established by the Lord when He delights in his way [and He busies Himself with his every step] (Ps. 37:23).

Trust Him With Your Destiny

Divine

Choices

Are

Always

The

Best

❧

Heaven's Mate Are Matchless

Heaven's Timing Is Perfect

Heaven's Ordered Steps Are With Precision

Heaven's Purpose/ Destiny Is Glorious

Heaven's Fruit Of The Spirit

Character/ Attribute Of Christ

Heaven Never Makes A Mistake

Purpose / Fulfillment
And For Their Personal Inspiration

Pastor Phil and Aunt Gladys Johnson
Married 45 years

❧

Uncle Emory and Aunt Emma Davis
Married 40 years

❧

Uncle Steve and Mary Dickerson
Married 45 years

❧

Uncle Joe and Aunt Sadie Dogan
Married 40 years

❧

Uncle Eddie and Aunt Patsy Blunt
Married 40 years

❧

Pastor Herman and Aunt Lucille Matthews
Married 40 years

❧

Pastor Jordan and Nancy Johnson
Married 50 years

❧

Rev. Thomas and Aunt Willie M. Moore
Married 35 years

❧

Dear Uncles, Aunts, and Cousins, Friends

GIVE ME HEAVEN'S MATE
By Joanne Williams

You waited for Heaven's best . . . you allowed Him to be your matchmaker as you waited for His perfect timing to bring you both to each other. Marriage is the plan of God. He never intended for man to be alone. Marriage is a covenant commitment - a vow made to God and the partner, not only to love, but also to be faithful, to become one, endure and enjoy this lifelong relationship. Man's wisdom, knowledge, and revelation concerning the holy union of marriage will never supersede the wisdom of God, who not only created the creature, but also created and ordained the institution of marriage.

This book will help you understand God's plan for marriage. Not knowing, understanding, and selecting God's divine plan for marriage have caused many to miss the enjoyment, pleasure, and fulfillment a true, loving marriage relationship is in the lives of two people who love God and each other. It will scripturally reveal examples of Heaven's selection and satanically influenced selections. The revelation itself will stir and provoke you to make a life destiny decision: *I Choose To Wait On Heaven's Mate*. Waiting on and marrying Heaven's mate is a blessing to you and your entire family. It positions you and your family to receive Heaven's blessings, releases, and divine overflows as you individually submit to His will and purpose for your lives, marriages, families, homes and ministries. *Give Me Heaven's Mate* is God's plan for marriage for Christians living in the twenty first century. It is a marriage based on God's plans and purposes, not man's traditions, cultures, or man made vows. Scripturally, it provides the wisdom, knowledge and understanding for establishing divine principles and guidelines, to establish a solid foundation for marriage, children, and the family. In following God's scriptural plan for marriage, divine principles will be outline for establishing, maintaining, enjoying your marriage, and fulfilling His purpose in your life.

This book unveils the wisdom and revelation of God's Word to assist unmarried singles, married couples, widows, widowers, divorcees, children, families, and parents for teaching and instructing their children to submit to the scriptural principles and guidelines for enjoying a healthy, loving, relationship in their marriage, family and home.

The Author is the Co-founding Pastor of Jubilee Christian Center in Clinton, Maryland, where she serves with her husband, Bishop Frank J. Williams, senior pastor. Her upcoming book, the *Power Of Endurance* will provoke many in Heaven's Mate Waiting Room to learn how to wait, the purpose of the enduring process, and divine preparation during the waiting process, and how to develop a closer, more meaningful relationship with our heavenly father during the waiting process.

Love,
Joanne Williams

Introduction

Marriage is the oldest relationship in the world, established by a sovereign creator in the Garden of Eden. In that beautiful, perfect setting, God organized the home by assigning roles and defining responsibilities to Adam and Eve. It has been defined as a divine institution designed to form a permanent union between a man and woman, that they might be helpful to one another. Moses presents it as the deepest corporeal and spiritual unity of man and woman.

In marriage, two hearts are grafted together, making them dependent on one another for life. This is depicted in John 15 with Jesus as the vine and believers as the branches. Through the baptism of the Holy Spirit and His control in the life of both partners, this picture of marriage and the parallel relationship of Christ and His bride come into focus. The Holy Spirit fills and fulfills both. God's plan for marriage is introduced in the book of Genesis, repeated in the Gospels and in the epistles. Marriage was perfect in its establishment: one man and one woman in a lifetime commitment.

God never intended man to be alone. The very bone from which woman was crafted came from man. Woman was taken out of man, and then presented to man in order to complete him. God created the man and the woman in His image with physical and emotional needs that only another human being could meet.

No parents were in Eden, but God's plan extended to the future with His formula for oneness in marriage. The partners are to leave their parents and "be joined" in order to become one. They are to be willing to lay aside all that pertains to their old loyalties, past goals and plans, lifestyles, and be joined to one another. This joining refers to a strong enduring bond made by a unit bound together by unconditional commitment, love and acceptance. It results in a combined unit that is much stronger than either individual had been separately.

Marriage is a threefold miracle. It is a biological miracle by which two people actually become one flesh; it is a social miracle through which two families are grafted together; it is a spiritual miracle in that the marriage relationship mirrors the union of Christ and His bride, the church. God clearly intended transparency and openness as part of His plan for marriage relationships–vulnerability without shame (Gen. 2:25).

Man's rejection of the Creator's plan at the time of the "fall" and the sentences passed on man and woman affected their relationships to God, nature, and each other. However, sin did not force God to cancel His plan: rather sin perverted and hindered man's response to His plan. As a result, pain has been added to childbirth, tyranny to headship, rebellion to submission, and problems to work, as well as separation to the fellowship of the marriage union.

There are consequences of sin in the male-female relationship, because both the man and woman chose to ignore God's plan and do things their own way. The complimentary roles of men and women, which had originally functioned to produce unity and harmony, would henceforth be a source of friction. The curse is not just a judgment rendered, but also is an explanation of the relationship between the man and the woman after the "fall." Alienation has come between the man and woman and between the couple and God, which ultimately means a distortion of God's plan. God has not changed or cancelled His plan. Sin perverted and hindered man's response to His plan. God does not make His plans dependent upon perfect people or the right circumstances, but destiny and purpose for His creation.

Scripture is replete with vivid examples of man's manipulation of people and situations. Manipulation is rooted in pride and selfishness, and involves viewing others as objects, not as individuals. It is an invasion of an individual's dignity because it seeks to limit freedom through control. The tools of manipulation are position, power, deception, and distortion. The results, even if perceived as successful, are always a denigration of God's best, or the manipulative individual believes that he or she knows more than God does.

Sarah manipulated her husband Abraham and her servant Hagar in order to grasp in her own time what God had promised; Rebekah manipulated her husband Isaac, as well as her son Jacob, in order to achieve her personal goal for her favorite son; David manipulated the battle to take another man's wife. In these instances and countless others, the manipulation brought more sorrow than joy.

Hence, *"Give Me Heaven's Mate"* is a "must" for every man, woman, and family. Wisdom is the principal thing. Therefore, get wisdom, and with all thy getting, get understanding. This book is a guide to your soul and a window to your heart.

Man's lifestyle, visions, missions and purposes have created great havoc and deterioration in the family, thus totally destroying the very foundation of marriage, family and home that God intended it to be. The mate selection process, along with Christian values, principles and examples intended for our use, even before the beginning of this world, have been severely misguided and misinterpreted. They can only be reconciled and restored when Christians arise, walk in line with the word, repent, pray, seek God's face and return unto the standards and principles established by God before the foundation of the world.

Believing God For Your Mate

Seek you out of the book of the Lord, and read; no one of these shall fail, NONE SHALL WANT HER MATE; for my MOUTH IT hath commanded, and His spirit it hath gathered them (Isaiah 34:16).

Marriage Still Takes Three

I once thought marriage took
Just two to make a go
But now I am convinced
It takes the Lord also.
And not one marriage fails
Where Christ is asked to enter
As lovers come together
With Jesus at the center.
But marriage seldom thrives
And homes are incomplete
Till He is welcomed there
To help avert defeat.
In homes where God is first
It is obvious to see
Those unions really work
For marriage still takes three.

Perry Tanksley

Marriage Covenant
MY COVENANT COMMITMENT

This marriage covenant is written on my heart and sealed by the Holy Spirit. I promise to love, honor, cherish in relationship, and be in all things a true and faithful partner as long as we both so live.

_____
YOUR NAME

_____
PARTNER'S NAME

_____

Therefore a man shall leave his father and his mother and shall become united and cleave to his wife, and they shall become one flesh. (Gen. 2:24 KJV).

Wherefore they are no more twain, but one flesh. What therefore God hath joined together, let not man put asunder. (Matt. 19:16 KJV).

And they twain shall be one flesh; so then they are no more twain, but one flesh. (Mark. 16:8 KJV).

Part One
PERSONAL ENCOUNTER SALVATION

Personal Response To God's Action

Confession:

And it shall be that whoever call upon the name of the Lord [invoking, adoring, and worshiping the Lord-Christ] Christ shall be saved
(ACTS 2:21 TAB).

Repentance:

And saying, the [appointed period of] time is fulfilled (completed) and the Kingdom of God is at hand; repent (have a change of mind which issues in regret for past sins and in change of conduct for the better) and believe (trust in, rely on; and adhere to) the good news (the Gospel). (Mark 1:15 TAB).

Faith:

For God so loved the world, that he gave his only begotten Son, that whosoever believeth in him should not perish, but have everlasting life.
(John 3:16 KJV).

Regeneration:

Not by works of righteousness, which we have done, but according to his mercy he saved us, by the washing of regeneration, and renewing of the Holy Spirit
(TITUS 3:5 KJV).

Holy Scripture:

And that from a child thou hast known the holy scriptures, which are able to make thee wise unto salvation through faith which is in Christ Jesus
(2 TIM. 3:15 KJV).

All scripture is given by inspiration of God, and is profitable for doctrine, for reproof, for correction, for instruction in righteousness
(2 Timothy 3:16 KJV).

You must know who Christ is, what he has done, and what he is able to do.

Developing A Relationship With Jesus
Salvation: God's Deliverance

Can two walk together, except they be agreed?
(Amos 3:3 KJV).

And what agreement hath the temple of God with idols? For ye are the temple of the living God; as God hath said, I will dwell in them, and walk in them, and I will be their God, and they shall be my people.

Wherefore come out from among them, and be ye separate, saith the Lord, and touch not the unclean thing; and I will receive you.

> And I will be a Father unto you, and ye shall be my sons
> and daughters, saith the Lord Almighty
> (II Cor. 6:16–18 KJV).

When both husband and wife have acknowledged Jesus as Saviour and Lord, the Holy Spirit lives in their hearts. As they submit to His Lordship, they are enabled to follow His directions. The husband will be empowered to love his wife as Christ loved the church (Eph. 5:25), and the wife will be inspired to submit as unto the Lord (Eph. 5:22–24). The atmosphere of the home will become one of joy (Eph. 5:19–21), as hurtful attitudes are laid aside, forgiveness and kindness become house rules, and divine principles to govern their relationship and marriage union. (Eph. 4:25–32).

Couples are enabled to overcome temptations with faithfulness to each other. When husbands and wives submit their expectations unto God and focus on the good, the spirit of peace will rule in their hearts and in their home (Phil. 4:6–8).

Salvation requires not only God's initial action, but also our response. There are basically three aspects of God's salvation or deliverance: justification, sanctification, and glorification. Justification is God's deliverance from sin and being justified freely by His grace through redemption that is in Christ Jesus (Rom. 3:24). When a person accepts Christ into his or her life, they become totally free from the penalty of sin and spiritual death (Rom. 3:23–25 KJV). The penalty for sins that have been committed in the past or sins that will be committed in the future has been paid through the death of Jesus Christ on the cross.

Sanctification is God's progressive deliverance of a believer from sin's power (Eph. 5:26; 1 Thess. 5:23 KJV). God's desire is that a believer mature and become more Christ like, and that they become free from sin's control in their life. But, if believers sin because of their fallen nature, God has made provision (1 John 1:9). God has given His Holy Spirit to aid believers in the process of sanctification.

Glorification is God's ultimate deliverance of the believer from sin's presence. Glorification will not be actualized until the Lord returns for his children (1 Cor. 15:51–57 KJV).

A couple's personal response to God's action is also of utmost importance in salvation.

> They must know who Christ is, what He has done, and what He is able to do.

They must have a conviction that his knowledge about Christ is true.

They must act upon the knowledge and conviction, trusting Christ only.

Jesus, in all His teaching, pointed to the Father's original plan for Christian marriage, in which the wife was to be an equal partner, loved, and protected (Matt. 19:4–6 KJV). Husbands and wives were given instructions on how they were to relate in the home. God never gives a command to His children unless He makes provision for them to obey. He has given the power of the Holy Spirit to help believers withstand temptation (2 Peter. 2–9 KJV) and the presence of Christ that becomes their spiritual armor in withstanding the enemy's fiery darts (Eph. 6:10–18 KJV). He also extends His presence through loving and supportive fellow believers in the church. And of course, he prepares for protection from abuse through establishing civil authorities.

Part Two
LOVE IS MORE THAN A FEELING

Love Is A Decision

Love is patient and kind.
Love is not jealous or
boastful or proud or rude.
Love does not demand its own way.
Love is not irritable, and keeps no record
of when it has been wronged.
It is never glad about injustice but rejoices
whenever the truth wins out.
Love never gives up, never loses faith,
is always hopeful, and endures
through every circumstance.
(1 Cor. 13:4–7 NLT)

LOVE IS MORE THAN A FEELING

Love Is A Decision

Though I speak with the tongues of men and of angels, and have not love, I am become as sounding brass, or a tinkling cymbal.

And though I have the gift of prophecy, and understand all mysteries, and all knowledge; and though I have all faith, so that I could remove mountains, and have not love, I am nothing.

And though I bestow all my goods to feed the poor, and though I give my body to be burned, and have not love, it profiteth me nothing.
Love suffereth long, and is kind, love envieth not, love vaunteth not itself, is not puffed up.

Doth not behave itself unseemly, seeketh not her own, is not easily provoked, thinketh no evil;

Rejoiceth not in iniquity, but rejoiceth in the truth.

Beareth all things, believeth all things, hopeth all things, endureth all things.

Love never faileth: but whether there be prophecies, they shall fail; whether there be tongues, they shall cease; whether there be knowledge, it shall vanish away.

For we know in part, and we prophesy in part.

But when that which is perfect is come, then that which is in part shall be done away.

When I was a child, I spoke as a child; I understood as a child, I thought as a child; but when I became a man, I put away childish things.

For now we see through a glass darkly; But then face to face; now I know in part; but, then shall I know, even also as I am known.

And now abideth, faith, hope, love, these three, but the greatest of these is love (1 Cor. 13: 1–13 KJV).

The scriptures declare and have assured us of God's love, reminding us that the proof of God's boundless love is that Christ died for us (Rom. 5:8; 1 John 4:9, 10 KJV). Love is not simply meant to make us feel good, but rather to motivate us to respond in ways that emulate His goodness. Love is action and sometimes demands that we act in very practical, and even uncomfortable ways.

- Love is not optional (1 John 3:11; 4:11). We are commanded to love one another.
- Love is demonstrative (1 John 3:14, 4:7, 20). Our love for God is shown to the degree we show love to others.
- Love is active, an act of the will (1 John 3:17). We are commanded to do the acts of love. If we shut our eyes to the needs of others, our love for God is called into question.
- Love is responsive (1 John 4:19). We are able to love because we have been and are loved by God. This love causes us to respond lovingly to others (1 John 4:21).

In both Hebrew (Ahab) and Greek (Agape), the word "love" is an action word, indicating conscious acts on behalf of a beloved. Essentially, scriptural love demands going beyond a particular behavior to include making a decision to love.

However, while several Greek words describe specific types of love, the Greek word agape expresses Christ like, selfless love; unselfish, loyal, benevolent concern for the well being of another; and is called by Paul the greatest gift of all (1 Cor. 13:13 KJV). Christian love is a fruit of the Holy Spirit, a virtue of godly living (Gal. 5:22 KJV).

Types of Love

Agape (GK) Indicates a choice to serve God, to love neighbors, to accept self without expecting something in return (Matt. 22:34–40).

Phileo (GK) Refers to esteem and affection reflected in the loving concern friends have for one another (John 21:15–17; Titus 2:4).

Eros (GK) Describes appetitive, self centered love, including sexual desire and physical craving.

Stergos (GK) Alludes to affection, especially among family members.

Characteristics of Love

The fruit of the spirit begins with love, and all of the other characteristics are really "An Outgrowth of Love" (Gal. 5:22 TAB).

Love (vs.1) If I (can) speak in the tongues of men and (even) of angels, but have not love (that reasoning, intentional, spiritual devotion).

Faith (vs. 2) And though I have all faith.

Joy (vs. 6) Rejoice not in iniquity, but rejoice in the truth.

Peace (vs. 4) Charity sufferereth long, and is kind; charity envieth not; charity vaunteth not itself, is not puffed up.

Longsuffering (vs. 4) Charity sufferereth long, and is kind; charity envieth not; charity vaunteth not itself, is not puffed up.

Gentleness (vs. 4) Charity is kind; charity envieth not; charity vaunteth not itself, is not puffed up

Goodness (Vs. 7) Beareth all things, believeth all things, hopeth all things, endureth all things

The attributes of love reflect both feelings and loving acts (1 Cor. 13:4–8). True love is characterized as:

- Patient And Slow To Anger
- Kind And Gentle To All
- Unselfish and Giving
- Truthful And Honest
- Hopeful And Encouraging
- Enduring And Without End

Love (vs. 7–8) -Beareth all things, believeth all things, hopeth all things, endureth all things. Charity never faileth; but whether there be prophecies, they shall fail; whether there be tongues, they shall cease; whether there be knowledge, it shall vanish away.

Faith (vs. 7–8) Beareth all things, believeth all things, hopeth all things, endureth all things. Charity never faileth; but whether there be prophecies, they shall fail; whether there be tongues, they shall cease; whether there be knowledge, it shall vanish away.

Meekness (vs. 4) Charity sufferereth long, and is kind; charity envieth not; charity vaunteth not itself, is not puffed up.

Temperance (vs. 5) -Doth not behave itself unseemly, seeketh not her own, is not easily provoked, thinketh no evil;

Characteristics Of The Unsaved Mate

- Natural/sensual/ worldly kind of love
- Unsaved (have not acknowledged Jesus as Lord and savior of their life; worldly minded; careth not for the things of God)
- Selfish/self willed (concerned about pleasing self more than God, you or family)
- Pleasure/lustful (given to fleshly gratification/satisfaction)
- Proves/walks in what is acceptable to flesh/man/world
- Misguided/confused values

Works Of The Flesh

- Now the works of the flesh are manifest, which are these, adultery, fornication, uncleanliness, and lasciviousness
- Idolatry, witchcraft, hatred, variance, emulations, wrath, strife, sedition, heresies
- Envying, murders, drunkenness, revellings, and such like; of the which I tell you before, as I have also told you in time past, that they which do such things shall not inherit the kingdom of God
- But the fruit of the spirit is love, joy, peace, long-suffering, gentleness, godliness, faith
- Meekness, temperance, against such there is no law
And they that are Christ's have crucified the flesh with the affections and lusts

- If we live in the spirit, let us also walk in the spirit
- Let us not be desirous of vain glory, provoking one another, envying one another (Gal.5: 19–21 KJV)

What Is Love?
God Is Love - An Attribute Of God

> For God so loved the world, that He gave His only begotten Son, that whosoever believeth in Him should not perish, but have everlasting life (John 3:16 KJV).

God is love - without Him, love does not exist (John 3:16; 1 John 4:8–10 KJV). Love is not the definition of God - God is infinitely more - but God is the definition of love.

Scriptural love (Gk. Agape) is active, yet selfless. Agape love is God's pattern for our love for Him (1 John 4:19 KJV) and for our love for one another (Eph. 5:25; 1 Pet 1:22 KJV). Its basis is God's deliberate, active, sacrificial giving of His Son for our redemption. To be loved by God means that He has set His sights on us, and is actively wooing us toward Himself at all times.

God's love is self-starting (1 John 4:10 KJV), indestructible (Rom. 8:38, 39 KJV), undeserved (Rom. 3:23 KJV), compassionate (Isa. 49:15 KJV), constant (Jer. 31:3 KJV), immeasurable (Eph. 3:18,19 KJV), voluntary (Rom. 5:8 KJV), and a gift (John 3:16 KJV). He did not begin loving at the cross, nor will He love us more tomorrow than He does today. There is nothing we can do, think, or say that will change His love, because there are no surprises for God–He knows us totally and loves us anyway (Ps. 139:1–5 KJV).

The goal of God's love is to have us with Him throughout eternity (1 John 4:16 KJV). He presented and made possible the accomplishment of this goal through Jesus and His sacrifice on the cross (John 1:14–18 KJV).

The Law Of Love Is Giving

God is love and God is a giver (1 John. 4:8, 16 KJV). He who does not love has not become acquainted with God (does not and never did know Him, for God is love) . . . ."God so loved the world that He gave his only begotten Son, that whosoever believeth in Him shall not perish, but have everlasting life." . . ."as my Father hath sent me, so send I you" (John 3:16; 20:21 TAB).

We can't give what we don't have. Many enter relationships full of fantasies, illusions, dreams, and delusions. Disappointments, pain, bitterness, and sorrow grip the hearts of many. True love is not based on man's fantasies; it is founded and based on Agape love, because love never fails.

We know that we cannot love as we should, or as we would like to, because it is not within our human ability to do so. In man's search for love, a lasting or eternal love is what we all are looking for. The core of our love must come from true love itself - God's Agape love. When we realize our selfishness and inability to love, we ask for God's love, to flow through us, empowering and enabling us to love those around us. Man, in his quest for true love, feels secure in believing that the love he thinks he feels is eternal. However, only God's Agape love carries with it the promise that Jesus has already fulfilled on the cross. "I love you enough that I would die for you".

Heaven's Mates need no reminders of the limitations of our human loving. Fortunately, they discovered their need for God's love and understood the difference between God's love and their own love. Therefore, man's definition and understanding of love can be divided into four categories. Herein do we define and illustrate the meaning of the stages of love for relationship clarification; for friends, lovers, children, and families.

The Stages Of Love

The following definitions of the four types of love will clarify the meaning of human ways of loving.

There are several aspects of love, and each is designed to be an integral part of a marriage relationship. There is the magnetic drawing of two people together, which is termed desire (Gen. 29:18 KJV), and should remain a very important facet of every marriage (Prov. 5:17–19 KJV). This progresses to romantic, sentimental love, which is strong, sweet, and absorbing, but cannot alone sustain the relationship (Gen. 26:8,9 KJV). The next stage is one of contentment with each other. It is a sense of assurance and belonging that enables partners to care for one another, and to give the promise of total loyalty (Ruth 3:9–11 KJV). The fourth facet of love is friendship, with an emphasis on communicating and being close, sharing thoughts and feelings, and dreaming together (Song 2:14 KJV).

These four aspects of love are held together with God's love, which is absolutely essential if the marriage is going to endure. God's love is unconditional; it is given with no thought of response. Self sacrificing love (Gk. Agape) is an act of the will and not emotions (1 Cor. 13:48 KJV). Agape, the God-kind of love is unselfish and undemanding. It realizes the value of the loved one, recognizes responsibility for the beloved, continues to grow, never fades, and is pure (1 Cor. 13:12,13 KJV).

God demands permanence in marriage (Mal. 2:16 KJV), but He intended for it to be a growing, loving relationship from beginning to end (Ecc. 9:9 KJV). This is a truth found in God's Word, and thus it is possible for Christians to accomplish it.

Permanence is assured as all five aspects of love come to find expression in a marriage. The house will be built, established, and filled with precious and pleasant riches (Prov. 14:1:24:3, 4 KJV).

Romance: The Acts Of Love

He brought me to the banqueting house, and his banner over me was love. (for love waved as a protecting and comforting banner over my head when I was near him).

Sustain me with cakes of raisins; refresh me with apples, for I am sick with love.

(He said) I charge you, O you daughters of Jerusalem, by the gazelles or by the hinds of the field (which are free to

follow their own instincts) that you not try to stir up or
awaken (my) love until it pleases
(Song of Solomon 2: 4–7 TAB).

The Shulamite bride loved and loved passionately. Every fiber of her being echoed with responsive, adoring and affection. She rejoiced in her husband's commitment to her (Song 2:4 KJV); she was enraptured by his desire for her (Song 7:10 KJV); and she was secure in her husband's pledge of enduring commitment (Song 8:6,7 KJV). The Shulamite is God's portrait of bridal bliss to be found within a permanent monogamous relationship.

The scripture approves of romance unreservedly. Marriages, even when arranged, were often recorded as love matches (Gen. 24:67 KJV), and Proverbs 30:19 speaks wonderingly of the mystery of romance. Romance provides a balanced picture of God's calling of the soul. The beloved is not forced to respond, but desires to respond willingly to the love offered.

Romance offers the lover an opportunity to focus on responsibilities rather than privileges. Rather than dwelling upon selfish needs and what others should do, the romantic lover is ever conscious of what he or she can do to show love for the other person (Matt. 16:24–26). Everyone needs the acts of love for life and growth. Romance moves beyond the needs of the lover to minister to the beloved. Love flows directly from the heart, radiating with the beautiful intensity of what fills the heart.

Love is one of the most powerful forces on earth. Proverbs 30:18–19 states: There are three things which are too wonderful for me, yes four which I do not understand:

- The way of an eagle in the air
- The way of a serpent on a rock
- The way of a ship in the midst of the sea
- And the way of a man with a virgin

The way of a man with a virgin is perhaps an overwhelming experience enrapturing his soul to the ecstasy of the pleasure of romance.

It is refreshing, beautiful and a joy to experience and see couples who keep the passion and excitement of romance alive in their marriage relationship. The love, joy and passion for each other is so powerful, it refuses to allow the trials, tests, and tribulations of life to interfere with the romantic pleasures shared between each other during the marriage. Couples must make a commitment and continue to "learn to make time for each other," enjoying the life God has given them together, and knowing that God has given us all things richly to enjoy (1 Tim. 6:17 KJV).

The quality of the celebration of sexual intimacy depends on the quality of the total marriage relationship. There can be very little fulfillment in the realm of physical intimacy if there is little closeness in the overall union. Since God designed male and female to fit together, and instilled within each a desire for the other, no problems are exclusively sexual in nature. Difficulties in physical intimacy are nearly always a symptom of problems in other areas of the relationship.

The act of marriage is the highest form of the communication of love for one another and the ultimate expression of intimacy. It provides a language that can express love without words. Indeed, there are no words to express all that is felt. Faith in God is the bond of the marriage covenant; sexual intimacy is the Holy Spirit's seal.

Part Three

CHOICES IN CHRISTIAN LIFESTYLES

And if it seems evil to you to serve the Lord, choose for yourselves this day whom you will serve, whether the gods which your fathers served on the other side of the River or the gods of the Amorites in whose land you dwell; but as for me and my house, we will serve the Lord (Joshua 24:15 TAB).

Life Lived In Relationship With God And Each Other

How shall a young man cleanse his way? By taking heed and keeping watch (on himself) according to Your Word (conforming his life to it).

With my whole heart have I sought You, inquiring for and of You and yearning for You; oh, let me not wander or step aside (either in ignorance or willfully) from Your commandments.

Your Word, have I laid up in my heart, that I might not sin against You (Ps. 119:9–11 TAB).

And if we are (His) children, then we are (His) heirs also; heirs of God and fellow heirs with Christ (sharing His inheritance with Him): only we must share His suffering if we are to share His glory (Rom. 8:17 TAB).

Priorities: Planning Your Days

> Thy word is a lamp unto my feet, and a light unto my path. Unfolding of your words gives light; it gives understanding to the simple (Ps. 119, 105, 130 NIV).

Life is full of opportunities, occasions, possibilities, challenges, and things to do. Singles can become overwhelmed with too many things to do (Luke 10:40 KJV). There are many good choices concerning how to apportion their time (Eccl. 3:1–8 KJV). To establish priorities is to determine what is important to you and how your time is to be apportioned–that is, who and what will take precedent over other parts of life.

Christian singles whose purpose and mission is to fulfill their God ordained destiny are not challenged in this area of their walk with God. They have learned the scriptural guidelines for God's divine order in maintaining a healthy relationship with Him are (Ps. 119:105,130 KJV):

- Your personal relationship to Jesus Christ. (Matt. 6:33 KJV).
- Develop and maintain a regular quiet time with our Heavenly Father (Ps. 55:17 KJV)
- Your commitment to home and family, especially spouse and children (Gen. 2:24; Ps. 127:3; Ep. 5:22, 25; 6:4; 1 Tim. 3:25; 58, 8 NIV)
- Examine your heart and your faith (1 Cor. 11:28; Psalms 26:2 NIV)
- Pray, meditate upon God's Word (Psalms 119:97 NIV)
- Maintain your spiritual fitness (Luke 9:62 NIV)
- Study God's Word daily (2 Tim. 2:15 NIV)
- Prepare yourself for the challenges of each day (Luke. 5:15, 16 NIV)
- Examine your Christian walk (1 Cor 11:28 NIV)

We are often overwhelmed by too many things to do. Like Martha, we become distracted by all preparations to be made (Luke 10:40 NIV) and fail to manage our time properly. To set priorities means to determine what is important to us, and how to best apportion our time.

Many single believers allow prayerlessness to become a part of their life-style, rather than prayerfulness. Time management is very important in every aspect of our life, especially our walk with God. Divine instructions were given to many standing idle in the market place in the scriptures. When our priorities and goals are in divine order, purpose and destiny meet, enabling us to set and accomplish first things first. Maintaining consistency in setting and accomplishing your priorities is a challenge for most singles and married couples. However, consider these admonitions in developing and maintaining your priorities.

- Allow His word, which is eternal to stand firm in your heart (Ps. 119: 89 KJV)
- Walk daily in His precepts and ponder His statutes in your heart (Ps. 119:94 KJV)
- Learn to let His praise dwell continually in your heart and soul (Ps. 119:164 KJV)
- Delight in the unfolding of His word which gives light and understanding to the simple (Ps. 119:130 KJV)
- Develop and maintain an intensified prayer life to determine daily priorities and prepare for each day (Luke 5: 15, 16)
- Follow His precepts, statutes and decrees daily to establish your steps and direction (Ps. 119:168 KJV)
- Rejoice in His promises, precepts, and righteousness (Ps. 119:159 KJV).
- Know that He directs your footsteps according to His word (Ps. 119:133 KJV).

The key principle in determining priorities is to always put first thing first. We must always learn to put spiritual values before worldly pursuits (2 Cor. 4:18 TAB). Learning to follow the example of Jesus is the key to setting and keeping our priorities in order. He met with the father in intense prayer and meditation to determine His priorities and prepare himself for each day (Luke 5:15-16 TAB). Learn to be led by the Holy Spirit.

Do not limit your investment in those you love, and others who cross your path, to money and gifts. Seek or look for ways to invest yourself, your time, and your energies. Family must be more important than occupation. As the scriptures declare, there is no success if the family is lost (2 Tim. 3:5, 5:8; Titus 2:4, 5 TAB). Learning to say "No, " as even Jesus did, even when some seemingly good requests for your time does not fit the overall plan of your life and ministry (Luke 4:42, 43 TAB).

Your Help Is Within You

And I will pray the Father, and He shall give you another comforter, that He may abide with you forever; even the spirit of truth; whom the world cannot receive, because it seeth Him not, neither knoweth Him; but ye know Him; for He dwelleth with you, and shall be In you . . .
(John 14:16 KJV).

But the Comforter, which is the Holy Ghost, whom the Father will send in my name, He shall teach you all things, and bring all things to your remembrance, whatsoever I have said unto you" (John, 14:26 KJV).

For I am full of words; the spirit within me constrains me
(Job 32:18 TAB).

Create in me a clean heart, O God, and renew a right, preserving, and steadfast spirit within me
(Ps. 51:10 TAB).

Peace be within thy walls and prosperity within thy palaces (Ps. 122:7 TAB).

Christian unmarried singles, divorcees, widows, widowers and all who are believing God for a mate, must know that their help, strength, deliverance, and "all" that they need are within–even the spirit of truth, which the world cannot give. Joy, peace, and happiness in the Lord come from the indwelling spirit of Christ, and not from without. The help, deliverance, and salvation (love, care and comfort) will not come from without. The Father raised Jesus from the dead, but the Father was within Jesus! Your help will come from within. Your help is within you.

- ❧ "Is not my help in me?" (Job 6:13 KJV).
- ❧ "Is not my help with me?" (Young's literal translation).

The victory in learning to live from within and not from without is the *spoken word*. The words you speak, filled with faith and in agreement with His Word, will release the Kingdom of God within you. Reflect upon this:

"For this *commandment* . . . it is not hidden from thee, neither is it *far off.* It is *not* in heaven, that thou shouldest say, 'Who shall go up for us to heaven, and bring it unto us, that we may hear it, and do it?' Neither is it beyond the sea, that thou shouldest say, 'Who shall go over the sea for us, and bring it unto us, that we may hear it, and do it?' But the *word* is *nigh* unto thee, in thy *mouth,* and in thy *heart,* that thou mayest do it . . . But the righteousness which is of faith *speaketh* on this wise . . . The *word* is nigh thee, even in thy *mouth,* and in thy *heart:* that is, the *word* of faith which we preach" (Deut. 30:11–14; Rom. 10:6–10 KJV)

> That if thou shalt confess with thy mouth the Lord Jesus, and shalt believe in thine heart that God hath raised him from the dead, thou shalt be saved.

> For with the heart man believeth unto righteousness; and with the mouth confession is made unto salvation.

> For the scripture saith, Whosoever believeth on him shall not be ashamed (Rom 10: 6–11 KJV).

> "Near you the word is, in your mouth and in your heart" (Wuest).

Every one of us must study the Word of God, learn to encourage ourselves, speak, and decree our own deliverance daily. The anointing is within you. During the process of waiting, and in your place or places of testing, the many passages of scriptures are birthed in your spirit. The power and authority of the *faith filled words* you speak will empower you to press through your test unto victory in the name of Jesus.

> You shall also decide and decree a thing, and it shall be established for you: and the light (of God's favor) shall shine upon your ways (Job 22:28 TAB).

Countless unmarried singles, divorcees, widows and widowers are trying to go through life without experiencing the ministry of the comforter. Many are still in need of spiritual growth and maturity to overcome unprofitable works within their flesh. They continue to struggle within and have not learned to submit unto the deliverer to receive overcoming power. They are still insensitive to the needs of others, and have not reached out in mercy and comfort because they are void of His comfort. They have not learned what it means to be comforted by the Holy Spirit. When hard places come, the carnal mind drags them further into spiritual, emotional, and mental bondage. We must learn to come in the unity of the faith, and of the knowledge of the Son of God unto a perfect man, unto the measure of the stature of the fullness of Christ (Eph. 4:13 KJV).

> And you are in Him, made full and having come to fullness of life (in Christ you are filled with the Godhead–Father, Son and Holy Spirit–and reach full spiritual stature). And He is the head of all rule and authority (of every angelic principality and power) (Col. 2:10 TAB).

The comforter is the Holy Spirit. We get to know Him in the hard and dry places of the experiences we go through in the world. We learn to hear His still, small voice in the silence of the desert. In the loneliness of the dealings of God, we learn to hear the voice of the holy spirit. He is the comforter. Our help is within us, the power of His Holy Spirit, strengthening, encouraging, and sustaining us daily in our walk with Him.

A Choice in Lifestyles

The Works of the Flesh	*The Fruit of Spirit*
(Gal 5:19-21)	(Gal 5:22-23)
Adultery	Love
Fornication	Joy
Uncleanness	Peace
Lewdness	Long-Suffereing
Idolatry	Kindness
Sorcery	Goodness
Hatred	Faithfulness
Contentions	Gentleness
Jealousies	Self Coontrol
Outburts of Wrath	
Selfish Ambitions	
Dissensions	
Heresies	
Envy	
Murders	
Drunkeness	
Reveries	

Loneliness: Never Alone

Now the Lord said, It is not good (sufficient, satisfactory) that the man should be alone; I will make him a helper meet (suitable, adapted, complementary) for him (Gen. 2:18 TAB).

Before God created Eve, He told Adam, "It is not good that man should be alone" (Gen. 2:18 KJV). Though not actually alone (for the animals were there), Adam was incomplete without human companionship. Central to God's purpose for His people are relationships with Him and with others (1 John 1:3, 7 KJV). When we disobey God, breaking fellowship, we become like Adam and Eve. Loneliness and a sense of isolation caused them to lose fellowship with God (Gen. 3:22–24 TAB).

Loneliness has been defined as without companion and fellowship, dejected from being, and without companion. It is part of every human life, not just that of the single person.

The scripture instructs us that man is a spirit. He lives in a body and possesses a soul. Man was made to be in continuous fellowship with God.

Loneliness, the result of a broken relationship, is not the same as aloneness. Jesus was never alone. He was always one with the Father, because He sought to walk in, be in, follow, and obey the perfect will of the Father (My Father and I are one). To develop and have a deeply intimate relationship with Christ, we must learn to withdraw continuously from human companionship, to dwell in His presence, and to meet with Him. This type of aloneness with Christ is desirable, and should be a part of every believer's life, especially before and during marriage. Believers who have developed a personal walk with Jesus and learned how to dwell in His presence are never truly alone because of our friend Jesus (Prov. 18:24; John 15:15).

Jesus experienced aloneness when He was tempted in the wilderness (Mark 1:12, 13), when He traveled (Matt. 8:19, 20), and when His disciples forsook Him (Mark 14:50). However, He experienced loneliness on the cross and was made sin for us (Matt. 27–46).

Singles and all believers should never entertain the state of idleness, because God's destiny and purpose for our life is full of pursuits, exploits, missions, and divine focus to fulfill His will on earth.

Always There

Hello God, I called tonight
To talk a little while . . .
I need a friend, who'll listen,
To my anxieties and trials . . .
You see, I can't quite make it
Through a day just on my own . . .
I need your love to guide me,
So I'll never feel alone.
I want to ask you please to keep
My family safe and sound.
Come and fill their lives with confidence,
For whatever fate they're bound.
Give me faith, dear God, to face
Each hour throughout the day,
And not to worry over things,
I can't change in any way.
I thank you God, for being home,
And listening to my call,
For giving me such good advice,
When I stumble and fall.
Your number, God, is the only one
That answers every time.
I never get a busy signal,
Never had to pay a dime.
So thank you, God, for listening,
To my troubles and sorrow.
Good night, God, I love You, too,
And I'll call again tomorrow!

˷

Author Unknown

> But as the One who called you is holy, you yourselves
> also be holy in all your conduct and manner of living.
>
> For it is written, you shall be holy, for I am holy
> (1 Pet. 1:15–16 TAB).
>
> For God has not called us to impurity, but to consecration
> (to dedicate ourselves to the Most High through purity
> (1 Thess. 4:7 TAB).

Holiness is described as a way to live, a lifestyle. Christians are called to live according to the principles and standards of God's Word, and to lead a pure life in accordance with God's call, commandments, and consequences. In terms of an individual's relationship to God, it means, "set apart." This "set apart" life of righteousness is of God and from God (1 Cor. 1:2; 3:16, 17 TAB). A holy life is a life that always chooses to do what God desires.

Holiness describes the character of God and the principles for Christian conduct. The scripture reveals the holiness of God and expresses God's desire for His children to develop a similar holiness (Ex. 19:6; Lev. 11:44, 45, 19:2; 1 Pet. 1:15 TAB).

There is a beautiful Christian song entitled "I've Learned How to Live Holy, And I Am Learning How to Live Right." It depicts the walk of holiness for all believers. We are learning how to live holy; we are learning how to live right. We cannot make ourselves holy, but, if we desire to become holy and set our will toward following the Lord, He will make us so. He never commands us to do something that He does not enable us to do (Rom. 4:12 NIV).

True holiness is exemplified only in God, through the Holy Spirit, which empowers His children to pursue holiness (1 Thess. 4:7, 8 TAB). The good news is that as we seek to be holy and invite the Holy Spirit to do His work in us, the Lord responds.

He cleanses us, leads us into His righteous and holy paths, and strengthens us to withstand the temptation to return to our former ungodly lives.

Part Four
SINGLE AND ENJOYING IT

The eye is the lamp of the body. So if your eye is sound, your entire body will be full of light (Matt. 6:22 TAB).

Your eye is the lamp of your body; when your eye (your conscience) is sound and fulfilling its office, your whole body is full of light; but when it is not sound and is not fulfilling its office, your body is full of darkness (Luke. 11:34 TAB).

And they said to one another, "Were not our hearts greatly moved and burning within us while He was talking with us on the road, and as He opened and explained to us (the sense of) the scriptures (Luke 24:32 TAB)?

My soul waits only upon God and silently submits to Him, for my hope and expectations are from Him (Ps. 62:5 TAB).

With God rests my salvation and my glory; He is my Rock of unyielding strength and impenetrable hardness, and my refuge is God (Ps. 62:7 TAB).

You will show me the path of life: in your presence is fullness of joy, at your right hand there are pleasures forever more (Psalms 16:11 TAB).

Single And Enjoying It

Behold that which I have seen: it is good and comely for one to eat and to drink, and to enjoy the good of all his labour that he taketh under the sun all the days of his life, which God giveth him: for it is his portion (Eccl. 5:18 KJV).

> And the Lord shall guide thee continually, and satisfy thy soul in drought and make fat thy bones: and thou shalt be like a watered garden, and like a spring of water, whose waters fail not (Isa. 58:11 KJV).

Not that I speak in respect of want: for I have learned, in whatsoever state I am, therewith to be content (Phil. 4:11 KJV).

Singleness can be an enjoyable, beautiful, and a fruitful state, depending on the person's outlook on life. The scriptures admonish believers to learn to be content in whatsoever state they find themselves. Singles, who are purpose, mission, and destiny oriented, learn to be happy in the Lord. Each day they are focused on pursuing and fulfilling their God ordained purpose. Singles are called to develop a deep love relationship with the Lord, and to channel their love to pure, productive, and generous ways to the service of others. A vibrant spiritual life can be the anchor for chastity, and a source of stability in an evil and perverse generation (Luke 9:41; 11:29 NIV).

The single person can experience great freedom to devote themselves to work, friendship, and service. All of these can contribute greatly to the ministry God has in their life, church, and the extension of God's kingdom on earth. Singleness is a permanent state of life for some people, and a temporary state in life for most. Adam had experienced solitude in the garden before God created Eve. Most teenagers and young adults today experienced a similar period of aloneness. The response of faith is to see singleness as a call to committed life, not a lonely life. Made in the image of God, the single person ideally lives in a covenant relationship with God and is called to develop their gifts - human and spiritual–and to contribute to the building up of the church (1 Cor. 12:7 TAB).

The greatest challenge many unfocused singles experience today is idleness. Not only idleness, but tattlers and busybodies, speaking things, which they ought not (1 Tim 5:13 NIV) and inappropriate challenges as well. Idleness, restlessness, and lack of focused spiritual pursuits have caused many singles to turn after Satan.

The world is full of recreational, leisurely, and enjoyable things to do. The question singles should ask themselves daily is, "Father, what would you have me to do today?" Too much idle time has created severe problems and unpleasant circumstances for many singles.

Singles, like many today, have allowed the state of being single to create a distraction for them, instead of using this precious time to develop a relationship with God and to understand His purpose and destiny for their life. Some believe they are created to live a life of celibacy or become eunuchs. In teaching his disciples, Jesus said "For there are eunuchs who were born thus from their mother's womb: and there are some eunuchs which were made eunuchs of men; and there are eunuchs which have made themselves eunuchs for the kingdom of heaven's sake (Matt. 19:12 KJV). Jesus employs the term figuratively, with a reference to the power; either possessed as a natural disposition or acquired as a property of grace, for maintaining and attitude of indifference toward solicitation of the desires of the flesh.

Singleness is a time when every single person should learn to make the most of their lifestyle. This should be a time to learn to be thankful and appreciative, and to enjoy every day God gives. I believe Adam enjoyed his experience of solitude before God created Eve. He enjoyed his fellowship and communion with God. He appreciated the joy of the Garden. Learn to appreciate the joy of your garden and experience rich, beautiful fellowship time with God.

The single person has an opportunity to give a unique level of service to the church and to those in need. It is a level of service that is unfettered and without distraction (1Cor. 7:35 TAB). The single person does not have the practical cares of a mate to keep them from responding wholeheartedly. His or her energy should be focused on meeting the needs that are divinely revealed, and which they feel compelled to address. An attitude of serving others should be in imitation of the Lord Jesus "who being in the form of God, did not consider it robbery to be equal with God, but made himself of no reputation, and took upon him the form of a servant, and was made in the likeness of men (Phil. 2:6, 7).

Identity In Christ—who Am I In Christ?

> In this [union and communion with Him] love is brought to completion and attains perfection with us, that we may have confidence for the day of judgment [with assurance and boldness to face Him], because as He is, so are we in this world (1 John 4:17 TAB).

> But in your hearts set Christ apart as holy [and acknowledge Him] as Lord. Always be ready to give a logical defense to anyone who asks you to account for the hope that is in you, but do it courteously and respectfully (1 Pet. 3:15 TAB).

Man's search for direction, purpose, and destiny leads him down many pathways in life–some positive, some negative. But all lead to the same direction. Man is empty, unhappy, miserable, and incapable of loving anyone until the emptiness within is filled with the spirit of the Lord. Recognizing and acknowledging the need for salvation (God's deliverance–justification, sanctification, and glorification) is the first and most important step toward salvation.

Salvation can best be described as "snatching" someone from danger. Just as a child is snatched from an oncoming automobile to save his life, the Lord snatches every individual who trusts in Him from the pathway that leads to eternal death in hell (Rom. 6:23 TAB). Salvation can be understood as God's deliverance.

Salvation is a process that requires not only God's initial action, but also our response. Man is empty and alienated from God, without foundation, until he acknowledges Jesus as Savior and Lord of his life. There are three aspects of God's salvation or deliverance: justification, sanctification, and glorification. Justification is God's deliverance from sin's penalty. When we accept Christ into our life, we become totally free from the penalty of sin and spiritual death (Rom. 3:23–25). The penalty for sins that have been committed in the past, or will be committed in the future, has been paid through the death of Jesus Christ on the cross.

Salvation is progressive. We must lay the foundation for our walk with the Lord and then begin to grow. Sanctification is God's progressive deliverance of a believer from sin's power to a meaningful, viable relationship with Jesus Christ (Eph. 5:26; 1 Thess. 5:23 TAB). God's desire is that a believer mature and become more Christ-like, that he or she become free from sin's control in their life. But if the believer sins because of the fallen nature, God has made provision (1 John 1:9). God has given us His precious Holy Spirit to help in the process of sanctification.

We must have a personal experience with Christ, surrendering our life to the Lord. It is at this point that salvation, or "deliverance" occurs. From that point throughout eternity, the power of Christ in the believer is greater than the power of sin over the believer (2 Tim. 81:12). Christ, in turn, covers our sins by having paid the penalty for those sins through His death on the cross. We then are challenged to live for Him and grow in His grace.

When God first made Adam, there was life in Adam's spirit. This was revealed because Adam communed with God (Gen. 1:26–31, 2:15–16, 3:8). God is a spirit, and we must worship Him in the realm of spirit and truth (John. 4:23–24). We cannot worship God in the realm of our soul (or mind). God bypasses our intellect, emotions, and will. We cannot understand God with our human reasoning, or the mind of carnality. We cannot understand the Book that He wrote, for that, too, must be spiritually discerned (1 Cor. 2:9–14)! He that comes to God must believe that He Is God (Heb.11: 6). That is not logical. Faith is contrary to reason, and faith is a spiritual force! The Bible makes no attempt to prove the existence of God . . . it assumes it! Therefore, before the transgression and the fall of man, Adam communed with God in the realm of the spirit. The spirit of man is that part of man that is God-conscious. We cannot know God in our mind. We must know Him in our spirit.

Thus, salvation is a complete deliverance, or spiritual maturity, and leads us into glorification, the third dimension of salvation. The scripture states, "who delivered us from so great a death, and doth deliver; in whom we trust that He will yet deliver us" (2 Cor. 1:10). When we acknowledged Jesus as Savior and Lord (initially saved), God delivered our spirit. Scriptural knowledge reveals a person is a sinner without God, and is a person who lives in a state of spiritual death. That describes those who have yet to taste of the blood atonement of Jesus Christ to cover their sin. There is death in the realm of the spirit . . . spiritual death!

Glorification is God's complete deliverance of the believer from sin's presence. Glorification will not be actualized until the Lord returns for His children (1 Cor. 15:51–57). While we are living on this earth, we will always be in the presence of sin. However, those of us who are trusting in Christ will one day be free from sin completely.

Our personal response to God's action is of utmost importance in salvation.

- We must know who Christ is, what He has done, and what He is able to do
- We must have a conviction that the knowledge about Christ is true
- We must act upon that knowledge and conviction, trusting in Christ daily

Salvation is the foundation of a couple's relationship. If mates are unequally yoked, or joined unto an unbeliever, division, dissension, and discord have already entered the relationship.

- "Can two walk together, except they be agreed" (Amos 3:3 TAB)?
- "Do two men travel together, unless they have planned it" (Amos 3:3 Moffatt)?
- "For how can we walk together with your sins between us" Amos 3:3 LB)?

If we agree with the words of the devil, we walk with the devil. If we agree with the Words of God, we walk with God. We are walking and talking with the one that we agree with . . . choosing a covenant of death or a covenant of life.

The joy of a progressive salvation is that the couple grows, matures, and overcomes together in the Lord. They learn to speak the same thing (God's Word), mind the same thing (the mind of Christ–"Let this mind be in you which was also in Christ Jesus" (Phil. 2:5 KJV); and are like-minded in the faith (Phil. 2:2). Salvation is progressive. The soul is the intellect, emotion, and will. Our intellect is what we think. It is our opinion. We have heard people say, "Let me tell you what I think! This is what I think about. . . ." For married couples, that saying changes into "Let us tell you what the Word declares what; Christ thinks about it!" That's the mind of Christ . . . His mind and thinking. God does not think the same way that man does.

> "Seek ye the Lord while He may be found, call ye upon Him while He is near: Let the wicked forsake His ways and the unrighteous man His thoughts . . . for My thoughts are not your thoughts, neither are your ways My ways, saith the Lord. For as the heavens are higher than the earth, so are My ways higher than your ways, and My thoughts than your thoughts" (Isa. 55:6–9 KJV).

The joy of the Lord is our strength. He gives us living water and we thirst no more. When we are born again of the water and of the spirit, we learn to grow up in Him in all things. We learn to worship Him in spirit and truth and be like-minded in the faith, overcoming the works of the flesh. We learn to walk in the character and integrity of the Word of Jesus Christ, declaring, "As He is, so are we in this world" (1 John 4:17).

The Importance Of Prayer
Developing And Maintaining Your Prayer Life

And this is the confidence (the assurance, the privilege of boldness), which we have in Him (we are sure) that if we ask anything (make any request) according to His will (in agreement with His own plan), He listens to and hears us. And if (since) we (positively) know that He listens to us in whatever we ask, we also know (with settled and absolute knowledge that we have (granted us as our present possessions) the requests made of Him (1 John 5:14–15 TAB).

Confess to one another therefore your faults (your slips, your false steps, your offenses, your sins) and pray (also) for one another, that you may be healed and restored to a spiritual tone of mind and heart. The earnest (heart felt, continued) prayer of a righteous man makes tremendous power available (dynamic in His working) (James 5:16 TAB).

But the face of the Lord is against those who practice evil (to oppose them, to frustrate, and defeat them (1 Peter 3:12 TAB).

Praying always with all prayer and supplication in the Spirit, and watching thereunto with all perseverance and supplication for all saints (Eph. 6:18 KJV).

There is a necessity for every believer to establish the foundation of prayer in his or her personal life, marriage, home, and family. The scripture instructs us to "Put on God's whole armor (the armor of a heavy-armed soldier which God supplies), that you may be able successfully to stand up against (all) the strategies and the deceits of the devil" (Eph. 6:11).

Prayer is fellowship with the Father–an open line of communication between God and man. Taking time to pray, staying before Him with all prayers, supplications and faith, and believing His Word, brings victory. We pray to the Father in the name of Jesus, through the Holy

Spirit, according to the Word of God. He moves as a result of prayers in faith–believing and knowing that "the effectual fervent prayer of a righteous man availeth much" (James 5:16).

Prayers that bring results must be based on God's Word. He did not leave us without His thoughts and His ways, for we have His word–His bond. He has instructed us to call unto Him, and He will answer and show us great and mighty things. As we pray the Word of God, it declares to put him in remembrance: let us plead together: (Isa. 43:26). He has promised us that the Word that goeth forth out of His mouth, shall not return unto Him void (without producing any effect, useless), but it shall accomplish that which He pleases and purposes, and it shall prosper in the thing for which He sent it (Isa. 55:11).

The power of personal prayers and confession of the Word of God for self, others and the Body of Christ is a necessity for every believer. Prayer empowers us to be changed from faith to faith, from glory to glory, always abounding in the wisdom, knowledge and understanding of our Lord. Christians' first priority is to love the Lord our God with our entire being, and our neighbor as our self. We are called to be intercessors, men and women of prayer. We are instructed to seek our Lord with all prayers and supplications; inquiring, meditating, and listening to His voice and directions for our lives.

Many believers have needs that are not met simply because they do not pray (James 4:2). While God does not promise to provide all we want, He does provide all we need (Phil. 4:19). He is our Jehovah-Jireh, our all sufficient provider. Every believer, married couple, and Christian needs to know that God promises to provide for the needs of His children. He provides for our physical needs of food, clothing, and shelter.

He provides for our spiritual needs through prayers, bible study, and ministries in His name. He provides for our personal needs through intimate relationships with God and other believers. He will provide for us as we seek Him through prayer. He provides for our total well-being–spiritually, physically, and materially. His source is unlimited.

The will of the Lord for our life and every true believer, "God's set-apart ones" is to . . . seek ye first the kingdom of God, and His righteousness; and all these things shall be added unto you (Matt. 6:33).

Dating: Relating To One Another

> Lean on, trust in, and be confident in the Lord with all your heart and mind, and do not rely on your own insight or understanding.
>
> In all your ways know, recognize, and acknowledge Him, and He will direct and make straight and plain your paths (Prov. 3:5–6 TAB).

The twenty first century is full of self-help books, techniques, guidelines, and principles on dating. However, dating relationships are not described in scripture. Consequently, we must stand on the principles and guidelines of God's Word pertaining to these relationships. God gives guidelines for relating to each other in every aspect of our life: The Word of God is profitable for instruction, for reproof and conviction of sin, correction of error, discipline in obedience for training in righteousness (holy living) and conformity to God's will in thought, purpose and action (2 Tim. 3:16)

- Dating teens must honor their parents and respect their counsel (Eph. 6:2 TAB).
- The dating partner must be considered. God's Word is very clear when it says, "Do not be unequally yoked together with unbelievers. You are wise to ask whether or not your date has a personal and growing relationship with the Lord. Also, you should consider whether that relationship is evident in your date's lifestyle (II Cor. 6:14 TAB).
- You must examine yourself. Are you spending time with the Lord? Are you depending on the Lord to meet your needs of love and security? Are you an example for Christ to all those with whom you have contact? (I Tim. 4:12 TAB).

The Lord has called you to have a loving relationship, and commitment unto Him that supersedes any dating relationship.

The Abstinence Principle
Passion Held By Principle

> For this is the will of God, that you should be consecrated (separated and set apart for pure and holy living): that you should abstain and shrink from all sexual vice.

> That each one of you should know how to possess (control, manage) his own body in consecration (purity, separated from things profane) and honor (1 Thess. 4:3–4 TAB).

> But to the unmarried people and to the widows, I declare that it is well (good, advantageous, expedient, and wholesome) for them to remain (single) even as I do (1 Cor. 7:8 TAB).

The love life of a Christian is governed by nothing less than the principle of God's Word. Christians must consider the authority of Christ over human passions and set their hearts on purity. Chastity means abstention from sexual activity outside of marriage. It is a Christian obligation. For the Christian there is one rule and one rule only: total abstention from sexual activity prior to marriage and total faithfulness within marriage (1 Cor. 7:1–9).

Christians are to value the sanctity of sex. This means to say no to unbridled passions and desires that arise from time to time. The Spirit of God is able to control all emotions, lusts, vile affections, and degrading passions once surrendered on the altar of prayers and supplications unto Him (James 5:17). For this is the will of God, that you should be consecrated (separated and set apart for pure and holy living) that you should abstain and shrink from all sexual devise (1 Thess. 4:3)

Purity in heart, having sincerity of heart, involves inner cleansing. The inner cry of the heart is "create in a me clean heart, O' God, and renew your right spirit within me (Ps. 51: 10).

To equate any personal sexual desire as natural, healthy, and God-given is a powerful lie. God does not give desires that cannot be fulfilled according to His standards of holiness, wholeness, and purity. Sexual purity is one of the foremost means of safeguarding a marriage from that which pollutes, infects or destroys physically, emotionally, or spiritually.

Purity means freedom from contamination from anything that would spoil the taste or pleasure, reduce the power, or in any way adulterate what a thing is meant to be. Within marriage, sexual union is natural, healthy, and pleasurable, not only for the moment, but for marriage life togetherness. Sexual intimacy is natural in the sense in which the original Designer created it to be. When virginity and purity are no longer protected and esteemed, there is dullness, monotony, and sheer boredom. By trying to grab fulfillment everywhere, you find it nowhere.

❧

There are three things too wonderful for me,
yes, four which I do not understand

The way of an eagle in the air
The way of a serpent upon a rock
The way of a ship in the midst of the sea;

(PROVERBS 30:18-19 TAB)

❧

Purity before marriage consists of giving ourselves to each other in obedience to God. Passion must be held by principle. The principle is love–not merely erotic, sentimental, or sexual feeling. There is no other way to control passion and no other route to purity and joy. If you choose to avoid the sin of sexual immorality, that is God's ideal. If you have already given away your virginity, the message of the gospel proclaims new birth, a new beginning, and a new creation (2 Cor. 5:17).

❧

Scarcely had I passed them,
found the one my heart loves.
I held him and would not let him go,
til I had brought him to my mother's house

(SONG 3:4 NIV)

❧

Part Five

HAPPINESS IS A CHOICE

Leah's servant Zilpah bore Jacob a second son. Then Leah said how happy I am! The women call me happy. So she named him Asher (Gen 30:13 NIV).

Happy and bless are the people who are in such a case; yes, happy (blessed, fortunate, prosperous, to be envied) are the people whose God is the Lord (Ps. 144:15 TAB).

He that handleth a matter wisely shall find good: and whoso truseth in the Lord, happy is he (Prov. 16:20 KJV).

Happy is the man that feareth always: but he that hardeneth his heart shall fall into mischief (Prov. 28:14 KJV).

Blessed (happy, fortunate, to be envied) is everyone who fears, reveres, and worships the Lord, who walks in His ways and lives according to His commandments (Prov. 29:18 KJV).

For you shall eat (the fruit) of the labor of your hands, happy (blessed, fortunate, enviable) shall you be, and it shall be well with you (Ps. 128:1–2 KJV).

They shall be abundantly satisfied with the fatness of thy house; and thou shalt make them drink of the river of thy pleasures.

For with thee is the fountain of life: in thy light shall we see light (Ps. 36:8–9 KJV).

Whom have I in heaven but thee? And there is none upon earth that I desire beside thee.

My flesh and my heart faileth: but God is the strength of my heart, and my portion forever (Ps. 73: 25–26 KJV).

I'm So Happy

I'm so happy, that I know the Lord.
Now I can fight satan with God's sword.
No more in darkness, will I have to be.
My God has most definitely set me free!
I'm so happy, my mind is finally clear.
No more my enemies, do I have to fear.
With God by my side, I know I'm ok.
When in trouble, all I need is to pray.
I'm so happy, He has forgotten my sins.
Satan thought he had me, But God wins.
My sins were oh so many, and terrible.
But God's forgiving nature, how lovable.
I'm so happy, I have Christian friends now,
They love me, but I don't know how.
Their love for me must be through God,
I'd think on me, they'd want to use a rod.
I'm so happy I have a church to attend,
Now my life, I know it will start to mend.
Hearing God's word, will begin the process,
And daily my sins, to the Lord, I will confess.
I'm so happy I have a better life awaiting.
Where there will be no more hating.
This earth below if full of much darkness,
The life hear after, will be full of kindness.
I'm so happy, heaven one day I will see,
Love, peace and joy will be for me.
It's so hard to imagine, but it's so true,
This is also available to you.
I'm so happy to be able to tell you,
That Jesus has a home for you too.
If you only ask Jesus to forgive your sins.
In your heart, He will come in.
I'm so happy that you ARE praying now.
Jesus is with you, as on your knees you bow.
Always trust in Him, and let Him lead you,
This I'm praying, you will do.

೩

Elaine Ables

Happiness Is A Decision

> Happy is the man that findeth wisdom, and the man that getteth understanding (Prov. 3:13 KJV).

> He that handleth a matter wisely shall find good; and whoso trusteth in the Lord, happy is he (Prov. 16:20 KJV).

> Happy is that people, that is in such a case; yea, happy is that people, whose God is the Lord (Ps. 144:15 KJV).

Happiness can be defined as a state of spiritual contentment that will carry you through the triumphs, pitfalls, or even heartaches of life with serenity and tranquility (Matt. 5:3–12). Happiness is a choice or act of the will (Ps. 144:15). We all have things "happen" in our lives that give us reasons to be unhappy, but we have the power through Christ to choose our response to those happenings. Happiness is a decision. Happiness may or may not be related to the circumstances in your life.

The scripture declares "that the kingdom of God is within us; it is peace, happiness and joy in the Holy Ghost" (Rom. 14:17). Happiness does not depend on external responses and forces that happen as a result of people, and would cause many to be unhappy, but upon the inner joy and peace of the indwelling Christ. However, when we learn to draw water out of our own cistern (or the Christ within), then and only then will our happiness spring up within us like rivers of living water (John 4:10).

Jesus had the Spirit without measure. Happiness is one of the fruit of the Spirit. Christians are happy because Christ- the Spirit of joy dwells with us. The Kingdom of God is peace, joy and righteousness in the Holy Ghost. He is our joy and happiness. He was anointed . . . with the oil of gladness above His fellows. Would He not deserve distinction as the happiest man that ever lived (Ps. 45:7)?

He gives some attributes that promote a response of happiness (meekness, righteousness, merciful, peacemakers (Matt 5:6–11). Believers must not concentrate on doing, but on being happy, living epistles read, seen and heard of all men. Total commitment to the Lord will result in a believer's instinctive Christ like response to various circumstances as they occur. In order to pursue happiness, we must appropriate the tools God has given–specifically, prayer, His word the gifts of the spirit, fruit of the spirit and His indwelling spirit (Prov. 3:13; 29:18). When a believer's faith and conduct are balanced, happiness will always result.

The scriptures declare, "He has given us all things richly to enjoy" (1 Tim. 6:17). Therefore, when faith and conduct are balanced, happiness will always result. Happiness is enjoying where you are; enjoying everything the Lord has given you, and not fretting about the things that have been taken away or withheld (Matt. 6:33–34). Happiness is trusting God's sovereignty and omniscience. You must believe that in every circumstance, God will work for your good (Rom. 8:28). Happiness comes from daily obedience and faith in the Lord.

Enjoying Your Walk With God

> Until the Lord have given your brethren rest, as he hath given you, and they also have possessed the land which the Lord your God giveth them; then ye shall return unto the land of your possession, and enjoy it, which Moses the Lord's servant gave you on this side Jordan toward the sunrising (Josh. 1:15 KJV).

> And also that every man should eat and drink and enjoy the good of all his labor, it is the gift of God (Eccl. 3:13 KJV).

> Charge them that are rich in this world, that they be not highminded, nor trust in uncertain riches, but in the living God, who giveth us richly all things to enjoy (1 Tim. 6:17 KJV).

Believers are blessed and should be full of the joy of the Lord, enjoying their personal walk with Jesus, and proclaiming daily that "Jesus is the best thing that ever happened in my life." Developing and maintaining a personal walk with Jesus is peace, joy, and happiness in the Holy Spirit. Surrendering, yielding, and saying yes to His will, way, and word is "experiencing that mountaintop experience," knowing that the satisfaction, joy, and excitement He brings in our life is the greatest gift God can give unto man.

A continual flow of His Holy Spirit is, the oil of gladness which gives great enjoyment to all life's day- to- day activities. Life is full of challenges, disappointments, frustrations, and concerns, but the Joy of Jesus and enjoying His presence is the oil that lessens the wear and tear of mundane frictions.

After the Israelites returned from exile, and came to observe the Feast of Tabernacle, they were sad because of the desolation of Zion. However, Nehemiah told them not to mourn, "For the joy of the Lord is your strength" (Neh. 8:10). Joy gives us strength to live day-by-day, to enjoy our walk with God, and to perform His Will.

Learning to fulfill God's Will is followed by the spirit of joy. The spirit of joy and gladness strengthens believers to obey God's leadings and promptings. The disciples of Jesus were filled with great joy and gladness as they obeyed and submitted to His divine will. The joy of the Lord strengthened, provoked, and stirred them for every good work.

God has given us all things richly to enjoy (1 Tim. 6:17). He maketh His sun to rise on the evil and on the good, and sendeth rain on the just and on the unjust (Matt. 5:45). Through His grace, God gives salvation and multiple spiritual blessings. Some of these blessings are peace, joy, happiness, sunshine, rain, health, happy marriages, and children.

Enjoying our walk with Jesus is the manifestation of His Word in our lives, which states, "He came that we might have life, and that we might have it more abundantly" (John 10:10). There is and can never be an enjoyment of life, and enjoying it more abundantly without the presence of "life itself." Jesus is The Way, The Truth and The Life; that eternal life that giveth life unto the world, abiding within us, and springing up into everlasting life.

Enjoying Your Family

And if it seems evil to you to serve the Lord, choose for yourselves this day whom you will serve, whether the gods which your fathers served on the other side of the river, or the gods of the Amorites, in whose land you dwell; but as for me and my house, we will serve the Lord" (Josh. 24:15 TAB).

For this cause I (seeing the greatness of this plan by which you are built together in Christ) bow my knees before the Father of our Lord Jesus Christ,

For whom every family in heaven and on earth is named (that Father from whom all fatherhood takes its title and derives its name) (Eph. 3:14–15 TAB).

Webster has defined family as parents and their children: a group of people connected by blood or marriage and sharing common ancestry; the members of a household. We as believers are members of the Family of God–the household of faith. A Christ-centered home provides unlimited potential for growth and maturity as they continuously give themselves to the principles of God's Word through prayer, fasting, Bible study, and fellowship.

It is an absolute example to be admired and followed in the family as we read and follow Joshua's example. He knew scripturally the necessity of establishing divine order and structure in his home. Family leadership and parenthood is needful in every generation that will enjoy the life our God has given. Parenthood brings joy. Three biblical mothers proved this through their reactions. Eve at the birth of her first exclaimed, "I have gotten a man from the Lord" (Gen. 4:1). Sarah, at ninety years old, finally bore a son, called Laughter (Isaac). Hannah was very excited and exuberant after Samuel's birth. She praised the Lord saying "My heart rejoiceth in the Lord" (1 Sam. 2:1).

> Then God said to Abraham, As for Sarai your wife, you shall not call her name Sarai, but Sarah shall be her name. And I will bless her and give you a son also by her; yes, I will bless her, and she shall be a mother of nations; kings of peoples shall come from her.
>
> Then Abraham fell on his face and laughed, and said in his heart, Shall a child be born to a man who is a hundred years old? And shall Sarah, who is ninety years old, bear a son (Gen. 17:15–17 KJV)?

Isaac's birth was connected with laughter. He not only alluded to the laughter of Abraham and Sarah (Gen. 18:12; 21:6), but also implied that God will smile and show favor to this son.

The enemy, Satan, has deceived and robbed many of their rich family heritages. In a fallen world, there is no such thing as a perfect family. Children have many needs; physical needs (food, shelter, clothing); emotional needs (love, acceptance, affirmation); intellectual needs (the opportunity to learn daily skills and to develop intellectually); and spiritual needs (guidance in how to know God personally and to mature in that relationship). However, a dysfunctional family is one which is consistently inadequate in meeting some or all of these needs.

Dysfunctional families have common patterns. They do not

talk, keeping the family secrets. They do not see, ignoring inappropriate behavior as well as altered perceptions of reality. They do not feel, disrespecting legitimate emotions. They do not trust, living in isolation and fearing more broken promises. The children strive desperately to be perfect, trying to meet all parental expectations.

We've got good news. Jesus desires to repair the breach for families in which children have been maligned or afflicted (Isa. 58:9–12). Perhaps Jesus is bringing and has brought many of Heaven's mates together for such an hour and time as this. He is repairing the breaches and introduces them to the joy of living according to the principles of His Word. And most importantly, revealing and exposing them to the reality of faith in God's Word. Providing the evidence that faith in God's Word turns hopeless circumstances, family living problems and dysfunctional family conditions around. He came to provide healing, deliverance and salvation for hurting families.

Enjoying Your Marriage

> Come with me from Lebanon, my spouse, with me from Lebanon: look from the top of Amana, from the top of Shenir and Hermon, from the lions' dens, from the mountain of the leopards.

> Thou hast ravished my heart, my sister, my spouse; thou hast ravished my heart with one of thine eyes, with one chain of thy neck.

> How fair is thy love, my sister, my spouse! How much better is thy love than wine! And the smell of thine ointments than all spices!

> Thy lips, O my spouse, drop as the honeycomb; honey and milk are under thy tongue; and the smell of thy garments is like the smell of Lebanon.

> A garden enclosed is my sister, my spouse; a spring shut up, a fountain sealed.

> A fountain of gardens, a well of living waters, and streams from Lebanon (Song 4:8–15 KJV).
>
> Let thy fountain be blessed; and rejoice with the wife of thy youth.
>
> Let her be as the loving hind and pleasant roe; let her breasts satisfy thee at all times; and be thou ravished always with her love (Prov. 4:17–18 KJV).

A woman whose husband passed away lamented, What joy is it now to live, enjoy and experience happiness in life. Heaven's mates are taught and learn how to be a wife, mother, friend with and without a mate; during and in the midst of hardships. He teaches and has taught us that the joy of the Lord is our straight. Learning and flowing with the ministry of the Holy Spirit enables us to grow up in Him in all things.

This is a daily process. Growth in the spirit and truth accentuates loneliness, boredom, restlessness, and rejection. She quickly acknowledged and stated she would yield and surrender to be a better wife if she could have him back again. Life's experience is a good teacher.

The book of Proverbs is a beautiful source of wisdom for all who would seek the mind of Christ in all areas of their life. We all should learn to "rejoice with the wife or husband of our youth . . . and be ravished always with their love" (Prov. 5:18–19). God's timing, love, grace, and care was timely manifested in the life of Isaac. Rebekah came into his life at the right time and brought comfort to him after his mother's death (Gen. 24:67). Jacob's love for Rachel was so great and delightful that his seven years of labor (increased to another seven years as a result of his father-in-law cunning deceit and manipulations) to earn her hand seemed but a few days (Gen. 29:20).

When we learn to receive and appreciate Jesus, then and only then, do we learn how to be grateful, thankful, knowing that He has given us all things richly to enjoy.

Enjoying your marriage, children, and family comes through maintaining a right relationship with Christ and obedience unto His precepts. Jesus said, "If ye know these things, happy are ye if ye do them" (John 13:17). Enjoying our marriage does not come when we pursue it, but when we pursue to fulfill our responsibility in Christ. Happiness or joy is not a goal, but is one of the fruit of the Spirit; which is the result of disciplined walking in God's pathway of obedience.

The fruit grower must follow the farmer's guide of good farming if he wants a healthy crop of apples. He prunes his trees, sprays against insects, fertilizes, and waters the soil; and when frost threatens, he builds smudge pots. Likewise the fruit of joy, produced by the Holy Spirit, becomes more abundant after God prunes our lives with spiritual discipline.

It is a wonderful, beautiful, and awesome blessing to enjoy our marriage and Christian walk.

Enjoying Your State Of Being

> But godliness with contentment is great gain. For we brought nothing into this world, and it is certain we can carry nothing out (1 Tim. 6:6–7 KJV).

> Not that I speak in respect of want; for I have learned, in whatsoever state I am, therewith to be content (Phil. 4:11 KJV).

Contentment has been defined as the ultimate acceptance of yourself, your surrounding, your past, and your future. We as believers are blessed, because the scripture tells us Jesus has paid the price for our sin and gives us a secure future of eternity in His presence, free of all pain and sorrow (Eph. 2:8,9; Rev. 21:4). The challenges, trials, and sufferings we experience now should be viewed in light of an eternity to be spent with the Savior (Rev. 21:7). God has provided a way for us to be rescued from an eternity in hell, and is sufficient to meet our needs in the world He created (Phil. 4:13, 19).

Contentment is not a God given gift. We are taught contentment as we yield and surrender unto Him to be Savior and Lord in our life. We learn how to be content in whatsoever state we are in. We trust God's gifts to be sufficient and His assignments to be appropriate. You can accept the way you look, the means you have been given, the family in which you are living, the struggles through which you have gone through, and be content and fulfilled in all (2 Cor. 3:5,6; 12:9).

Reaching this blessed state of contentment is not an easy task. Satisfaction when you have urgent needs, freedom from worry when you have overwhelming concerns, patience and letting God work when pressures abound–these seem the impossible dream. Happiness is not merely a human pursuit, but demands spiritual resources found in the indwelling Holy Spirit.

However, acceptance does not mean stagnation. Dissatisfaction with areas in your life that can be changed may help you to see that something is missing. When this happens, we dare not adopt the "Canaan" syndrome of complaining. Remember that God's people were not allowed to enter the Promised Land because of their murmuring (Josh. 5:6). Rather, to take that dissatisfaction to the Lord and see what He would challenge you to do, and be willing in the meantime to be "content as you walk toward the ultimate goals." This is the balance between, "I have learned to be content," and, "I can do all things through Christ which strengtheth me (Phil. 4:11, 13).

We all must trust that God has given us everything we need for this moment in time. As you depend on the Lord, you learn to be content as you pursue His goals for your life (1 Tim 6:8).

Part Six

SINGLES BELIEVING GOD FOR A MATE

Seek out of the book of the Lord and read: not one of these (details of prophecy) shall fail; none shall want and lack her mate (in fulfillment). For the mouth (of the Lord) has commanded and His Spirit has gathered them (Isa. 34:16 TAB).

For therein is the righteousness of God revealed from faith to faith: as it is written, The just shall live by faith (Romans 1:17 KJV).

And whatever you ask for in prayer, having faith and (really) believing, you will receive (Matt. 21:22 TAB).

For whatever is born of God is victorious over the world, and this is the victory that overcometh the world, even our faith (1 John 5:4 TAB).

Therefore I say unto you, what things soever ye desire, when ye pray, believe that ye receive them, and ye shall have them (Mk 11:24 KJV).

And this is the confidence that we have in Him, that, if we ask any thing according to His will, he heareth us.

And if we know that he hear us, whatsoever we ask, we know that we have the petitions that we desired of Him (1 John 5:14, 15 KJV).

Singles Believing God For A Mate

Therefore I say unto you, What things soever ye desire, when ye pray, believe that ye receive them, and ye shall have them (Mark 11:24 KJV).

Look in the scroll of the Lord and read: none of these will be missing, not one will lack her mate. For it is His mouth that has given the order, and His Spirit will gather them together (Isa. 34:16 NIV).

And this is the confidence that we have in him, that, if we ask any thing according to his will, he heareth us:

And if we know that he hear us, whatsoever we ask, we know that we have the petitions that we desired of him (1 John 5: 14–15 KJV)

The desire to be married is experienced by many in the Christian world. The desire for marriage is recognized from childhood to adulthood- when little girls began playing house, imitating mommy from the care of the baby to household cleaning, cooking and parental instructions (children providing leadership- giving instructions like mommy). However, as we reflect on "children playing house," there was always an absent of the father. The living story today is, little girls have spent much time imitating mother, playing house, etc. The family balance in the "children playing house scenario", was and is incomplete without the father. A father figure is absent in their conception of God's plan for the family. The desire for marriage and family began as early as childhood or child's play.

The preparation for marriage is planted in the mind of the child at an early age, leaving he or she void of the knowledge, wisdom, and understanding about marriage and the family to include the marriage union. Consequently, depending on our open mindedness to life and the challenges that come with growth and maturity, we marry and- often miss the divine purpose for the union. This causes us to be unprepared to experience the joy, pleasures, and fulfillment marriage brings.

We marry, often not knowing how to be a wife (the God- kind-of- wife) and husband (the God- kind- of- husband). As Christians we have read the letter of the Word, and did not understand the letter without the spirit of wisdom, knowledge, and revelation of the hidden mystery of the gospel of Christ (the true meaning). The scripture declares that the letter killeth, but the Spirit makes alive (2 Cor 3:6).

Essentially, once married, we don't know how to relate to the God- kind of wife or the God- kind of husband. We have read, studied the Word, prayed, and realized that marriage demands that each person grow in the wisdom, knowledge and understanding of God's Word to include loving, sharing, and growing up in Him in all things. However, we are still missing the key element. The family balance in "the children playing house scenario," was, and is incomplete without the father. The key element is married partners compliments each other strengths and weaknesses in the marriage. They grow together through daily life challenges, experiences, and problems.

The first and most important step for singles is to learn to submit their lives, purpose, and destiny unto God. Learn to develop a meaningful, viable relationship with Him before you marry. In order to enjoy the fulfillment of life and marriage, a meaningful relationship with Him must be developed before the marriage. In the union of husband and wife, two distinct, different people, make a lifetime commit to each other. They are dedicated, and must learn to follow God's principles, guidelines, and Word for their lives, require further growth, development, and maturity through trusting, waiting and obeying Him. Growth is a continuous life process that should not cease until we go on to be with our Lord and Savior Jesus Christ.

When singles realize that they are complete in Christ (Col. 2:10), He will enable each person to enter and maintain a healthy, balanced relationship, growing spiritually, emotionally, naturally and in every area of their life.

Believing and finding a mate is one of the second most important decisions we make in life. This decision should never he made impulsively or in haste. He is knowledge, wisdom, and understanding. He is our all and all, and should never be left out of our relationships or decisions. He alone knows who your mate is, where he is, why He has chosen to bring the two of you together, and when this meeting will take place.

If you are truly believing God for your mate, submit yourself entirely unto Him in all ways, and strive sincerely to please Him. He has your best interest at heart- to include, enjoying your walk with Him, your marriage, family, and home.

Part Seven

SINGLES PREVAILING IN PRAYER

If my people, who are called by my name, shall humble themselves, pray, seek crave, and require of necessity, my face and turn from their wicked ways, then I will hear from heaven, forgive their sin, and heal their land
(2 Chr. 7:14 TAB).

Ask, and it shall be given you; seek, and ye shall find; knock, and it shall be opened unto you:

For every one that asketh receiveth; and he that seeketh findeth; and to him that knocketh it shall be opened.

Or what man is there of you, whom if his son ask bread, will he give him a stone?

Or if he ask a fish, will be give him a serpent?

If ye then, being evil, know how to give good gifts unto your children, how much more shall your Father which is in heaven give good things to them that ask him?

Therefore all things whatsoever ye would that men should do to you, do ye even so to them: for this is the law and the prophets (Matt. 7:7–12 KJV).

And this is the confidence that we have in him, that, if we ask anything according to his will, he heareth us:

And if we know that he hear us, whatsoever we ask, we know that we have the petitions that we desired of him
(1 John 5:14–15 KJV).

The earnest (heartfelt, continued) prayer of a righteous man makes tremendous power available (dynamic in the working) (James 5:16 TAB).

Be unceasing in prayer (praying, perseveringly) (1 Thess. 5:17 TAB).

Prevailing In Prayers

Seek ye out of the book of the Lord, and read: no one of these shall fail, none shall want her mate: for my mouth it hath commanded, and his spirit it hath gathered them (Is. 34:16 KJV).

Ask, and it shall be given you; seek, and ye shall find; knock, and it shall be opened unto you:

For every one that asketh receiveth; and he that seeketh findeth; and to him that knocketh it shall be opened.

Or what man is there of you, whom if his son ask bread, will he give him a stone?

Or if he ask a fish, will be give him a serpent?

If ye then, being evil, know how to give good gifts unto your children, how much more shall your Father which is in heaven give good things to them that ask him.

Therefore all things whatsoever ye would that men should do to you, do ye even so to them: for this is the law and the prophets (Matt. 7:7–11 KJV).

Prevailing in prayer brought great deliverance to the widow in the city. The Greek word "nikao" means "to subdue, conquer, overcome, prevail, get the victory." Webster's definition of prevail means "to gain ascendance through strength or superiority; triumph; to be or become effective." "The effectual fervent prayers of a righteous man availeth much" (James 5:16 KJV).

One of the greatest problems twenty-first century Christianity is experiencing is that of prayerlessness. Unmarried singles, families, and believers must learn the necessity of praying without ceasing. The scripture declares that "men ought always to pray and not to faint" (Luke 18:1). Many of the things we call prayer mean prayerlessness unto God. Sincerely praying with all prayers and supplication unto God takes commitment and dedication unto God.

Prayer is the God given opportunity to become intimately acquainted with Him. As a conversation with God, prayer enables the believer to build a personal relationship with the Lord. Prayer is an expression of a believer's dependence on God and, at the same time, an affirmation of God's promise to the redeemed for spiritual power.

While many believers desire to spend time with God in prayer, few actually do. Spiritual discipline is necessary to make prayer a priority in our lives. God however, has made prayer a priority, directing His children to pray daily and without ceasing. Prayer should be a daily priority in our lives.

Singles must acknowledge the necessity of laying the foundation of prayer in their lives. Prayerlessness has caused a great impact on the lives of many singles to include impulsiveness, confused values, lack of character, and the necessity of living a God fearing and Christian life on earth.

There is a global call and necessity for every unmarried single to return unto the altar of prayer and supplication. The scriptures speak repeatedly of the importance of prayer. Paul admonishes believers to pray about everything (Phil 4:6). Singles and believers should make all their requests known unto God. In addition, believers are admonished to pray regularly and frequently. David went as far as to promise the Lord, "Evening, morning and noon, I will pray" (Ps.55:17).

Jesus prayed for extended periods of time, especially when making important decisions (Luke 6:12).

Prayer should occupy a place in the heart and life of all singles and believers. An altar or place of prayer should be in every life and home. Singles should plan a special time and place as a part of their daily prayer schedule (Luke 15:1).

Singles are admonished to develop and focus on the necessity and priority of prayer in their life. They should develop and grow in prayer through sharing their commitment to pray for each other, encouraging, and supporting each other during times of life challenges, trials and tests.

There is a necessity for every unmarried single to lay, develop, and maintain an altar of prayer in their life. The altar of prayer is needed in every singles life. They are missing the most viable source of power, deliverance and healing in their life by allowing prayerlessness to be a part of their life.

Learning to develop and maintain their prayer life early or prior to marriage, not only prepares, but strengthens the foundation of prayer in their life. Prayer is needed as they make the transition from a single lifestyle to married. The sweet communion and fellowship with God is a most rewarding and glorious experience for all who willingly submit and surrender unto Him.

The scripture declares that the Lord knoweth them that are His. The spirit of prayer and supplication enables us to draw closer unto Him- assuring us that He knows and hears our prayers.

Praying unceasingly is not something that comes naturally. This is learned and developed during a process of time. The flesh is not interested in prayer, and has to be trained to pray. Learning to bring your flesh in submission to prayer entails commitment and sacrifice unto God. Developing discipline in prayer means you are not controlled by your fleshly desires, circumstances and distractions, but you have established and will maintain this posture in prayer because it is needed in your life.

If we wait for the ideal time to pray, or pray when we feel like praying, we will never pray. Our flesh has no desire to develop the discipline and rewards that prayer brings into our lives. If we do not establish a daily time of prayer and supplication, something else will always come up we think is more important.

> "Present your case," says the Lord. Set forth your arguments, saith the king of Jacob (Is. 41:21).

> And Abraham drew near, and said, wilt thou also destroy the righteous with the wicked (Gen. 18:23)?

> Abraham illustrated the principle of learning to plead your case before the Lord. He said, suppose there are fifty righteous people within the city. Will you also destroy the fifty righteous people and not spare them? He said, "Far be it from you to do such thing to slay the righteous with the wicked! So that the righteous fare as

> do the wicked. Far be it from you! Shall not the judge of
> the earth execute judgment and do righteously
> (Gen 18:24–25)?

He pleaded his case beginning with the number fifty and decreasing unto to ten. And the Lord said, I will not destroy it for the ten righteous sake.

Our Heavenly Father encourages us to produce our cause and bring forth strong reasons for our petition with fervency. He encourages us to lay our petition before Him. We serve a mighty God. He is touched with the feeling of our infirmities (Heb. 4:15). He loves us and careth for us. He has not forgotten or overlooked the unmarried singles believing Him for a mate. He hears your case. He sees your petition, and will answer as you submit to His destiny and purpose for your life.

Abraham's pleading could not save Sodom and Gomorrah, but it saved his family. Singles prevailing in prayers, praying without ceasing, are destroying the works of the enemy (1 John 5:17).

And shall not God avenge his own elect, which cry day and night unto him, though He bear long with them (Luke 18:7).

Singles learning how to pray day and night are declaring war on the enemy. Jesus compared His own elect to a widow harassed to quit. Singles must believe "they have no reason not to receive their mate." The scripture has declared, none shall want their mate (Isa. 34:16). The woman could not find any reason to fail, so she unashamedly pleaded her case before the judge. Singles should continue prevailing in prayer, (praying without ceasing), your Heavenly Father heareth and will reward you openly.

Singles Prevailing In Prayer

> The earnest (heartfelt, continued) prayer of a righteous
> man makes tremendous power available
> (dynamic in its working) (James 5:16 TAB).

> For the eyes of the Lord are upon the righteous (those
> who are upright and in right standing with God), and His
> ears are attentive to their prayer . . . (1 Peter 3:12 TAB).

> For the Word that God speaks is alive and full of power (making it active, operative, energizing, and effective); it is sharper than any two-edged sword, penetrating to the dividing line of the breath of life (soul) and (the immortal) spirit, and of joints and marrow (of the deepest parts of our nature), exposing and sifting and analyzing and judging the very thoughts and purposes of the heart (Hebrews 4:12 TAB).

God Alone Is The Perfect Matchmaker
Confession

Isaiah 34:16: Seek ye out of the book of the Lord, and read; no one of these shall fall, none shall want her mate: for my mouth it hath commanded and his spirit it hath gathered them.

Luke 1:37: For with God nothing shall be impossible

Rev. 12:11: And they overcame him by the blood of the Lamb, and by the word of their testimony, and they loved not their lives unto the death.

Jer. 32:17: Oh Lord God; behold, thou hast made the heaven and the earth by thy great power and stretched out arm, and there is nothing too hard for thee.

Matt. 9:29: According to your faith be it unto you.

Eph. 5:17: Wherefore be ye not unwise, but understanding what the will of the Lord is.

Ps. 32:8: I will instruct thee and teach thee in the way which thou shalt go and I will guide thee with mine eye.

Job 14:14: All the days of my appointed time will I wait till my change comes.

Ps. 121:2: My help cometh from the Lord, which made heaven and earth.

Prayer Points

1. I receive my right match in the name of Jesus.

2. I thank God because He alone is the perfect matchmaker.

3. I thank God for empowering me to wait to on my mate.

4. Father, release the man/woman You have preordained as my husband/wife in the name of Jesus.

5. Father, release the divine match You have chosen for my life in the name of Jesus.

6. Father, let it be a person who loves You wholeheartedly, is committed and dedicated to fulfilling Your purpose and destiny on earth.

7. Father, establish our relationship and home in accordance with the Scriptures (Eph. 5:20–28).

8. Father, let all satanic spirits of distractions and hindrances keeping me from meeting my mate be dissolved in the name of Jesus.

9. Father, release your ministering angles to guard and watch over all that concerneth my meeting, my mate, relationship, and marriage.

10. Father, I believe You have created a special man/woman of God for me in the name of Jesus.

11. I stand in the gap and call him/her out of obscurity into my life, in the name of Jesus.

12. I reject the provision of satan's counterfeit spouse by the enemy, in the name of Jesus.

13. I cut off the flow of any inherited marital problems into my life, my mate, and children, in the name of Jesus.

14. Let patience reign in my life until the right person comes, in the name of Jesus.

15. Father, in the name of Jesus, just as Abraham sent his servant to find his son, Issac, a wife, send the Holy Spirit to bring my future wife/husband to him/her in Jesus name.

16. Father, your word has declared that "none shall want their mate; I stand in agreement with your word and purpose for my life."

17. I thank God for His rainbow of unfailing promises; for His Word is yes and amen (2 Cor. 1:20).

18. I reject Satan's counterfeit. I receive God's original today, in the name of Jesus.

19. In the name of Jesus, I submit my own will to receive God's will for my life in Jesus name.

20. No weapon that is formed against my marrying the mate God has chosen for me shall prosper in the name of Jesus.

Part Eight

SPIRITUAL INCOMPATIBILITY

The sons of God saw that the daughters of men were fair, and they took wives of all they desired and chose (Gen 6:2 TAB).

You shall not make marriages with them; your daughter you shall not give to his son nor shall you take his daughter for your son,

For they will turn away your sons from following Me, that they may serve other gods; so will the anger of the Lord be kindled against you and He will destroy you quickly (Deut 7:3–4 TAB).

Ye shall keep my statutes. Thou shalt not let thy cattle gender with a diverse kind: thou shalt not sow thy field with mingled seed: neither shall a garment mingled of linen and woollen come upon thee (Lev. 19: 19 KJV).

Can two walk together, expect they be agreed (Amos 3:3 KJV)?

Do not be unequally yoked with unbelievers (do not make mismated alliances with them or come under a different yoke with them, inconsistent with your faith). For what partnership have right living and right standing with God with iniquity and lawlessness? Or how can light have fellowship with darkness?

What harmony can there be between Christ and Belial (the devil)? Or what has a believer in common with an unbeliever?

What agreement (can there be between) a temple of God and idols? For we are the temple of the living God; even as God said, I will dwell in and with and among them and will walk in and with and among them, and I will be their God, and they shall be My people
(2 Cor. 6:14–16 TAB).

Now I beseech you, brethren, mark them which cause divisions and offences contrary to the doctrine which ye have learned: and avoid them (Rom. 16:17 KJV).

Know ye not that the friendship of the world is enmity with God? Whosoever therefore will be a friend of the world is the enemy of God (James 4:4 KJV).

Incompatible Relationships
Letting Go of Mismated Relationships

A very rich man was in Maon, whose possessions and business were in Carmel. He had 3,000 sheep and 1,000 goats, and he was shearing his sheep in Carmel.

The man's name was Nabal and his wife's name was Abigail; she was a woman of good understanding, and beautiful. But the man was rough and evil in his doings; he was a Calebite (1 Sam. 25: 2–3 TAB).

And he came up and told his father and mother, I saw one of the daughters of the Philistines at Timnah; now get her for me as my wife.

But his father and mother said to him, Is there not a woman among the daughters of your kinsmen or among all our people that you must go to take a wife from the uncircumcised Philistines? And Samson said to his father, Get her for me, for she is all right in my eyes
(Judges 14: 2–3 TAB).

For it came to pass, when Solomon was old, that his

wives turned away his heart after other gods: and his heart was not perfect with the Lord his God, as was the heart of David his father.

For Solomon went after Ashtoreth the goddess of the Zidonians, and after Milcom the abomination of the Ammonites (1 Kings 11: 4–5 KJV).

And Rebekah said to Isaac, I am weary of my life because of the daughters of Heth: if Jacob take a wife of the daughters of Heth, such as these which are of the daughters of the land, what good shall my life do me (Gen 27:46 KJV)?

Incompatibility affects the entire family. The effects are escalated greater when there are additional problems like alcoholism, drugs or hidden deviant sexual behaviors.

Passionate desires and temporal pleasures have and are creating severe problems in our families today. In essence, not only the couple, but the children are hurt; and for some it takes years to heal the hurt, pain, and wounds resulting from such mismated relationships.

Incompatibility has been defined as unable to exist together in harmony; not suited for combination or association: inconsistent (Random House Webster's College Dictionary; Webster's Dictionary and Thesaurus).
There are twelve myths about spiritual incompatibility, which causes many singles to compromise their Christian principles and values; and marry outside the will of God:

- My faith in God is strong enough to carry my mate unto deliverance
- I am strong enough to forbear in love for their salvation and deliverance
- Our love is strong else to make the marriage work
- He is a good provider, that's the main thing- children will make our marriage better
- My church is a praying church- my mate will experience salvation and deliverance
- We love each other

- Marriage will bring about change
- Praying together will bring salvation and deliverance
- My Christian family will pray us through
- God will forgive me
- God understands
- God will see us through this marriage

Single believers, believing, and waiting upon God for their mate knows that you are the main target on satan's incompatibility list. Many unbelievers are discerning and know you love God, are sincere about your walk, and striving to live in righteousness. You are chosen because you are special, royalty and mates in whom the spirit of God lives. Spiritual Incompatibility keeps you in the valley of decision, constantly confronted with choosing to serve and please God's or serving and pleasing your mate.

The scripture declares, what fellowship hath righteousness with unrighteousness? And what communion hath light with darkness (2 Cor 6:14)? The questions are asked in the scripture, what has a believer in common with an unbeliever? In what areas are you compatible? You have acknowledged Jesus as Savior and Lord. The unbeliever is still walking under the influence of the God of this world. You have repented of your sins and have been forgiven. The unbeliever has not repented and is unforgiven.

> What harmony can there be between Christ and Belial (the devil)? Or what has a believer in common with an unbeliever?

> What agreement (can there be between) a temple of God and idols? For we are the temple of the living God; even as God said, I will dwell in and with and among them and will walk in and with and among them, and I will be their God, and they shall be My people
> (2 Cor. 6: 15–16 TAB).

God loves you. He has given you the opportunity to choose; to make the right decision for your life. The scripture declares "let no man say when is tempted, I am tempted of God; for God cannot be tempted with evil, neither tempteth he any man" (James 1:13). Compromising or forfeiting your principles to receive less than God's perfect will for your life, is disobedience unto the Word of God.

Incompatibility will be evident in every facet of the marriage. Decisions will have to be made daily in reference to the marriage, home, family and your personal growth and development. The scripture declares, "Can two walk together, except they be agreed (Amos 3:3)? You are positioning yourself to lose the fellowship or closeness of your walk with God when you compromise your walk for temporal pleasures.

Samson, a mighty man of God, went to Timnath one day and fell in love with one of the daughters of the Philistines (Judg. 19:2). His parents said, "is there never a woman among the daughters of thy brethren, or among all my people that thou goest to take a wife of the uncircumcised Philistines?

The incompatibility problem did not stop with the woman he married in Timnath, but followed him to Gaza. In Gaza, he met a harlot. The scripture declares he loved a woman in the valley of Sorek, whose name was Delilah, whom the lord of Philistines recruited and placed on special assignment (every one of them gave her eleven hundred pieces of silver to entice Samson and find out wherein his great strength lieth. She accepted the offer.

This incompatibility relationship cost him everything; to include his eye sight; breaking his Nazarite vow and flow of God's power in his life and ministry. Delilah made him sleep upon her knees, called for a man, caused him to shave off the seven locks of his head; and began to afflict him, and his strength went from him. Samson told Delilah all his heart. Samson trusted his enemy, got comfortable with the enemy, laid his head on the enemy's lap and enjoyed sleeping with the enemy. The enemy's strategy is subtle. He is keenly aware of what flesh desires and works diligently to fulfill, fleshly passions (Judges 16: 4–30).

This incompatible relationship was these greatest down fall Samson had experienced, eventually causing him death. It caused the spirit of God to depart from him, the Philistines put out his eyes, bound him with fetters of brass, and left him grinding in the prison house (Judges 16: 10–22). The penalty of our sins can cause great tragedy and chaos in our lives.

Incompatibility has caused much unnecessary pain and sufferings for many singles. Many have neglected sound biblical counseling, spiritual nurturing, mentoring and care provided by the family and mature Christian leadership.

> The thief cometh but for to steal, and to kill, and to destroy. I am come that they have life, and that they might have it more abundantly.
>
> And the Lord said, Simon, Simon, behold, Satan hath desired to have you, that he may sift you as wheat:
>
> But I have prayed for thee, that thy faith fail not: and when thou art converted, strengthen thy brethren (Luke 22: 31–32 KJV).

The scripture declares, "he who finds a wife, findeth a good thing, and obtaineth favour of the Lord" (Prov 18:22). Singles who are trying creative ways to meet and marry their mate, from speed dating, hiring matchmakers, your friends and others to fulfill God's plan in your life- are missing the mark, erring in the faith and piercing themselves with many sorrows (1 Tim 6: 10). Men are hunters, and are said to enjoy the thrill of hunting for their prey. Many singles wearing the look of desperation and over anxiousness on their face. They are frightening, God fearing, sincere, committed, dedicated men away. Women and men who are after God's heart are seeking those who are committed and like-minded in the faith (Phil. 2:2).

Incompatibile relationships result from restlessness, boredom, and agitation. The scripture declares, "they that wait upon the Lord shall renew their strength; they shall mount up with wings as eagles; they shall run, and not be weary; and they shall walk, and not faint (Isa. 40:41).

Today, countless Christian singles are seeking, looking, scanning internet websites, and cybersurfing daily in search of the perfect mate or their soul mate; as it is referred to in the twenty first century. Many singles are obviously in the wrong place, at the wrong time, and doing the wrong thing. They have left the scriptural principles of God's purpose, plan, and destiny for their life, and have willfully planned or established their own life destiny or legacy for their lives.

The scriptures explicitly focus our mindset in the area of spiritual compatibility; keeping us in check that spiritual compatibility is the first principle in choosing your mate or "Heaven's Mate." Compatibility for Christians should always be in line with God's Word. Any deviation from the principles and guidelines of the scriptures positions Christians to miss the mark or error during the selection process. Jesus the author and finisher of our faith should be the center and Lord of the relationship or decision. The scriptures and experience in marriage have proven that "marriage still takes three." Without Jesus as the center of our relationship, success and true fulfillment is void in the marriage.

In searching for the chosen mate or soul mate, God alone chooses the time and the seasons. When we patiently, humbly, and diligently learn to wait upon him, we will reap the rewards of patience and endurance.

Spiritual incompatibility marriage to an unbeliever means first of all, our spiritual fellowship is out of sync (darkness vs. light); we don't share the same faith; are not liked minded in the faith; are not on one accord; are not of one mind, and cannot walk in the spirit or power of agreement.

Can two walk together except they be agreed (Amos 3:3)?

Many Christians have purposely joined or yoked themselves up to an unbeliever, compromising the principles of the Word of God with the promise that their mate will walk with God. Spiritual deliverance is a process; it is progressive and takes time.

Marrying an unbeliever is a mismated joining or alliance. Your choice of deliverance is "Jesus is the Way," and theirs is, "leave my demonic influence or demons alone." Right living and right standing with God is your lifestyle- iniquity and lawlessness is theirs.

But ye shall destroy their altars, break their images, and cut down their groves. We are called to destroy the works of the devil. The scripture declares, "for this purpose the son of man was manifested that He might destroy the works of the devil" (1 John 3:8).

Singles who are determined to wait upon the Lord for the mate He has chosen, are positioned for victory, success and fulfillment of their petition. The scripture declares, "He watcheth over His word to perform it (Ezek. 37:14). The following points will strengthen and assist you in remaining focused during your journey.

- Sincerely submit your life and destiny unto the Lord
- Develop your prayer life
- Develop your faith through studying, meditating and confessing the word of God
- Fast and pray
- Let God lead and guide you daily

- Learn to listen and obey the voice of God
- Learn to trust the three-fold confirmation of God
- Learn to be anxious for nothing- be patience
- Dating is not scriptural- let the Holy Spirit lead you according to His Word
- Be sincere and honest
- Communicate honest and forth right
- Do not compromise sound Christian principles/ standards/ values
- Develop effective communication
- Like-mindedness in the faith is determined through the Holy Spirit, His word and faith based communication
- Yield, surrender, submit to the Holy Spirit to assist you in developing discipline to maintain your walk with God and remain steadfast in the faith.
- Discernment is one of the gifts of the spirit- flow in it.

Part Nine

MARRIAGE DELAYS/ LATENESS/ HINDRANCES

Seek ye out of the book of the Lord, and read: no one of these shall fail, none shall want her mate: for my mouth it hath commanded, and His spirit it hath gathered them (Isa. 34:16 KJV).

For the vision is yet for an appointed time, but at the end it shall speak, and not lie: though it tarry, wait for it; because it will surely come, it will not tarry (Hab. 2:3 KJV).

Nevertheless, David took the stronghold of Zion, that is the City of David (2 Sam. 4:7 KJV).

Come down from your glory, you inhabitants of the Daughter of Dibon, and sit on the ground among the thirsty! For the destroyer of Moab is advancing against you, he will destroy your strongholds (Jer. 48:18 TAB).

For the weapon of our warfare are not physical (weapons of flesh and blood), but they are mighty before God for the overthrow and destruction of strongholds (2 Cor. 10:4 TAB),

For we wrestle not against flesh and blood, but against principalities, against powers, against the rulers of darkness of this world, against spiritual wickedness in high place (Eph 6:2 KJV).

Marriage Delays / Lateness / Hindrances

Seek ye out of the book of the Lord, and read: no one of these shall fail, none shall want her mate: for my mouth it hath commanded and His spirit it hath gathered them (Isa. 34:16 KJV).

Come down from your glory, you inhabitants of the Daughter of Dibon, and sit on the ground among the thirsty! For the destroyer of Moab is advancing against you, he will destroy your strongholds (Jer. 48:18 TAB).

For the weapons of our warfare are not physical (weapons of flesh and blood), but they are mighty before God for the overthrow and destruction of strongholds (2 Cor. 10:4 TAB),

For we wrestle not against flesh and blood, but against principalities, against powers, against the rulers of darkness of this world, against spiritual wickedness in high place (Eph 6:12 KJV).

The scripture declares when Zion travailed, the sons and daughters of God came forth. Many unmarried singles desiring to marry are concerned about the apparent lateness or delay in their time for marriage. This has concerned many to the extent of allowing relatives, friends, believers, and others to mislead or misguide them in the faith; thinking God has forgotten or has not heard their prayer.

It is comforting to know that the God we serve cannot lie. He not only watcheth over His word to perform it, but His Word shall not return unto Him void, but it shall accomplish that which He please, and prosper in the thing where unto He send it (Isa. 55:11). Believers who are confident, know that His word has promised us that He will never leave us, nor forsake us. He is with us always even unto the end of time (Heb. 13:5).

His destiny and purpose for our lives to include marriage has not changed. God instituted marriage and performed the first wedding ceremony in Genesis chapter 2. He has a mate for all who would dare believe and stand upon His Word. Even if you think you have missed His perfect will for your life, His plans and purpose remains the same.

If you believe you have opened the door to the enemy through the lust of the eyes, lust of the flesh and pride of life, ask God's for forgiveness; then forgive yourself. God's mercy endures forever. Sincerely ask God to position you to unseat the strong-man that may have, and is holding you captive—delaying the release of your mate. If the strong-man has held you captive for years, and you have allowed fear, doubt, and unbelief to bind you further, remember to stand steadfastly upon the scripture, which declares "for this purpose, the son of man was manifested, that he might destroy the works of the devil (1 John 3:8). The anointing destroys the yoke (strongholds of the devil) (Isa. 10:27).

Singles who are determined to destroy the works of satan must realize, following His will does not come without a price. You must arise and determine within yourself that you will "not only believe God to meet your mate, but that the both of you will walk hand- in- hand, and fulfill His destiny and purpose on earth together. He is waiting for you to proclaim His Word- "this is the victory that overcometh the world, even our faith," and "fight the good fight of faith" (2 Tim 4:7).

Delays in marriage can come as a result of many reasons- from sin to divine timing. However, know of a certainty, God has not forgotten you. Have you forgotten and taken your eyes off the plans God has for you? Have you allowed your self-esteem to hit an all time low; allowing self pity, fear, rejection, and pride to lock you into "believing you will never get married; no one wants to marry you, you are too old to marry, and you are not marriage material"? Arise today in the inward man, and be renewed in the spirit of your mind, knowing that "there is nothing to hard for God" (Gen. 18:14). Marriage for you can and will bring a flow of love many have lost, refusing to nurture and minister unto each other daily the precious gift God has given unto them.

The book of Ecclesiastes 3:11 declares that God makes all things beautiful in time. He will reverse all the works of satan, and draw you and your mate unto each other (Isa. 34:16). His timing is perfect. Look unto Him who has power to hasten His Word to bring your marriage into manifestation and perform all that He has promised (Jeremiah 1:12). Declare unto yourself in faith and confidence in the Word of God; "the best is yet to come." Declare as King David when he received revelations that he had carried the Ark of the Covenant wrong, resulting in the death of one of the sons of God. In hearing of the overflow of blessings in Obededom's house, he told his wife Michal who observed him dancing in the spirit and under the anointing (paraphrased,) "you haven't seen nothing yet," I am going to dance even more than this (2 Sam. 6: 20–23).

Delays and lateness in marriage enables the processing of God to release an even greater deliverance and cultivation of character and integrity in your life. Your completeness in Him has positioned you for His extreme makeover, manifesting more of the character of God in your personal walk and fulfillment of His destiny and purpose in your life.

Part Ten
God's Plan For Marriage

And the Lord God said, It is not good for the man to be alone; I'll make him a helper, a companion (Gen. 2:18 MSG).

So God formed from the dirt of the ground all the animals of the field and all the birds of the air. He brought them to the man to see what he would name them. Whatever the man called each living creature, that was its name (Gen. 2:18–19 MSG).

Honor marriage, and guard the sacredness of sexual intimacy between wife and husband. God draws a firm line against casual and illicit sex. (Heb. 13:4 MSG)

And said, for this cause shall a man leave his father and mother, and shall cleave to his wife: and they twain shall be one flesh (Matt. 19:5 KJV).

Wherefore they are no more twain, but one flesh. What therefore God hath joined together let not man put asunder (Matt. 19:6 KJV)

Marriage Is A Gift
Principles Of Marriage

Marriage is a covenant, a vow made unto God and the partner not only to love, but also to be faithful and to endure in this lifelong exclusive relationship.

And said, For this cause shall a man leave father and

> mother, and shall cleave to his wife: and they twain shall be one flesh.
>
> Wherefore they are no more twain, but one flesh. What therefore God hath joined together, let not man put asunder (Matt. 19:6 TAB).

Marriage is the oldest relationship in the world, established by a sovereign Creator in the Garden of Eden. In that beautiful, perfect setting, God organized the home, and blessed roles and responsibilities to Adam and Eve.

Adam was to be the provider ("to tend" the garden), the protector ("and keep" the garden), and the leader ("the Lord commanded the man"). His assigned occupation was to care for the garden and those in it (Gen. 2:15–17). This demanded the type of servant leadership emulated by Jesus (Eph. 5:21; 23).

The woman had several responsibilities. She was to be a "helper" (Gen. 2:18), a comforter, (Gen. 24:67) and an encourager (Prov. 31:12). Eve was Adam's partner for carrying out God's purpose to multiply and replenish the earth (Gen. 1:28). She was created to be his closest earthly companion, relieving his loneliness (Gen. 2:18).

When sin entered the world, chaos followed. God's plan did not change, but was distorted by the sinful choices of Adam and Eve and their descendants. God let Adam and Eve choose to sin, but He did not let them choose sin's consequences (Gen. 3:10). They were cast out of their idyllic home with this foretelling. Adam's work became difficult he would have to contend with thorns and thistles (Gen. 3:17–18), and Eve would suffer pain in childbirth (Gen. 3:10). Adam, Eve, and their posterity would have spiritual warfare until the end of time.

Despite the failure of Adam and Eve, God's principles for marriage have remained the same. According to their God-defined roles, husbands are to use their God given authority to provide, to protect, and to love (Gen. 2:15–17; Eph. 5:25). Wives are to help their husbands and submit to their God- directed leadership (Gen. 2:18; Eph. 5:23–24). Husbands and wives can ignore God's program for the home, but when a spiritual principle is violated, division is the result. They can seek to redefine God's plan according to heir own desires and circumstances, but ultimately human wisdom cannot compete with an all- wise God. There can be no unity, no contentment, and no peace- only a house divided- in a marriage that defies God's principles. Husbands and wives are challenged to spend time, energy, and creatively looking for ways to conform to divinely directed leadership and Christ like submission.

Marriage Joins Two People In The Circle Of Its Love

Marriage is a commitment to life,
the best that two people can find and bring out in each other.
It offers opportunities for sharing and growth
that no other relationship can equal.
It is a physical and an emotional joining that is promised for a lifetime.

Within the circle of its love,
marriage encompasses all of life's most important relationships.
A wife and a husband are each other's best friend,
confidant, lover, teacher, listener, and critic.
And there may come times when one partner is heartbroken or ailing,
and the love of the other may resemble
the tender caring of a parent or child.

Marriage deepens and enriches every facet of life.
Happiness is fuller, memories are fresher,
commitment is stronger, even anger is felt more strongly,
and passes away more quickly.

Marriage understands and forgives the mistakes life
is unable to avoid. It encourages and nurtures new life,
new experiences, new ways of expressing
a love that is deeper than life.

When two people pledge their love and care for each other in marriage,
they create a spirit unique unto themselves which binds them closer
than any spoken or written words.
Marriage is a promise, a potential made in the hearts of two people
who love each other and takes a lifetime to fulfill.

❧

Edmund O'Neill

Marriage Is A Covenant

Now therefore swear unto me here by God that thou will not deal falsely with me, nor with my son, nor with my son's son, but according to the kindness that I have done unto thee, thou shalt do unto me, and to the land wherein thou hast sojourned (Gen. 21:23 KJV).

> Therefore, a man shall leave his father and his mother and shall cleave unto his wife and they shall be one flesh (Gen. 2:24 KJV).

> Wherefore he called that place Beer-sheba: because there they swore both of them (Gen. 21:31 KJV).

> Marriage is a covenant. The book of Malachi 21:14 states, "She is thy companion and the wife of thy covenant." Genesis 15 gives a beautiful picture of the marriage covenant. God's confirmation with Abraham was divided into five parts.

- God reminded Abram of His faithfulness in the past (v. 7)
- God gave a sign to confirm His promise (v. 8–12)
- God specified the provisions of the covenant (v. 13–16)
- God ratified the covenant by a divine appearance (v. 17)
- God concluded the covenant with an unconditional promise (v. 18)

When God made a covenant with Abraham, the father of all the faithful, God commanded circumcision as a sign of that faith relationship (Gen. 17:11). This act of obedience also represented the putting away of evil (Deut. 10:16; Jer. 4:4). Because God's covenant promises to Abraham were fully realized by Jesus Christ, the apostle Paul taught that every Christian, both male and female is circumcised, not by human hands, but in Christ. The sinful nature is replaced by Christ's presence.

The Marriage Covenant Is Divided Into Three Parts:

- To leave the father and mother, a reference to the wedding ceremony or time of public commitment.
- To be joined, suggesting tender affection and faithful commitment in a permanent relationship of growing love.
- To "become one flesh" in physical union, which notes the deepest and most exclusive intimacy.

Marriage
A Picture Of Unity

So by whatever (appeal to you there is in our mutual dwelling in Christ by whatever) strengthening and consoling and encouraging (our relationship) in Him (affords) by whatever persuasive incentive (we share) and by whatever depth of affection and compassionate sympathy.

Fill up and complete my joy by living in harmony and being of the same mind and one in purpose, having the same love, being in full accord and of one harmonious mind and intention (Phil. 2:1–2 TAB).

Wives, be subject (be submissive and adapt yourselves) to your own husbands as a service to the Lord.

For the husband is head of the wife as Christ is the Head of the Church, Himself the Savior of (His) body (Eph. 5:22–23 TAB).

In marriage, two hearts are grafted together, making them dependent upon one another for life. This is depicted in John 15, with Jesus as the vine and believers as the branches. Through the infilling of the Holy Spirit and His control in the life of both partners, this picture of marriage and the parallel relationship of Christ and His bride come into focus. The Holy Spirit fills and fulfills both.

Throughout scripture, the marriage union is a metaphor or picture of the relationship between God and His people. In the Old Testament, Israel is pictured as the wife of Yahweh. When Israel became unfaithful and worshipped other gods, she was described as a harlot (Jer. 3:11; Ezek. 23). Her spiritual adultery became so despicable in God's sight that He issued a writing of divorcement (Jer. 3:8). Actually, this was a separation, as God and His great love for His chosen people could not bear to cut off Israel without a promise of renewal (Hos. 2:14–20; 5:15).

The whole focus and course of life is changed both by marriage and a personal experience with Jesus Christ. Marriage and becoming a child of God both demands death to self, accountability unto God and to each other. A wife or husband cannot be faithful to more than one partner, as a Christian cannot serve any other God. Believers should have no hesitation in giving themselves in totality unto God because of His great love, care, provision and the high price He paid for us (I Pet. 1:18, 19).

> Seek ye out of the book of the Lord and read: No one of these shall fall, None Shall Want Her Mate; for my mouth it hath commanded and His spirit it hath gathered them (Isaiah 34:16 KJV).

> Many of the handmaidens, daughters of Zion, and sons and brothers in the faith have not learned how to wait upon God for their mate. God's Word is backed by His authority and power, and cannot return unto Him void. The God we serve cannot lie. The dreams, visions, and Word He has spoken concerning us will surely come to pass.

> He instituted the first marriage ceremony in Genesis, chapter two.

> And the Lord God said, It is not good that the man should be alone; I will make him an help mate for him.

> And out of the ground the Lord God formed every beast of the field, and every fowl of the air, and brought them unto Adam to see what he would call them, and whatsoever Adam called every living creature, that was the name thereof.

> And Adam gave names to all the cattle, and to the fowl of the air, and to every beast of the field, but for Adam, there was not found a help mate for him
>
> And the Lord caused a deep sleep to fall upon Adam, and he slept; and He took one of his ribs, and closed up the flesh instead thereof; And the rib, which the Lord God had taken from man, made He a woman, and brought her unto the man.
>
> And Adams said, This is now bone of my bones, and flesh of my flesh, she shall be called woman, because she was taken out of man
>
> Therefore shall a man leave his father and his mother, and shall cleave unto his wife: and they shall be one flesh (Gen. 2:18–22 KJV).

God's principle for relationships, marriages, and the home establishes the foundation and road map for developing and maintaining healthy Christ centered families and examples from generation unto generation.

The Word of God is the divine blueprint and healthiest guideline for Christians to model their day-to-day living and examples for living. Christians are admonished to teach, train, and instruct their children the way in which they should live.

Learning to examine our walk with God, according to the principles of His word, enables us to live the abundant life outlined in the scriptures. The scripture declares He came that we might have life and have it more abundantly (John 10:10).

There are many women today with the spirit and attitude of Vashti, the Queen (Esther. 1:9–22). She experienced a quick and rude awakening concerning her decision not to honor the king's request and appear before the king, as was the custom for the queen. She chose to publicly dishonor and humiliate her husband. If you truly and honestly love your spouse, you will seek ways to compliment him/her, and be determined to make your marriage work, dismissing all the works of the enemy working against your relationship. The scriptures declare "love is as strong as death" . . . only death can break the power of love.

Queen Vashti's behavior was inappropriate and disrespectful to her husband. Love chooses to forgive, apologize, and repent quickly. Love is priceless and a gift from God. Our prayers should be to ask God to teach us how to love our spouse and meet his/her needs (emotional, financial, material, physical and spiritual).

Queen Vashti's disrespect, dishonor, and lack of submission unto the king caused her to forfeit her royal position. The king sent out a royal commandment, and had it written among the laws of the Persians and the Medes, that Queen Vashti not be allowed to come any more before King Abasuerus; and let the king give her royal estate unto another that was better than she.

The king sent letters unto all the king's provinces and to every man to rule his own house.

God's principles and guidelines for relationships, marriages, and the home, establishes the foundation and road map for developing and maintaining healthy Christian homes, relationships, and marriages, from generation to generation.

Contentment And Marriage

Let your conversation be without covetousness; And be content with such things as ye have: for he hath said, I will never leave thee, nor forsake thee
(Heb. 13:5 Scofield Ref.).

Not that I speak in respect of want: for I have learned in whatsoever state I am, therewith to be content
(Phil. 4:11 KJV).

Remove far from me vanity and lies: give me neither poverty nor riches; feed me with food convenient for me. Lest I be full and deny thee, and say, who is the Lord? Or lest I be poor and steal, and take the name of my God in vain (Prov. 30:8–9 Scofield Ref).

But godliness with contentment is great gain.

For we brought nothing into this world, and it is certain we can carry nothing out.

And having food and raiment let us therewith be content
(1 Tim. 6:6–8 KJV).

Contentment has been defined as "sufficiency," and is so rendered in II Cor. 9:8. It is the disposition of mind through grace, in which one is independent of envious circumstances (Phil. 4:11), so as not to be moved by envy (James 3:16), anxiety, and repining (I Cor. 10:10).

Contentment is the ultimate acceptance of yourself, your surroundings, your past, and your future. Finding contentment for believers should be effortless. Jesus has paid the price for our sin and has given us a secure future of eternity in His presence, free of all pain and sorrow (Eph. 2:8- 9; Rev. 21:4). The challenges, tests, and trials we experience now should be viewed in light of an eternity to be spent with the Savior (Rev. 21:7). God provided a way for you to be rescued from an eternity in hell. He is sufficient to meet our needs in this world that He created (Phil. 4: 13- 19).

Reaching this blessed state of contentment is not an easy task. Satisfaction when you have very real unmet needs, freedom from wrong when you have overwhelming concern, patience in letting God work when pressures abound–seem like impossible dreams. But the peace of God that surpasses all understanding shall keep your hearts and minds through Jesus Christ. Happiness, despite headaches caused by the past, and in the midst of tragedies experienced in the present, is based on a promise trusted for the future. It is not merely a human pursuit, but demands spiritual resources only found in the indwelling Holy Spirit.

God chose not to give us contentment as a gift. He chose rather to teach us to be content as we allow Him to be the ruler in our life. Contentment is learned (Phil. 4:11). As you trust God's gifts to be sufficient and His assignments to be appropriate, you can accept the way you look, the means you have been given, the family in which you are living, the struggles through which you have gone, the job you have, and be content and fulfilled in all (II Cor. 3:5–6; 12:9).

Job humbly positioned himself in faith during times of great trials and testings. He said, "All the days of my appointed time will I wait till my change come" (Job 14:14). He trusted that God had given him everything he needed for that moment in time. We must learn to be content with family, surroundings, job, current state, and ourselves. As we continue to trust God, we can be content as we pursue His goals for our life, marriage, children, family and ministry.

Confidence: Inward Peace

For the Lord shall be thy confidence, and shall keep thy foot from being taken (Prov. 3:26 KJV).

It is better to trust and take refuge in the Lord than to put confidence in man (Ps. 118:8 TAB)

Confidence in an unfaithful man in time of trouble is like a broken tooth, or a foot out of joint (Prov. 25:19 TAB).

For thus saith the Lord God, the Holy One of Israel; in returning and rest shall ye be saved; in quietness and in confidence shall be your strength; any ye would not (Isa. 30:15 KJV).

Cast not away therefore your confidence, which hath great recompense of reward (Heb. 10:35 KJV).

In the Old Testament, the words "confidence" and "assurance" are different forms of the same Hebrew word. Isaiah adds the concept of quietness. In quietness and confidence (Isa. 30:15 KJV) shall be our strength. Isaiah tells us that "quietness and assurance" are the effects of righteousness (Isa. 32:17 KJV). In our Christian walk, we must learn through daily walking by faith and not by sight, that standing and believing firmly in the Word of God is a great source of inner peace, confidence, and joy in Him.

Assurance is not based on optimism about your own abilities. Rather it is an inward peace based on God's righteous work in you. Such confidence is not self-confidence, for that would be false security and reliance on something unreliable. The scripture declares that those who have confidence in their own strength, beauty, or righteousness are to be considered fools (Prov. 28:26).

True confidence–rooted in the Lord's capabilities and His relationship with His children–is a quiet strength that brings great reward and a lasting security that is fully satisfying.

In man's search for security and safety in today's world, he has learned to place confidence and assurance in uncertain wealth, this world's system, and in everything but the Word of God. The word confidence has been defined by Webster as "a feeling of self assurance; a feeling of trust in a person; reliance."

We are blessed as believers to know with all confidence and assurance that we have access, with boldness and confidence by faith in Him, and all things in heaven and on earth (Eph. 3:12). We are taught not to put our confidence in an unfaithful man or woman, but in Christ Jesus.

The essence of faith, reliance, and trust is confidence in Christ through His word; knowing that what He has promised, He shall surely bring to pass.

The Foundation

> At the beginning you existed and laid the foundations of the earth; the heavens are the work of your hands (Ps. 102:25 TAB).

> You laid the foundations of the earth, that it should not be moved forever (Ps. 104:5 TAB).

> When He gave to the sea its limit and His decree that the waters should not transgress (across the boundaries set by) His command, when He appointed the foundations of the earth (Prov. 8:29 TAB).

> Therefore shall a man leave his father and his mother, and shall cleave unto his wife; and they shall be one flesh (Gen. 2:24 KJV).

> For this cause shall a man leave his father and mother, and shall be joined unto his wife, and they two shall be one flesh (Eph. 5:31 KJV).

> And said, for this cause shall a man leave father and mother, and shall cleave to his wife and they twain shall be one flesh

> Wherefore they are no more twain, but one flesh. What therefore God hath joined together; let not man put asunder (Matt. 19: 5–6 KJV).

Marriage was designed by God, before there was any creative activity, to be a picture of His own relationship with His people. The fall introduced sin, and the relationship between husbands and wives was formed. Loving servant headship was replaced by tyranny and a desire for power, or by an indifference and unwillingness to offer spiritual leadership.

Countless people have gone forth to live their lives full of blind ambitions, desires, passions, visions, and dreams; essentially, they forget the Lord, their maker. To proceed in life pursuing the fulfillment of life's ambitions and desires without Jesus–the sure foundation - is equivalent to a house without a sure foundation that stretched forth the heavens, and laid the foundations of the earth (Isa. 51:13 KJV). In his instructions to the Corinthians Church, Paul stated as a wise master builder, he laid the foundation and let every man take heed how he buildeth thereupon (2 Cor. 3:10–11). Life experiences, challenges, and pursuits, reveal the quality of building materials, or foundation; if it is gold, silver, precious stones, wood, hay or stubble.

The Lord in the beginning laid the foundation of the earth because He knew that an earth without a foundation, specifically a solid foundation, cannot stand. It is empty and is a hull, whose builder and maker is not God. It is useless, fruitless and is destined to fail when God is not the Savior and Lord of the house. Man, in his wisdom, knowledge, and intellect, believes that "he can make it without God," and thinks he is in himself "his god." He has no need for God in his lifestyle. Jesus is the author and finisher of our faith. He is the Alpha and Omega, and all things that are made are made by Him. He sees the beginning and ending of all things, so how can the clay or creature say, "That's all right Jesus, I got it? Stand back; I know what I am doing." Indeed, the creature, like many today, has missed the mark. No house, lifestyle, or destiny can be successful without the master builder. Jesus alone has the blueprint for the house. He created the blueprint, and the heavens are the works of His hands. Can the house building process proceed without seeking instructions? The blueprints for the works are of His foreknowledge and plan.

The scripture declares that every wise woman buildeth her house; but the foolish plucketh it down with her own hands (Prov. 14:1). Meaningful, strong relationships must transcend the earth's temporal things. The foundation for meaningful relationships and the marriages is built upon the foundation of gold, silver, and precious stones- meaning the Word of God, faith, with Jesus being the Chief Cornerstone. This foundation will endure the test of time and endure until death do us part (Matt. 19:6).

Our prayers should be to ask God to teach us how to love our spouse and meet his/her needs (emotional, financial, material, physical and spiritual). We should also minister to each other according to knowledge of God's Word, and not according to this world's wisdom, man's fantasies, marriage solutions, and creative strategies. The wisdom of God that is from above is first pure, then peaceable, gentle, easy to be entreated, full of mercy and good fruits, without partiality, and without hypocrisy. And the fruit of righteousness is sown in peace of them that make peace (James 3:17–18).

> "If the foundation be destroyed, what can the righteous do (Ps. 11:3 KJV)?"

In architecture, the foundation is the most important part of a building. This is the part on which the whole building will rest. It has to be solid. The height of the building is determined by the foundation.

Life's accomplishments depend on the type of foundation we have. The ability to read is the foundation for further education. Our further education and graduation cannot be accomplished if we are illiterate.

During our developmental years, many of us did not experience the effect of a structured home environment, quality family life, time, or a foundation that would position us for success or a healthy lifestyle. The lack of foundation in many lives limits one to experience success in life. A well balanced; healthy home positions us to live a happy, joyous and fulfilled life during our Christian walk.

Believers are blessed and fortunate to have the good news of the gospel, knowing that our foundation is Christ. An imperfect foundation, or the lack thereof, can be developed, established, and corrected. The Word of God is profitable for all things. It is profitable for doctrine, reproof, correction, and for instruction in righteousness; that the woman/man of God may be perfect, thoroughly furnished unto all good works (2 Tim. 3:16).

> "Set me as a seal upon thine heart, as a seal upon thine arm; for love is as strong as death; Jealousy is cruel as the grave: the coals thereof are coals of fire which hath a most vehement flame. Many waters cannot quench love,

neither can the floods drown it; if a man were to give all the substance of his house for love, it would be utterly contemned (Song. 8:6–7 TAB).

Love is as strong as death . . . only death can break the power of love. Many waters cannot quench love . . . No matter how deep or turbulent the waters of tribulation and affliction are, they cannot drown love (Isaiah 43:2). Neither can the floods of crisis drown love . . . no disaster or satanic storm can destroy true love.

Love cannot be bought. Love is unconditional and it is priceless. It is a gift from God. The love of God is shed abroad in our hearts by the Holy Spirit, which is given unto us (Rom. 5:5).

- The Power of Love for Your Spouse
- Stir/motivate you to pray without ceasing
- Intercede for your spouse
- Pray with a heart of love
- Wise and understanding heart
- The Lord teach you how to love your spouse
- The Lord teach you how to meet his/her (emotional, material, physical and spiritual) needs

Marriage Reconciliation/Restoration

The hand of the Lord was upon me, and carried me out in the spirit of the Lord, and set me down in the midst of the valley which was full of bones.

And caused me to pass by them round about; and, behold, there were very many in the open "valley;" and, lo, they were very dry.

And he said unto me, Son of man can these bones live? And I answered, O Lord God, thou knowest.

> Again He said unto me, Prophesy upon these bones, and say unto them, O ye dry bones, hear the word of the Lord.
>
> Thus saith the Lord unto these bones; Behold, I will cause breath to enter into you, and ye shall live:
>
> And I will lay sinews upon you, and will bring up flesh upon you, and cover you with skin, and put breath in you, and ye shall live; and ye shall know that I am the Lord.
>
> So I prophesied as I was commanded; and as I prophesied, there was a noise, and behold a shaking, and the bones came together bone to his bone.
>
> And when I beheld, lo, the sinews and the flesh came upon them, and the skin covered them above; but there was no breath in them.
>
> Then said He unto me, Prophesy unto the wind, prophesy, son of man, and say to the wind, Thus saith the Lord God; Come from the four winds, O breath, and breathe upon these slain, that they may live.
>
> So I prophesied as He commanded me, and the breath came into them, and they lived, and stood up upon their feet, an exceeding great army (Ezek. 37:1–10 KJV).

The Word of God declares, "for with God nothing shall be impossible (Lk. 1:37)." Our God knows no impossibility. The word impossibility is not in His vocabulary. Sarah was asked the question by the angel "Is anything too hard for the Lord (Gen. 18:14)?"

Is anything too hard for the Lord? Is it impossible for God to restore your marriage? Is it impossible for God to restore the love, joy, and happiness you experienced when you first met? Is it impossible for God to heal, reconcile, and restore your marriage? The power of prayer, when embarked upon without ceasing, will call life into dead things, and call your marriage back to life.

The enemy has driven countless husbands and wives out of their homes and marriages, leaving them out of the will of God, and living without their God ordained mate. Our God turns hopeless circumstances around! As we surrender and yield unto Him with all prayer and supplications, He steps into our situation and restores the love between our spouse and us. Jesus is the resurrection and the life. He is the life within us. Cannot He restore broken marriages? Cannot He reunite the heart, ignite the fire, and let His love permeate in our heart? God specializes in "doing the impossible." He specializes in "making impossibilities possible."

Jesus said unto her, I am the resurrection, and the life, he that believeth in me, though he were dead, yet shall he live (John 11:25 KJV).

God is powerful and specializes in "making all things possible." He resurrected the dead womb, body, and fertility of a ninety nine year old woman. He strengthened and empowered an old body to conceive and bring forth a healthy son to the glory of God.

The Word of God empowered, overshadowed, and elevated Sarah's mindset until she laughed within herself, saying, "after I am waxed old, shall I have pleasure, my lord being old also" (Gen. 18:12 KJV)? The angel of the Lord spoke the Word of God to Sarah, and asked her a question. "Is there anything too hard for the Lord?" "At the appointed time I will return unto thee, according to the time of life, and Sarah shall have a son" (Gen. 18:14).

Life's trials, tests, circumstances, negative voices, environments, television programs, and music have disillusioned many. They have caused many to live a life of loneliness, bitterness, frustration, anxiety, and unnecessary suffering. He is the Lord God who healeth us of all of our infirmities, problems and all that concerneth us. Learn to trust, obey, and follow Him.

God Makes Everything Beautiful
"Beautiful House But Not A Home"

And the beauty of the Lord our God be upon us: and establish thou the work of our hands upon us; yea, the work of our hands establish thou it (Ps. 90:17 KJV).

O worship the Lord in the beauty of holiness: fear before him, all the earth (Ps. 96:9 KJV).

> For the Lord taketh pleasure in his people: he will beautify the meek with salvation (Ps. 149:4 KJV).

> He hath made everything beautiful in his time: also he hath set the world in thine heart, so that no man can find out the work that God maketh from the beginning to the end (Eccl 3:11).

> To appoint unto them that mourn in Zion, to give them beauty for ashes, the oil of joy for mourning, the garment of praise for the spirit of heaviness, that they might be called trees of righteousness, the planting of the Lord, that he might be glorified (Isa. 61:3 KJV).

> Awake, Awake, put on thy strength, O Zion; put on thy beautiful garments, O Jerusalem, the holy city, for henceforth there shall no more come into thee, the uncircumcised and the unclean (Isa. 52:1 KJV).

Beautiful Houses

Furniture, no one can set on, unoccupied rooms not lived in, unslept in beds, miserable bedrooms, and kitchens that are not enjoyed by the owners.

There is a law in musical tone, which says, "two instruments tuned to the same pitch are in tune with each other." A similar rule in mathematics, "two quantities equal to the same quantity are equal to each other."

> We love Him, because He first loved us (1 John 4: 19 TAB).

Two people in tune with God are in tune with each other. Two people in love with Christ have love for each other (1 John 4:19 TAB).

> Many, O Lord my God, are thy wonderful works which thou hast done, and thy thoughts which are to us- ward: they cannot be reckoned up in order unto thee; if I would

declare and speak of them, they are more than can be numbered (Ps. 40:5 KJV).

The key to spiritual satisfaction is being "in right standing with God." This happens when we are in the center of God's will, abiding in Him, and His Word abiding within us. It is when God's riches become our riches. When a proper relationship has been restored between us and God, then, and only then does true happiness, contentment, and peace of mind become a natural outgrowth of that restored relationship.

Discovering That Worldly Lusts Do Not Satisfy

They shall be abundantly satisfied with the fatness of thy house, and thou shalt make them drink of the river of thy pleasures.

For with thee is the fountain of life: in thy light shall we see light.

O continue the lovingkindness unto them that know thee and thy righteousness to the upright in heart
(Ps. 36: 8–10 KJV).

The trouble with most of us is that we made happiness our goal, instead of aiming at something higher, loftier, and nobler. Unhappiness is like pain–it is only the effect of an underlying cause. Pain cannot be relieved until the cause is removed. Pain and disease go together. Disease is the cause and pain is the effect.

Oh that thou wouldest rend the heavens, that thou wouldest come down, that the mountain might flow down at thy presence (Isaiah 64:1 KJV).

We are partakers of all God's heavenly blessings. The scripture declares, that God has blessed His children with all spiritual blessings in the heavenly places in Christ (Eph. 1:3).

An open heaven enables us to receive the breakthroughs we need in our daily lives. When the heavens open, the angels of God will begin to descend and ascend, bringing multiple blessings for the saints. These blessings include favor, power, promotion, breakthroughs, joy, peace, happiness, and joy in the Holy Spirit.

Sure Foundation

Therefore, thus says the Lord God, Behold, I am laying in Zion for a foundation a Stone, a tested Stone, a precious Cornerstone of sure foundation; he who believes (trusts in, relies on, and adheres to that Stone) will not be ashamed or give way or hasten away (in sudden panic) (Isa. 28:16 TAB).

But no weapon that is formed against you shall prosper, and every tongue that shall rise against you in judgment you shall show to be in the wrong. This (peace, righteousness, security, triumph over opposition) is the heritage of the servants of the Lord (those in whom the ideal servant of the Lord is reproduced); this is righteousness or the vindication which they obtain from Me (this is that which I impart to them as their justification) says the Lord (Isa. 54:17 TAB).

The scripture teaches us the difference between the wise and foolish builders in the parable of the house built on the rock (Matt. 7:24–27). It teaches that whosoever heareth the Word and doeth them, He would liken him unto a wise man which built his house upon a rock. The man dug deep and laid his foundation on a rock. When the rain descended, and the floods came, and the winds blew and beat upon that house, and it fell not; because it was founded upon a rock. The second man is like a foolish man who built his house upon the sand. He that heareth and doeth not is like a foolish man that without a foundation, built his house upon the sand. The rain descended, and the floods came, and the winds blew, and beat vehemently upon that house. It fell, and great was the fall of it. The two foundations reflect the quality of building materials used by many to build their relationships, marriages, and homes. When Christ is the center of our relationship and marriage, the building material is the Word of God. No weapon that is formed against our marriage shall prosper; and every tongue that shall rise against our marriage shalt be condemned. This is the heritage of the servants of the Lord, and their righteousness is of me, saith the Lord (Isa. 54:17).

Men and women are instructed in the Word to not make mismated alliances with unbelievers or come together with them, inconsistent with their faith (2 Cor. 6:14 AMP). Spiritual incompatibility, lack of harmony, lack of mutual understanding, and not being like mindedness in the faith- puts relationships in disarray and division from the beginning of the relationship. Incompatible in the relationship is unmistakable. The relationship is not in harmony. One of the singles has acknowledged Jesus as Savior and Lord of his life and is committed and dedicated to the principles and guidelines of His Word. He or she is knowledgeable of the scriptures which declare there can be no agreement between a believer and an unbeliever, (2 Cor. 6:15) admonishing them to re- examine their compatabilty decision.

Don't become partners with those who reject God. How can you make a partnership out of right and wrong? That's not partnership that is war. Is light best friends with dark? Does Christ go strolling with the devil? Do trust and mistrust hold hands? Who would think of setting up pagan idols in God's Holy Temple? That is exactly what we are, each of us a temple in whom God lives (2 Cor 6:14–18).

Failure to seek, wait upon God, and follow godly principles in selecting a mate has destroyed many families, marriages, relationships, and homes. The scripture clearly declares that the marriage union is ordained to succeed and prosper, creating a loving atmosphere to be fruitful, multiply, and replenish the earth.

Satan has deceived countless husbands and wives as a result of looking at the outerward person (flesh) and refusing to discern or see the inward person, who is created in the image and likeness of God. Men or women, who have not acknowledged Him as Savior and Lord of their lives, can never be happy with godly mates for many reasons. Among the major reasons are:

- Spirit of God - ungodly mates are not born again of the spirit and of the Word. The spirit of God dwells in one, and the spirit of Satan dwells in the other.

- Companionship - ungodly mates' desires are following Satan, worldly things, and pleasures of the world. Godly mates love God, heavenly things, the Word of God, prayer, and fellowship with God.

- Agreement - how can two walk together except they agree? Ungodly mate's interests cater to the flesh and worldly things. Godly mates seek to please God and follow His plans.

- Finances- Ungodly mates do not agree with the scriptural principles of giving and refuse to pay tithes. Godly mates know and obey His principles. They believe the Word of God, which states it's "He who gives us power to get wealth."

- Fellowship in the Body of Christ–Ungodly mates dislikes attending church, bible study, prayer, fasting, and meditating on the word of God. . Godly mates know their inheritance is among the saints of God. They love attending church, bible study, and Christian fellowships.

- Moral Values- Ungodly mates' moral values are misguided, confused, worldly, and satanic. Godly mates have been taught sound Christian values and principles, and have learned to live in simplicity and truth.

- Music–An ungodly person's interest in music is satanic, sensual, worldly, and lustfully inclined. A Godly mate's interest in music is for praise, fellowship, and worship unto God.

- Recreation - Ungodly mates enjoy movies, dances, worldly concerts, and activities. Godly mates' pleasures are Godly, peaceful, spiritually, and physically healthy.

When you make wrong choices, selections, and hurry into marriage, the chances are you will hurry out. Wrong foundations in marriage includes lust, sex before marriage, accidental pregnancies, marrying for money, marrying for sexual need, marrying for beauty, or because the person looks good. These are wrong reasons for getting married.

Marriage is a gift from God unto man. Marriage is honorable and the bed undefiled (Heb. 13:4).

Marriage Should Be Based On Four Principles:

Love- God has given you a deep and gentle love for the person. Love never fails. Your love will continue to grow as you both learn to relate sincerely and openly to each other; Your love for each other enables your marriage to grow and experience joy and happiness (1 Cor. 13: 1–13).

God has given you the spirit of wisdom and revelation in the knowledge of His will and purpose for your mate (Eph. 1:17).

God has guided and directed you in knowing His will concerning the mate He has chosen (Ps. 25:12).

God's Word has been confirmed by a threefold witness; You have received divine revelation through His Word; taken time to seek Him; heard His voice; and is confident and assured He is leading you to marry (Ps. 32:8).

When you build the foundation of your marriage on Christ, it will stand the test of time and conquer the storms of life. When you prayerfully and patiently wait upon the Lord for your marriage partner, He will confirm it with His seal of approval upon your union in marriage.

For this cause shall a man leave his father and mother, and cleave to his wife; and they twain shall be one flesh: so then, they are no more twain, but one flesh. What therefore God has joined together, let not man put asunder (Mark 10:7–9 KJV)?

Establishing A Godly Marriage Foundation

Godly mates and married partners learn to build the foundation of their homes on godly principles, faith, knowledge, wisdom, and understanding of God's Word. Division, dissension, discord, gaps in communication, and fleshy compromises are destroyed because of the Word of God. The satanic works of the enemy that destroy the unity, love, and peace in a marriage relationship of are:

- Sin
- Lack of submission
- Selfishness
- Interference by in-laws
- Adultery
- Evil family counsel
- Evil powers of conspiracy
- Demonic in-laws
- Spirit of fear
- Spirit of misunderstanding
- Spirit of misinterpretation
- Spirit of exaggeration
- Parental Attachments
- Financial failure
- External influences
- Suspicion

Jesus Christ is the Prince of Peace. He will bless, keep, and sustain any marriage as you seek Him through prayer, learning to wait upon Him, and abiding in His word.

The Word of God has outlined and gives understanding of His divine purpose for the institution of marriage. Lack of understanding of His principles for marriage causes people to abuse, neglect, and destroy the very gift God has given.

God's Threefold Ingredients For Marriage:

- A man will leave his parents and form a covenant with his wife
- The husband and wife will cleave together and become committed to each other.
- The husband and wife will take responsibility for nurturing an ministering unto each other.

The key to godly unions in marriage is establishing, developing, and maintaining a godly foundation. Foundations built and based upon God's Word cannot be destroyed or divided.

The satanic spirits of dissension and discord cannot enter Christ centered relationships that are given to prayer, fasting, bible study, and fellowship. A threefold cord is not quickly broken, because if one prevails against him, two shall withstand him. . You will always get a fraction or piece where there is division or separation, which hurts and damages lives that are fragmented.

Two Are Better Than One
A Threefold Cord Is Not Quickly Broken
The Power Of Agreement

"Two are better than one, because they have a good (more satisfying) reward for their labor; For if they fall, the one will lift up his fellow; But woe to him that is alone when he falls, and has not another to lift him up. Again, if two lie down together, then they have warmth; but how can one be warm alone? And though a man might prevail against him, who is alone, two will withstand him. A threefold cord is not quickly broken" (Ecc. 4:9–12 TAB).

The Scripture declares that a threefold cord is not quickly broken. One of the symbols of marriage is a triangle, with God at the top and the husband and wife at the bottom. This is symbolic of God holding the marriage together. There is a line joining the woman to God and a line joining the man to God. These lines signify their relationship with God. There is also a line joining the man and the woman. The threefold cord is not quickly broken. If the husband and wife can maintain these relationships - Give Me Heaven's Mate request is granted.

Two are better than one. There is power in prayer, and there is more power when two people pray in unity. When husbands and wives have learned how to pray without ceasing, they confirm the Word of God, which declares the earnest (heartfelt, continued) prayer of a righteous man makes tremendous power available (dynamic in its working) (James 5:16). Their bond is inseparable in the name of Jesus. The Word of God declares, "One shall chase a thousand and two ten thousand" (Deut. 32:30). The power of prayer is the answer for husbands and wives experiencing confusion, misunderstandings, petty and naïve differences, lack of willingness to follow godly principles and stand upon the Word of God. Prayer is the answer to destroy the works of the enemy.

> Follow peace with all man, and holiness without which no man shall see the Lord. Looking diligently lest any man fail of the grace of God; lest any root of bitterness springing up trouble you, and thereby many be defiled (Heb. 12:14–15 KJV).

Prince Of Peace Reigns

Husbands and wives, who have learned that the Prince of Peace, Jesus, abides within them, have learned to surrender their will and mind unto Him. Through prayer and submitting to His word blood, from the spirits of confusion, frustration, misery, distress, and every evil thing that will try to enter within the home and marriage.

The peace of God ruling and reigning within us creates and releases a sweet smelling aroma within our lives, homes, and wherever we go.

The scripture declares, "Where there is envying and strife, there is confusion and every evil work. The wisdom that is from above is first pure, peaceable, gentle, and easy to be entreated, full of mercy and good fruits, without partiality, and without hypocrisy. And the fruit of righteousness is sown in peace of them that make peace.

The peace of God affects everything we do in life. Love, decisions, attitudes, and the actions of man are all affected by the spirit of peace or the lack thereof. Sadly to say, couples who do not have the peace of God cannot richly enjoy each other, their children, and the joy of their marriage. Jesus is the Prince of Peace, and when He is ruling and reigning in our lives, their marriage, home, and relationship.

Whatever happens in our relationships, we must seek to walk in and maintain peace. When there are disagreements, discord, and strife, we should always seek a peaceful solution. When we are hurt, bruised, or battered in a relationship, there is a tendency for resentment. Every person, at some point in his or her life, experiences being wronged by another.

He or she must learn to quickly choose to forgive, or to dwell upon the wrong committed by another. Bitterness defiles all those it touches, and extends to other relationships. He or she not choosing to forgive and not dwell upon the wrong releases the spirit of healing and forgiveness within the relationship. Forgiveness is a choice- that builds character and integrity in each partner.

Bitterness can have far-reaching, long-lasting, and self-destructive effects. Bitter husbands and wives must first turn unto Christ (Rom. 5:8–10). Once they have accepted forgiveness, then, they are not only able, but are also commanded to forgive each other (Matt. 6:12). The divine way to forgive is to replace bitterness with love within your heart, especially by showing love to the one who has been wronged (1 Cor. 13:4–7; Gal. 5:22).

Husbands and wives often unnecessarily hurt each other by holding on to bitterness. The love of God will melt all the bitterness in your heart and enable you to reach a peaceable agreement with the one you disagree with. Let the spirit of peace rule and reign within your heart in the name of Jesus.

Until Death Do Us Part

He answered, "Haven't you read in your Bible that the Creator originally made men and woman for each other, male and female? And because of this a man leaves father and mother and is firmly bonded to his wife, becoming one flesh- no longer two bodies but one. Because God created this organic union of the two sexes, no one should desecrate his art by cutting them apart
(Matt 19:4–8 MSG).

Jesus said, "Moses wrote this command only as a concession to your hard-hearted ways. In the original creation, God made male and female to be together. Because of this a man leaves father and mother, and in marriage he becomes one flesh with a woman- no longer two individuals, but forming a new unity. Because God created this organic union of the two sexes, no one should desecrate his art by cutting them apart"
(Mark 10:5–9 MSG).

Marriage is a divine institution designed to form a permanent union between man and woman, that they might be helpful to one another. The presence of Jesus at the wedding in Cana happily illustrates the feeling and teaching of Christianity respecting marriage. Christ taught the divine origin and sacredness of duty. It is more then filial duty. It unifies the husband and wife to become one.

Weddings are much more than beautiful gowns, crowds of people, gifts, and expensive decorations. A wedding is a time of *commitment*. It should include worship and giving thanks unto God, as well as the celebration of the wonderful blessing God has given you in a spouse.

The wedding ceremony is an appropriate time to reflect on the example of unconditional love that God has demonstrated (Rom. 5:8). The couple must "commit" to follow the Lord in their home no matter what circumstances arise, and "till death do us part." The importance of this permanency of the union grows out of the fact that the vows are not merely between one man and one woman, but includes the heavenly Father Himself. It is also because such commitment is molded after Christ's commitment to the church.

In today's generation, weddings extend from formal, solemn ceremonies to informal and private gatherings. The type of ceremony is not necessarily important if it meets two Scripture criteria:

- The marriage must be established in the name of the Lord Jesus (Mark 10:9 KJV).
- Thanks must be given unto God (Col. 3:17 KJV).

A wedding should be a time of worship and celebration of each marriage partner's commitment grounded in the love of God.

Improper Marriage Confession

Now while Ezra prayed and made confession, weeping, and casting himself down before the house of God, there gathered to him out of Israel a very great assembly of men, women, and children; for the people wept bitterly.

> And Shechaniah (II) the son of Jehiel, (one of the congregation), of the sons of Elam, said to Ezra, "We have broken faith and dealth treacherously against our God and have married foreign women of the peoples of the land, yet now there is still hope for Israel in spite of this thing.
>
> Therefore, let us make a covenant with our God to put away all the foreign wives and their children, according to the counsel of my Lord and of those who tremble at the command of our God; and let it be done according to the Law. Arise, for it is your duty, and we are with you. Be strong and brave and do it.
>
> Then Ezra arose, and made the chiefs of the priests, the Levites, and all Israel swear that they would do as had been said. So they took the oath (Ezra 10:1–5 TAB).

There are many reasons, motives, and circumstances for entering the sanctity of marriage today. Many parents agree to the union of their sons and daughters with unbelievers, unsaved, and unequally yoked mates. Generational curses, sins, misguided values, immorality, and lack of godly principles are established as a result of mismated unions. Mismated unions cause a further deterioration of values and principles in the family when prayer, the Word, divine principles and guidelines are not established and practiced.

This is one of the main reasons it is a necessity for families to "pray without ceasing." The scripture declares, that the effectual fervent prayers of a righteous man availeth much (James 5:16). When families leave the principles of God's Word to follow that which is ungodly or unholy, the entire family experiences the impact of that decision.

Christians must look to the scriptures concerning God's plan for marriage and selecting a mate. The scriptures warn believers not to enter marriage with an unbeliever for one of the same reasons the Jews were not to do so - because it can weaken the faith of the believer, create division, and cause them to forsake their God. The Christian values, principles, love for God, and the Word of God cannot be shared with an unbelieving spouse (husband) (2 Cor. 6). The entire relationship from courtship to marriage should be Christ centered to fulfill the destiny and purpose of God for their lives.

Believers marrying outside of the will and purpose of God not only positions themselves, but the children birthed in that union, to many generational curses, sins, misguided values, and immorality. Ezra did as many should do today. He took a stand, instructing the chiefs of the priests', wives, and their children according to God's law.

Christians are not exempt from trials, tests, and temptation today. However, the scripture declares, "let no one say when he is tempted, I am tempted of God; for God is incapable of being tempted by (what is) evil and He Himself tempts no man (James 1:13).

But every person is tempted when he is drawn away, enticed, and baited by his own evil desire (lusts, passions).

Then the evil desire, when it has conceived, gives birth to sin, and sin, when it is fully matured, brings forth death (James 1:14–15).

Marriage is the cornerstone for the family upon earth. It gives a testimony of their lives and interactions with each other. A parent provides the example for their children to see how crucial the sanctification process is in their own lives. Joshua not only lived a Godly example before his family, but left a Godly principle and standard for his generation.

Joshua stated during the midst of much confusion, "and if it seems evil to you to serve the Lord, choose for yourselves this day whom you will serve, whether the gods which your fathers served on the other side of the River, or the gods of the Amorites, in whose, land you dwell; but as for me and my house, we will serve the Lord (Joshua 24:15).

The scriptures declare the time has arrived for judgment to begin with the household of God; and if it begin with us, what will (be) the end of those who do not respect or believe or obey the good news (The Gospel) of God.

And if the righteous are barely saved, what will become of the godless and wicked (1 Peter 4: 17–18)?

Many are knowingly disregarding and disobeying the scriptures. Following and obeying his or her desires suddenly becomes more important than obeying the Word of God. Wrong choices and decisions have consequences that often leave many generational curses for your children to live and deal with.

In order for our families to reap the rewards of their labor in the twenty first century, we must ask for the old paths; where is the good way, and walk therein, and find rest for our souls." (Jer. 6:16).

Families must restore the altar of prayer, personal relationship with Jesus, commitment, bible study, church fellowship, and righteous living before God They must walk before their families and children with love, longsuffering, knowledge, wisdom, and understanding. True love is not permissive, but corrective. God loves us so much He never ceases to correct us when we need it (Heb. 12:6–7). He loves us so much, He refuses to compromise His Word to satisfy our flesh. We love our children and love ones, but God loves them and us more, providing His standards and principles for us to live by.

For the Lord corrects and disciplines everyone whom He loves, and He punishes, even scourges every son whom He accepts and welcomes to His heart and cherishes.

You must submit to and endure (correction) for discipline; God is dealing with you as with sons. For what son is there whom his father does (thus) train and correct and discipline? (Heb. 12:6–7).

These I Can Promise

I cannot promise you a life of sunshine;
I cannot promise riches, wealth, or gold;
I cannot promise you an easy pathway
That leads away from change or growing old.
But I can promise all my heart's devotion;
A smile to chase away your tears of sorrow;
A love that's ever true and ever growing;
A hand to hold in yours through each tomorrow.

Yes, I'll marry you.

❧

Author Unknown

Marriage: Problem Solving

One of the most distressing facts of life is that every marriage will experience problems. These cannot be sidestepped but must be faced and resolved.

Children can be a great source of enjoyment, but they can also add stress to a marriage. The mothering instinct is so strong in many women that they tend to neglect their husbands as they care for their children (I Sam. 1:8). At times, a wife will even deceive her husband in favor of her children (Gen. 27:1–29). A wife must remember that her union with her husband is second only to her relationship with God.

Financial problems can also put undue stress upon a relationship if the couple quarrels over who is going to make what sacrifices. If a couple will seek God's direction on financial matters, He will be faithful to supply their needs (Matt. 6:33; Phil. 4:19).

Unresolved anger can build to resentment and bitterness, so that meaningful communication ceases (Heb. 12:15; Eph. 4:26).

The temptation and the opportunity to be unfaithful are ever present in any relationship and marriage (Prov. 7:6–23). An intimate and vibrant relationship with God will encircle the relationship between the husband and wife, and provide the strength and vitality to remain loyal and faithful during the marriage.

Isolation, the state of being excluded, is one of the more subtle maladies of marriage. Marriage can easily slip out of priority. People often take their mates for granted, giving their attention to other urgent matters, and soon warmth and communication have diminished. The remedy for isolation is to guard the marriage relationship tenderly and to give priority to your spouse, being open and honest and not keeping secrets from one another.

Problems can be negative weapons in a marriage, dividing hearts and destroying unity, or they can be positive things that help recommitment and renewal. Married couples who learn to cleave to each other during difficult and challenging times, and who have learned to pray, wait upon the Lord in all long suffering and patience, and experience a deeper bond and unity in their marriage. The love and harmony releases the quality of relationship enabling to enjoy and fulfill the pleasures of their marriage life with each other.

Marriage To An Unbeliever

Be not unequally yoked together with unbelievers; for what fellowship hath righteousness with unrighteousness? And what communion hath light with darkness?

And what concord hath Christ with Belial? Or what part hath he that believeth with an infidel?

And what agreement hath the temple of God with idols? For ye are the temple of the living God; as God hath said, I will dwell in them; and walk in them: and I will be their God, and they shall be my people
(II Cor. 6:14–16 KJV).

While knowingly marrying an unbeliever violates God's Word (II Cor. 6:14), the scripture provides very practical encouragement to those who find themselves the wives or husbands of unsaved spouses.

Win without a word. Do not preach to an unsaved mate. He/ She cannot comprehend spiritual truths (II Cor. 4:4; I Pet. 3:1–4). Regeneration is the work of the Holy Spirit. God desires repentance for all (II Pet. 3:8).

Cultivate a quiet and gentle spirit. A spouse who is saved will at all times disagree with an unsaved spouse. You may disagree but do not be disagreeable. Avoid agitation and harshness. Concentrate on being the best spouse possible. Relax and enjoy your spouse. Do not condemn your spouse. Mirror God's love through your pure character and generosity toward them.

Be submissive in your love. Demonstrate loving respect for your spouse. However, submission does not require agreeing to engage in sinful activities or living in fear (II

Tim. 1:7). If your spouse dangerously mistreats you or your children, seek protection from authorities.

Pray for your spouse's salvation. While their salvation is not guaranteed, your faith and prayers act as a catalyst, binding satan and opening your spouse's heart to the Holy Spirit (Acts 16:31).

There are countless Christian spouses who have endured the test of time, fought the good fight of faith, and beheld the manifestation of the results of their spouse being saved. But none are like the testimony of Mrs. Smith Wigglesworth and Abigail in the Bible (I Sam. 25).

The story of Smith Wigglesworth's wife is an astonishing testimony in itself. Brother Wigglesworth was a great man of God, and it was the life and testimony of his wife that got him saved. He told her not to attend Christian meetings anymore. Mrs. Wigglesworth went anyway. One night when she returned from a service, she found the door of the house locked. This woman wrapped herself in her coat and slept outside by the door the whole night.

When Wigglesworth opened the door the next morning, she jumped up and gave him a kiss and said, "Good morning, Smith. What can I fix you for breakfast?" She started rushing around to get his breakfast ready. The man was dazzled, because he thought that immediately when she entered, there would be a fight. This act of unconditional love broke his hardened heart, and he received Jesus as his Lord.

Abigail was the intelligent and beautiful wife of Nabal, a wealthy, foolish scoundrel who was harsh and overbearing (I Sam. 25:3, 17). Although many women are in unhappy marriages by their own choice, Abigail probably entered this union through no choice of her own, since most marriages in her day were arranged by parents. This woman of faith acted wisely in giving David and his men food to save the lives of her household.

Her husband Nabal rudely insulted the future King of Israel and his men. David reacted swiftly, intent on hotheaded vengeance. Forewarned by a servant, Abigail moved with precision to try to avert the extermination of her entire household. She knew that her husband had made a terrible decision. She used wisdom in how she responded to save her household:

Let not my lord, I pray you; regard this foolish and wicked fellow. Nabal, for as his name is, so is he–Nabal (foolish, wicked) is his name, and folly is with him. But I, your handmaid, did not see my lord's young men whom you sent.

So now, my lord, as the Lord lives and as your soul lives, seeing that the Lord has prevented you from blood–guiltiness and from avenging yourself with your own hand, now let your enemies and those who seek to do evil to my lord be as Nabal.

And now this gift, which your handmaid has brought my lord, let it be given to the young men who follow my lord (I Sam. 25:25–26).

Abigail moved with great precision, she intercepted David with humility and warm personality. This moved the heart of David and his men so greatly, that upon the death of her husband; he wasted no time in asking Abigail to continue to bless his life as his own wife. She was the one to whom David said, "I . . . respected your person" (I Sam. 25:35). She had earned from him respect, and illustrates vital principles of restraint and proper priorities for wives today. Let us learn from the great wisdom used by Abigail in reversing the works of the enemy in her marriage and family.

Part Eleven

GOD'S DESIGN FOR THE FAMILY

So God created man in His own image, in the image and likeness of God. He created him; male and female He created them.

And God blessed them and said to them, "Be fruitful, multiply, and fill the earth, and subdue it (using all its vast resources in the service of God and man) and have dominion over the fish of the sea, the birds of the air, and over every living creature that moves upon the earth (Gen. 1:27–28 TAB).

Now this is the instruction, the laws, and the precepts which the Lord your God commanded me to teach you, that you might do them in the land to which you go to possess it.

That you may (reverently) fear the Lord your God, you and your son and your son's son, and keep all His statues and His commandments which I command you all the days of your life, and that your days may be prolonged.

Hear therefore, O Israel, and be watchful to do them, that it may be well with you and that you may increase exceedingly, as the Lord, the God of your fathers, has promised you, in a land flowing with milk and honey.

Hear, O Israel: the Lord our God is one Lord (the only Lord).

And you shall love the Lord your God with all your (mind and) heart and with your entire being and with all your might.

And these words which I am commanding you this day shall be (first) in your (own) minds and hearts; (then)

You shall whet and sharpen them so as to make them penetrate, and teach and impress them diligently upon the (minds and) hearts of your children, and shall talk of them when you sit in your house and when you walk by the way, and when you lie down and when you rise up.

And you shall bind them as a sign upon your hand, and they shall be as frontlets (forehead bands) between your eyes.

And you shall write them upon the doorposts of your house and on your gates.

And when the Lord your God brings you into the land which He swore to your fathers, to Abraham, Isaac, and Jacob, to give you, with great and goodly cities which you did not build.

And houses full of all good things which you did not fill, and cisterns hewn out which you did not hew, and vineyards and olive trees which you did not plant, and when you eat and are full,

Then beware lest you forget the Lord, Who brought you out the land of Egypt, out of the house of bondage (Deut. 6:1–12 TAB).

God's Design For The Family

And God created man in His own image, in the image of God created he him; male and female created He them.

And God blessed them, and God said unto them, Be fruitful and multiply, and replenish the earth, and subdue it: and have dominion over the fish of the sea, and the fowl of the air, and over every living thing that moveth upon the earth (Gen. 1:27–28 KJV).

A family has been defined as a group of persons related by marriage and blood ties, and generally living together in the same household (Nelson Illustrated Bible Dictionary). In the Western world, the family traditionally consists of a man and his wife and their children. However, the family units were often much larger than the primary family, especially if the man had more than one wife.

The scripture reveals that not everyone in the old testament lived in line with God's divine principles. There were times when a man married more than one wife. Solomon is a perfect example. He had seven hundred wives, princesses, and three hundred concubines (1 Kings 11:3).

When God created Adam, He declared, "It is not good that man should be alone" (Gen. 2:18). He then created woman and united them; and they become "one flesh" (Gen 2:24). Consequently, the family was designed by God to provide companionship for the various members of the family. Additionally, the institution of marriage was approved and sanctioned by the Lord (Matt. 19:4–6).

God's ideal for the family is that it be a harmonious unit where love for God and neighbor are instituted into each member (Deut. 6:6–

9). When there is division with the couple, especially denominational beliefs, they can never have the harmony and serve the purpose that God desires. In the Old Testament believers were instructed not to marry foreigners who would hinder their faith and bring strife to the marriage (Ex. 34:13–16; Duet 7: 3–4).

The Apostle Paul commanded the New Testament believers, "Do not be unequally yoked together with unbelievers (2 Cor. 6:14).

The scripture describes the conflict that is carried in many families as a result of marriage to unbelievers, and to foreigners (Ex. 34:13–16; Deut. 7:3–4). Solomon is an example of a man who disobeyed God's command and married three hundred concubines (1 Kings 3:3–15). His final years can be summarized in one sentence "For it was so, when Solomon was old, that his wives turned his heart after other gods, and his heart was not loyal to the Lord his God, as was the heart of his father David" (1 Kings 11:4). These wives and their gods caused Solomon to take his eyes off the living God.

The family is very important in the plan of God. Christ-centered homes provides the spiritual and natural structure to assist the family circle in living a balanced loving, healthy, and Christian lifestyle in the home, community and the Body of Christ . In Exodus, each commandment of the Decalogue (Ten Commandments) touches upon behavior within the family circle. Joshua is described as the godly patriarch who led his family to follow Yahweh God (Josh. 24:15).

Families must join hand-in-hand and fight the good fight of faith as never before. satanic attacks on the home from drugs, alcohol, sexual immorality, financial problems, misguided values and other problems are attacking the Christian homes daily. Married couples have learned to guard their marriage, family, and children with prayer, the Word and Christian's fellowship. They have learned to walk and abide in the scriptural revelation, which declares, "and this is the victory that overcometh the world- even our faith"-, faith in the Word of God (1 John 5:4).

God commands husbands to love their wives as Christ loved the church by assuming and fulfilling their leadership responsibility in the family and home. Wives were created to be a helper to their husbands (Gen. 2:18), supplementing and not supplanting, complementing and not commanding.

Twenty first century Christian families must learn to follow and walk in line with the scripture which declares "stand by the road and look: and ask for the eternal paths, where the good, old way is; then walk in it, and you will find rest for your souls. But they said we will not walk in it (Jer. 6:16). Families must learn that the world's fashions; fads, styles and trends does and should not determine the values and lifestyle of the home. The home is established on Christ-centered values; to live and maintain godly living standards and principles according to God's Word.

Part Twelve

MARRIAGE RELATIONSHIPS

Friends And Lovers

Friends

Your own friend and your father's friend, forsake them not; neither go to your brother's house in the day of your calamity. Better is a neighbor who is near (in Spirit) than a brother who is far off (in heart) (Prov. 27:10 TAB).

A friend loves at all times, and is born, as is a brother, for adversity (Prov. 17:17 TAB).

I do not call you servants (slaves) any longer; for the servant does not know what his master is doing (working out). But I have called you my friends, because I have made known to you everything that I have heard from my Father. (I have revealed to you everything that I have learned form Him) (John 15:15 TAB).

His voice and speech are exceedingly sweet; yes, he is altogether lovely (the whole of him delights and is precious). This is my beloved, and this is my friend, O daughter of Jerusalem! (Song 5:16 TAB).

Lovers

I am my beloved's (garden), and my beloved is mine! He feeds among the lilies (which grow there) (Song 6:3 TAB).

I am my beloveds, and his desire is toward me! Come, my beloved! Let us go forth into the field; let us lodge in the villages

Let us get up early to the vineyards; let us see if the vine flourish, whether the tender grape appear, and the pomegranates bud forth; there will I give thee my love.

The mandrakes give a smell, and at our gates are all manner of pleasant fruits new and old, which I have laid up for thee, O my beloved (Song. 7: 10–11 KJV).

This Day I Married My Best Friend

This day I married my best friend

... the one I laugh with as we share life's wondrous zest,

as we find new enjoyments and experience all that's best.

... the one I live for because the world seems brighter

as our happy times are better and our burdens feel much lighter.

... the one I love with every fiber of my soul.

We used to feel vaguely incomplete, now together we are whole.

∞

Author Unknown

Relationship And The Woman

Withhold not good from them to whom it is due, when it is in the power of thine hand to do it (Prov. 3: 27 KJV).

Render therefore to all their due: tribute to whom tribute is due: custom to whom custom; fear to whom fear; honour to whom honour (Rom 13:7).

> If it be possible, as much as lieth in you, live peaceably with all men (Rom. 12: 18 KJV).

> And let us not be weary in well doing: for in due season we shall reap, if we faint not (Gal 6:9 KJV).

> Strive not with a man without cause, if he have done thee no harm (Prov. 3:30 KJV).

> But let it be the inward adorning and beauty of the hidden person of the heart, with the incorruptible and unfading charm of a gentle and peaceful spirit, which is not anxious or wrought up, but is very precious in the sight of God (1 Pet. 3:4 TAB).

The nature of the woman is femininity, a reality of God's design and making. Her femininity is God's precious gift to every woman–and, in a very different way, His gracious gift to man as well. The difference between men and women is not a mere matter of biology. The nature of the woman was designed to compliment the man in all aspects of the relationship and marriage. Yet, never as now have we more needed.

To know and understand God's *plan for marriage,* we must first begin with *the divine blueprint-,* which is His Word. We have seen and observed our parents, neighbors, friends, movies, read books, experienced our own personal fantasies, and scanned through beautiful photo albums about what we thought was *The Perfect Marriage.* His word is the divine principles, standards and blueprints for our marriage and the home.

Not knowing what the definition of a *Perfect Marriage* is, we proceeded to develop and design our plans for what we believe and want our *Perfect Marriage* to resemble. We planned and designed a beautiful and elaborate marriage, a *Picture Perfect Marriage,* meant for the movies. The wedding plans for many costed two million, one million, thousands, and to some, a simple, married by the Justice of the Peace. Only to discover, after the honeymoon and sometimes during the honeymoon, "we left *God completely out of the Marriage. We forgot to ask, seek and receive a threefold confirmation."* The scripture declares in the mouth of two or three witnesses shall every word be established (2 Cor. 13:1).

This threefold confirmation is the missing ingredient in both the

Christian and secular world. Currently, Christian marriages are experiencing an astonishing sixty percent divorce rate, exceeding that of the secular world. What the Christian and secular world both are experiencing and must awaken to is- *"Marriage Still Takes Three"*-. The successes or failures of our marriages is contigent upon how much we are willing to submit to His plans, Word, and the details of His blue prints.

Neither man nor woman is adequate to bear the divine image (Gen. 1:27 KJV). Rather, these two together represent the image of God– one of them in a special way as the initiator, the other as the responder. God made Eve from the man and brought her to the man whom Adam named Eve. He accepted responsibility to "husband" her–to provide for, protect, and lead her (Gen. 2:15–17, 21–22 KJV).

Surrender is a key ingredient of femininity. As a bride, a woman in marriage surrenders her independence, her name, her destiny, her will, and ultimately in the marriage chamber; her body to the bridegroom. As a mother, she surrenders in a very real sense her life for the life of the child. As a single woman, she surrenders herself in a unique way for service to her Lord and for service to family and community.

Femininity receives. It takes what God gives. In other words, women are to receive the given as Mary did (Luke. 1:38) and not to insist upon the not given, as Eve (Gen. 3:1–6). This does not imply a woman should surrender to evils, such as coercion or violent conquest.

The challenge for today's woman is to be the woman the scripture has declared her to be; holy through and through, asking for nothing but what God wants to give her; and receiving with both hands whatever that is. Femininity is a precious treasure to be guarded and nourished each and every day.

Part Thirteen

Marriage To An Unbeliever

For married people I have a command which is not my own but the Lord's: a wife must not leave her husband;

But if she does, she must remain single or else be reconciled to her husband; a husband must not divorce his wife.

To the others I say (I, myself, not the Lord): if a Christian man has a wife who is an unbeliever and she agrees to go on living with her, he must not divorce her.

And if a Christian woman is married to a man who is an unbeliever and he agrees to go on living with her, she must not divorce him.

For the unbelieving husbands is made acceptable to God by being united to his wife, and the unbelieving wife is made acceptable to God by being united to her Christian husband. If this were not so, their children would be like pagan children; but as it is, they are acceptable to God.

However, if the one who is not a believer wishes to leave the Christian partner, let it be so. In such cases the Christian partner, whether husband and or wife is free to act. God has called you to live in peace.

How can you be sure, Christian wife that you will not save your husband? Or how can you be sure, Christian husband that you will not save your wife.
(1 Cor: 7:10-16 TEV)

Marriage To An Unbeliever

And if you are married, stay married. This is the Master's command, not mine. If a wife should leave her husband, she must either remain single or else come back and make things right with him. And a husband has no right to get rid of his wife.

For the rest of you who are in mixed marriages- Christians married to non Christians- we have no explicit command from the Master. So this is what you must do. If you are a man with a wife who is not a believer, but who still wants to live with you, hold on to her. If you are a woman with a husband who is a believer but he wants to live with you, hold on to her. The unbelieving husband shares to an extent in the holiness of his wife, and the unbelieving wife is likewise touched by the holiness of her husband. Otherwise, your children would be left out, as it is, they also are included in the spiritual purposes of God.

On the other hand, if the unbelieving spouse walks out, you've got to let him or her go. You don't have to hold on desperately. God has called us to make the best of it, as peacefully as we can. You never know, wife: The way you handle this might bring your husband, not only back to you, but to God. You never know, husband: The way you handle this might bring your wife not only back to you but to God.

And don't be wishing you were someplace else or with someone else. Where you are right now is God's place for you. Live and obey and love and believe right there. God, not your marital status, defines your life. Don't think I'm being harder on you than on the others. I give this same counsel in all the churches
(1 Cor. 7: 10–16 MSG).

Although marrying an unbeliever violates the Word of God, the scriptures provide encouragement, comfort and wisdom to those who find themselves the husband or wife of an unsaved person.

Believers can find great comfort, strength and confidence in the Lord, knowing that He is touched with the feeling of our infirmities. The day-to-day challenge of life, nurtured with prayer, love, understanding and learning to patiently waiting on your mate to receive Jesus as Savior and Lord is a process. The process varies from one person to the next. However, our spiritual growth and development brings changes from faith-to-faith, and glory-to-glory, always abounding in the wisdom, knowledge and understanding of our Heavenly Father. It takes time, to submit to His process of healing and deliverance. Learn to let the fruit of patience develop and flourish in your life.

Marriage to an unbeliever is no doubt one of the most challenging trials, and tests in the Christian walk, for many believers. Believers who have experienced the initial salvation process, understands that salvation is progressive, and takes time to bring forth the fruit of the spirit in our lives; specifically love, patience, longsuffering, and the determination to submit to the deliverance process of God.

The salvation process brings with it an illumination that transcends the realm of darkness that we have never experienced before. We learn to no longer walk as unbelievers who walk in the vanity of their mind, having their understanding darkened, being alienated from the life of God through the ignorance that is in them; (Eph. 4:17), but to grow up in him in all things and learn to pray through unto the breakthrough in overcoming all our problems and challenges.

The challenge of marriage to an unbeliever is great and is an opportunity to draw closer to God, trusting Him to work all things according to the counsel of His will. Problems, circumstances, and issues experienced in marriage to an unbeliever are different from believer to believer. However, God's Word, power, and deliverance remains the same for all who dare to believe Him at His Word. Learn to trust Him for your deliverance, remembering that it is a process that takes time and patience.

Some are experiencing marriage to spouses with severe addiction problems like drugs, alcoholics, gambling, sexual perversion, low self-esteem, laziness and many other unprofitable works of the flesh. The question remains the same, Is there anything to hard for God? With man it is impossible, but all things are possible with God (Mark 10:27).

The key to having a healthy Christ centered marriage is the extent you are willing to submit yourself unto the inner workings of God and trust Him for the experience of salvation and deliverance in your spouse's life. Your commitment to submit to your spouse, your children and family, unto the Lord, and determined to pray through unto the breakthrough, determines the point of your family's healing and deliverance. The scriptures declare that the effectual fervent prayers of a righteous man availeth much (James 5:16).

Perhaps when you both married, you chose each other outside the will of God, as a result of unbridled passion and lust. There may have been a lack of discernment in facing the reality about the mate you have chosen. You may have thought your mate was a Christian, thought he or she knew God, but you did not know they did not have a personal relationship with Him; you may have thought your mate had a knowledge of the scripture, but denied the power thereof; you thought your mate was receiving the Word during fellowship meetings, when indeed it was only a ritual, void of actually hearing, receiving and applying the Word of God. Whatever the circumstance, reason, or motive, the scriptures declare "there is nothing too hard for God" (Jer. 32:17).

Faith in God's Word turns hopeless circumstances around. Satan, in the name of Jesus, you will not drive me out of my home, marriage, relationship, or family. The deliverer lives within me; and I decree my deliverance in the name of Jesus. The scriptures declare, we can decree a thing, and it shall be established unto us (Job 22:28).

To grow up in Him in all things challenges us to make decisions based on faith in His word. The scripture declares, "that faith in God's word turns hopeless circumstances around; "and according to your faith be it unto you (Matt. 9:29).

There is nothing to hard for God (Jer. 32:17). The love of God is one of the most powerful forces on this earth. Choose to believe the report of the Lord.

The power of a praying wife, and praying husband has turned many marriages; relationships, and family circumstances around. The power of prayer has positioned them to experience victory at all cost. In adhering to the scripture, they have chosen to cleave and not leave. Essentially, if you are married, stay married, and chose to believe the report of the Lord. The scriptures declare how can you be sure, Christian wife that you will not save your husband? Or how can you be sure, Christian husband that you will not save your wife (1 Cor. 7:16).

To say that this level of healing, deliverance, renewal and refreshing for your marriage comes without a daily challenge and surrendering of one's will and life unto God is unscriptural. The scriptures declare, many are the afflictions of the righteous, but the Lord delivereth them out of them all (Ps. 34:11). The joy of receiving healing for your marriage relationship and deliverance from a turbulent marriage is a result of the power of God in manifestation. The joy of experiencing unspeakable joy is the answer to prayer for many and a victorious testimonial for others. Many married couples become disillusioned in their walk of faith, put a time limit on God, and do not fight the good fight to save their marriage. However, faith in God's Word not only turns hopeless circumstances around, but also brings victory for the marriage believers, standing in faith confessing and decreeing "and this is the victory that overcometh the world even our faith (1 John 5:4).

We must learn to wait upon God. Job, in his furnace of afflictions, when none of his friends, to include his wife, understood the pain, hurt, disappointment and suffering he was experiencing, positioned himself to receive victory and deliverance. He proclaimed "all of my appointed days will I wait till my change come" (Job 14:14). He was determined to look unto Jesus the author and finisher of his faith. He realized that the tests and trials he was experiencing; only God could bring deliverance from one of the most devasting experiences in his life.

To the believer married to an unbeliever, change your posture through faith; choose to believe the Word of God. This is an opportunity to experience the miraculous, deliverance, and wonder working power of God in your marriage and relationship.

To the unmarried singles, remember you have a choice. If you choose to marry outside of the will of God, you are responsible for the decision you make. You have been enlightened by the Word of God, counseled and is afforded the opportunity to make the right choice.

While the plan of God for marriage remains the same, the experience of marriage to an unbeliever is challenging and is an opportunity for a greater witness in your life unto the glory of God.

The scripture declares, for what knowest thou, O wife, whether thou shalt save thy husband? Or how knowest thou, O man, whether thou shalt save thy wife (1 Cor. 7:16)? Being used as a vessel or source of life to change your mate will demand more than just reading and quoting the scriptures. It will require you to live a prayerfully, humble, God-fearing life, and be the man or woman God has called you to be. It will require you to love rather than talk love; be kind, rather than talk kindness (1 Cor 13:4). Living this type of life requires total dependence upon God, His Word, prayer, and learning to wait patiently upon Him.

The scripture declares, "Every wise woman buildeth her house, but the foolish plucketh it down with her hands" (Prov. 14:1). Often daily life problems and challenges causes us to reflect on how we think things should, could, or would be, if I had chosen a different direction. However, this type of thinking creates double mindedness and instability in all our ways. The scripture declares a double-minded person is unstable in all their ways, and shall not receive anything of the Lord (James 1:6–8).

The power of prayer is available to every person married to an unbeliever. The scripture declares that the effectual fervent prayer of a righteous man availeth much (James 5:16). The scriptural revelation is, I am going to continue with all prayer and supplication, praying through unto the breakthrough. In Genesis 18:14, the scripture declares that there is "nothing to hard for God." There is not a problem, disease, illness, behavior or circumstances that the blood of Jesus cannot heal, deliver, or set free.

The scripture gives the illustrations of several types of wives and the impact their behavior had upon their lives, husbands and families. These illustrations and different and types of behaviors are prevalent among women:

Types Of Behavior (Women)

- Disobedient- Eve . . . . Gen. 3:1–8
- Obedient- Sarah . . . . 1 Pet. 3:5–6
- Worldly- Lot's . . . . Gen. 19:26
- Humble- Manoah's . . . . . Judg. 13:22,23
- Prayerful- Hannah . . . . . . 1 Sam 1:1–15
- Prudent- Abigail . . . . 1 Sam 25: 3, 14–35
- Criticizing- Michal . . . . . .2 Sam 6:15,16
- Unscrupulous- Jezebel . . .1 Kin. 21:5–15
- Modest- Vashti . . . . .Esth. 1:11, 12
- Foolish- Job's wife . . . . . . Job 2:7–10
- Cruel- Herodias . . . . Matt. 14:3–12
- Righteous- Elisabeth . . . .Luke 1:5, 6
- Lying- Sapphira . . . . .Acts 5:1–10

The joy and happiness of the type of marriage you desire, is dependent upon your level of faith, and your willingness to exercise faith in the Word of God. He is willing to give you your expected end, as you trust Him. The scripture declares according to your faith be it unto you (Matt. 9:29). The duties and responsibilities of the wife and husband are according to His word.

In Luke 1:37, the scripture declares, "For with God nothing shall be impossible. Is it not impossible for God to save and change your unsaved mate? The answer you give to that question will not only determine the salvation of your mate, but the joy, and happiness you experience in your marriage. If you believe that there is nothing too hard for God, and that God can save your mate, you have positioned yourself to receive salvation and deliverance for your spouse and marriage. He has given you an expected end (Jer. 29:11). You can receive spiritual growth and development in your marriage and relationship. You can function in your marriage according to the duties and responsibilities outlined in the scriptures.

Duties Of The Wife

- Submit to her husband . . . . 1 Pet 3:5,6
- Reverence her husband . . . Eph. 5:33
- Love her husband . . . . Titus 2:4
- Learn from her husband . . . 1 Cor 14:34, 35
- Be trustworthy . . . . .Prov 31:11, 12
- Love her children . . . . Titus 2:4
- Be chaste . . . . .Titus 2:5
- Be a keeper at home . . . . . . Titus 2:5

Duties Of The Husband

- Love . . . . Eph. 5:25, 28
- Honor . . . . .1 Pet. 3:7
- Provide for . . . . .1 Tim 5:8
- Instruct . . . . 1 Cor 14:35
- Protect . . . . .1 Sam 30:1–19
- Not divorce . . . . 1 Cor 7:11

Part Fourteen

Heaven's Mate
None Shall Want Their Mate

Seek out of the book of the Lord and read: no one of these shall fail; none shall want her mate: for my mouth it hath commanded, and His spirit it hath gathered them (Isa. 34:16 KJV).

Look in the scroll of the LORD and read: None of these will be missing, not one will lack her mate. For it is his mouth that has given the order, and his Spirit will gather them together (Isa. 34:16 NIV).

Search from the book of the LORD, and read: Not one of these shall fail; Not one shall lack her mate. For My mouth has commanded it, and His Spirit has gathered them (Isa. 34:16 NKJV).

Search the book of the Lord and see all that he will do; not one detail will he miss; not one kite will be there without a mate, for the Lord has said it, and his Spirit will make it all come true (Isa. 34:16 TLB).

Search in the Lord's book of living creatures and read what it says. Not one of these creatures will be missing, and not one will be without its mate. The LORD has commanded it to be so; he himself will bring them together (Isa. 34:16 TEV).

Search the book of the LORD, and see what he will do. He will not miss a single detail. Not one of these birds and animals will be missing, and none will lack a mate, for the LORD has promised this. His Spirit will make it all come true (Isa. 34:16 NLT).

Seek Ye out of the book of Jehovah, and read: no one of these shall be missing, none shall want her mate; for my mouth, it hath commanded, and his Spirit, it hath gathered them (Isa. 34:16 ASV).

Seek out of the book of the Lord and read: not one of these [details of prophecy] shall fail, none shall want and lack her mate [in fulfillment]. For the mouth [of the Lord] has commanded, and His Spirit has gathered them (Isa. 34:16 TAB).

A Match Made In Heaven

Here's a tale that should be told
of what faith and love can do,
And what miracles are wrought
when the faithful "pray on through."

How a guy with a future
loves a girl with a past,
And his friends all warn him
it'll never last ...

For that girl craves the night-life
and she loves all the men,
So she'll break his heart ...
it's just s matter of when.

But the guy with a future
has a prayed-up aunt,
And she knows God can do
what a mortal man can't.

And the prayed-up aunt
has a Jesus-lovin' friend ~
And they prayed for days,
And for weeks on end.

And they prayed for that nephew

and his girlfriend with the past,
And they cast out demons
and they bind them fast.

And they pray loud and long
and they praise and shout,
Till their voices ring in Heaven,
till their voices give out!

Still, they hold this couple
before the throne,
And their tears flow freely
and they start to moan.

But they never give up ~
they stand on God's Word,
And a peace comes upon them
for they know He's heard.

And the guy with a future
falls down on his knees,
And he suddenly asks
would God save him, please.

And the same thing happens
to the girls with a past,
Who's been loose and easy,
who's lived hard and fast ...

She repents her lifestyle
that was full of sin,
And she gives her heart
and asks Jesus in.

And the devil rages!
'cause he lost this time;
But the angels rejoice!
as all Heaven's bells chime!

So, the guy with a future

weds the girl with a past,
And their hearts prove loyal
and their love steadfast.

They live happily ever after
to the very end ...

All for prayers of an aunt
and her Jesus-lovin' friend!

"Now faith is the substance
of things hoped for,
the evidence
of things not seen."
(Hebrews 11:1 KJV)

ഒ

CONNIE

Heaven's Mate
Is This The Mate God Has Chosen For Me?

And he made his camels to kneel down without the city by a well of water at the time of the evening, even the time that women go out to draw water.

And he said, O lord God of my master Abraham, I pray thee, send me good speed this day, and show kindness unto my master Abraham.

Behold, I stand here by the well of water; and the daughters of the men of the city come out to draw water;

And let it come to pass, that the damsel to whom I shall say, Let down thy pitcher, I pray thee, that I may drink; and she shall say, Drink, and I will give thy camels drink also: *let the same be she that* thou hast appointed for thy

servant Isaac; and thereby shall I know that thou hast shown kindness unto my master.
And it came to pass, before he had done speaking, that, behold, Rebekah came out, who was born to Bethuel, son of Milcah, the wife of Nahor, Abraham's brother, with her pitcher upon her shoulder.

And the damsel *was* "very fair to look upon, a virgin, neither had any man known her: and she went down to the well, and filled her pitcher, and came up.

And the servant ran to meet her, and said, Let me, I pray thee, drink a little water of thy pitcher.

And she said, Drink, my lord: and she hasted, and let down her pitcher upon her hand, and gave him drink.

And when she had done giving him drink, she said, I will draw water for thy camels also, until they have done drinking.

And she hasted, and emptied her pitcher into the trough, and ran again into the wall to draw water, and drew for all his camels.

And the man wondering at her held his peace, to wit whether the Lord had made his journey prosperous or not.

And it came to pass, as the camels had done drinking, that the man took a golden earring of half a shekel weight, and two bracelets for her hands of ten shekels weight of gold; (Gen 24:11–22 KJV).

We're finally at the chapter that unveils the divine purpose and reason for writing this book. The chapter where spiritual revelation and the spirit of wisdom and knowledge provides illumination to discern and know the mate He has chosen for you. This chapter will provide scriptural revelations of His Word and of divine purpose for marriage.

Marriage has been defined as a divine institution designed to form a permanent union between man and woman that they might be helpful to one another (Gen 2:18). Whether you're currently in a state of singleness, looking for your mate, recovering from a bad choice, committed to one, or positioned and determined to wait upon Him for the mate He has chosen; the contents of the information provided will enlighten, strengthen and provide the insight needed to make the right choice; the divine choice- Heaven's Mate for your life.

The questions many perhaps are asking are; what is Heaven's Mate? Is there such a mate as Heaven's Mate? Is it possible for me to marry Heaven's Mate? Where would I find such a mate? Does such a mate exist upon this earth? These are all valid questions for unmarried singles believing God for their mate.

Random House Webster' College Dictionary has defined the word mate as a husband or wife; spouse, one of a pair; to become mated; to join or associate suitably: couple. Consequently, as defined in the Three-In- One Concise Bible Reference Companion, the word mate refers to either member of a pair. There can never be Heaven's mate without spiritual compatibility. Heaven's mate can be defined as a mate who is born again, spirit filled, heavenly minded (1 Cor. 13:48), bearing the image of the heavenly (1 Cor. 15:49), a mate in whom the spirit and Word of God dwells. The scripture declares, "as He is, so are we in this world" (1 John 4:7). A mate who is heavenly minded, has learned to set their affection on things above, and not beneath (Col. 3:1–2).

> If then you have been raised with Christ (to a new life, thus sharing His resurrection from the dead), aim at and seek the (rich eternal treasures) things that are above, where Christ is, seated at the right hand of God.
>
> And set your minds and keep them set on what is above (the higher things), not on things that are on the earth (Col. 3:1–2 TAB).

Heaven's Mates are mates who are walking in obedience, surrendered unto Him, and are in love with Him. It's, in Him, they live, move, and have their being. They are after His heart, desires, pleasures, purposes and the things that please Him. They are committed, dedicated, consecrated, and are waiting to fulfill their divine assignment. Their level of discernment is as sharp as the eagle, which is the only bird that look towards the sun and his enemies or ungodly pursuers turn back. Heaven Mates have learned to run to Christ when being pursue, and their enemies or ungodly pursuers turn back. When they cry unto Him, their enemies turn back, because God is with them (Isa. 56:9). The eagle has sharp eyes and is able to see afar off.

- Singles pursuing Heavens Mates are called, ordained, and appointed to fulfill His will.
- Singles divinely assigned; purposes; called, appointed, and anointed to fulfill His purpose in their life.
- Singles are a blessing to the kingdom of God when they are divinely assigned to fulfill His destiny with Heaven's mate!
- Singles learn to be wise and make the right choices/ decisions positioning their families for generational blessings not curses.

Heaven's mate's, destiny, purpose and mission were ordained before the foundation of the world, before they were conceived in their mother's womb. They were called, chosen, and appointed by God to fulfill His purpose in their life (Jer. 1:5). They did not choose their destiny, calling or ministry. Their Heavenly Father foreordained their destiny before the foundation of the world, before he formed them in the womb and before they came forth, he sanctified them.

Heaven's Mates who are obedient unto the heavenly calling, and are in right standing with God have been taught to know the voice of God. They have the spirit of God abiding within, with the ministry of the Holy Spirit, confirming and reassuring them of the will and purpose of God for their life and ministry.

The world's wisdom is full of every creative match making technological approaches available, from cyber- surfing, graphologist (handwriting expert), common sense, intellectual strategies, palm readers, stimulating and exciting the mind and psych's daily. These mates have married outside of the will of God and reaped the consequences of that decision during their entire marriage and life on earth. Often during the longevity of the marriage, their chosen spouse never experienced salvation, or changed their unacceptable behavior. Consequently, causing them to learn to live with the consequences of their decision.

Many because of their love, consecration, and commitment unto God learn to endure all things until death; choosing to cleave and not leave. The spiritual incompatible marriage was an absolute hinderance for experiencing the joy and fulfillment that was foreordained for their marriage and family before the foundation of the world.

Single Christians, there are many mates who will hinder the fulfillment of divine destiny in your life. Their goals, ambitions, desires and purposes are not heavenly bound. In essence, the joy of dwelling in His presence, prayer, Word and fellowship is grievous and not pleasurable, unto them; it is not beautiful but repulsive. Salvation is a gift, not a burden. If by any chance you cast your eyes on a beautiful diva, and her heart dislikes or finds the things of God distasteful or disagreeable; learn to make your exit decision quickly; she is not Heaven's mate. The answer to your choice can perhaps be you have missed it; you are seeing through a glass darkly. You have positioned yourself to receive less than God's best for you.

During a time of severe testing and need in his life, David (1 Sam.30:6) encouraged himself in the Lord, because of the discouragement and disappointment of five hundred ninety-nine men. A great source of inner encouragement would be to ask yourself three questions. The first question is; "Is this the mate I believe God has chosen for me? Will this mate function in His divine plan in helping me to fulfill His destiny and purpose for my life? And finally- divine destiny- until death do us part- is my love for the person strong enough to spend the rest of my live with? These questions will not appeal to the joy and satisfaction that unbelievers seeks, relinquishing the need to seek the wisdom of God through His Word, prayer and waiting upon Him.

The wisdom of the world will never supersede the wisdom of God. The scriptures declare that your faith and trust should not stand in the wisdom of men, but in the power of God (1 Cor. 2:5). Daniel was a man of God in whom an excellent spirit, knowledge, understanding, interpreting of dreams, showing of hard sentences, and dissolving of doubts dwelled.

The glory and power rested upon Daniel so magnificently that he served four heathen kings; and was made master of the magicians, astrologers, chaldeans and soothsayers. The wisdom of the king's team of worldly leaders could not exceed the glorious power and anointing God had upon His anointed.

Heaven's Mate Character?

We're finally at the divine purpose for writing this book, the chapter where you should be able to sincerely examine where you stand scripturally in the mate selection process. Ask yourself the following questions:

- What is the definition of Heaven's Mate?
- Am I ready for Heaven's Mate?
- Can I appreciate Heaven's Mate?
- Am I compatible with Heaven's Mate?
- Do I need more deliverance to live with Heaven's Mate?
- Do I enjoy dwelling in the presence of the Lord?
- Can I live and walk in line with the divine destiny, purpose and mission for Heaven's Mate.
- Do I need to return to the altar and wait on the Lord?
- How much am I willing to submit my life, destiny, purpose and mission unto God?

Are You Ready For Heaven's Mate?

- Here are some questions to ask yourself to help you determine if you are ready for Heaven's Mate?
- Have you acknowledge Him as Saviour and Lord?
- Have you learned to put Him first in your life?
- Have you developed a personal relationship with Him?
- Are you learning to dwell daily in His presence in prayer, fasting, His Word, meditation, and loving communion?
- Do you delight yourself in fulfilling His purpose and will for your life?
- Do you enjoy heavenly pursuits, pleasures and fulfillment?
- Can you share your marriage to Heaven's mate with God and the Body of Christ?
- Can you learn to wait and work patiently with Him when He is fulfilling the will of God in his life?
- Can you agree with the will of the Father, the Holy Spirit and the Word for their life, ministry and work?
- Can you sacrifice your life, destiny and purpose to fulfill His will in their life?

Heavenly Glance
Heavenly Blissfulness

Purpose Of The Heavens

- To declare God's glory . . . . .Ps. 19:1
- To declare God's righteousness. . . . . Ps. 50:8
- To manifest God's wisdom . . . . Prov. 8:27

Believers Present Attitude

- Given foretaste of . . . . Acts 7:55, 56
- Earnestly desires . . . . 2 Cor. 5:2, 8
- Looks for . . . . 2 Peter 3:12
- Considers "far better" than now . . . . . . .Titus 2:5
- Puts treasures there . . . . .Titus 2:5

Description

- Home . . . . .John 14:2
- Kingdom . . . . Matt 25:34
- Abraham's bosom . . . . Luke 16:22, 23
- Paradise . . . . .2 Cor 12:2, 4
- Better Country . . . . .Heb 11:10, 16
- Holy City . . . . {Rev 21:2, 10–27; Rev. 22:11–5}

Positive Characteristics

- Joy . . . . Luke 15:7, 10
- Rest . . . . Rev 14:13
- Peace . . . . Luke 16:25
- Righteousness . . . . 2 Peter 3:13
- Service . . . . Rev 7:15
- Reward . . . . Matt 5:11, 12
- Inheritance . . . . 1 Peter 1:4
- Glory . . . . Rom 8:17, 18

Entrance Into

- Righteous . . . . Matt 23:34, 37
- Changed . . . . 1 Cor 15:51
- Saved . . . . John 3:5, 18, 21
- Called . . . . 2 Peter 1:10, 11
- Overcomers . . . . Rev 2:7, 10, 11
- Those recorded . . . . Luke 10:20
- Obedient . . . . Rev 22:14
- Holy . . . . Rev 19:8

Inhabitants

- God . . . . 1 Kings 8:30
- Christ . . . . Heb 9:12, 24
- Holy Spirit . . . . Ps 139:7, 8
- Angels . . . . Matt 18:10
- Just Men . . . . Heb 12:22, 23

Things Lacking In

- Marriage . . . . Matt 22:30
- Death . . . . Luke 20:36
- Flesh and Blood . . . . 1 Cor 15:50
- Corruption . . . . 1 Cor 15:42, 50
- Sorrow . . . . Rev 7:17
- Pain . . . . Rev 21:4
- Curse . . . . Rev 22:3
- Night . . . . Rev 22:5
- Wicked People . . . . Rev 22:15
- End . . . . Matt 25:46
  Rev 22:5

Heaven's Mate Comparison

In today's generation, many believe there is a God, have read, heard, or just know of God. Many are just somewhere in between? Many are waiting or can't wait for death to enjoy heaven or living in His presence forever. However, they are missing the joy of living the abundant life through Christ Jesus. The values and perspectives of Heaven should guide our lives daily in the things of God.

To learn to walk in, live in, and experience Heaven on Earth is far fetched for many. To believe we can enjoy and experience Heaven on Earth is too humanly powerful to conceive.

In reality, we are spirit filled believers are partakers of all of His heavenly blessings, in heavenly places in Christ Jesus. The scripture declares that God has blessed "His children with all spiritual blessings in the heavenly places."

Learning to live under and experience the outpouring of an open heaven enables us to obtain the breakthroughs and releases we need daily in our lives. When heaven opens, the angels of God will begin to ascend and descend, bringing multiple blessings for the believers. These blessings include love, peace, joy, favor, power, promotion, and breakthroughs.

Too often people fail to realize the effect walking under a closed heaven has upon their lives and those around them. One of the curses in Deuteronomy 28:23 declares, "And the heaven that is over your head shall be brass, and the earth that is under you shall be iron" (Deut. 28:23).

The scripture declare that "God will rend the heavens," and the angels of God will begin to ascend and descend upon our life (John 1:51). Daniel prayed and fasted for twenty-one days. When his angel of blessing came, he said, "Fear not Daniel, for the first day that thou did set thine heart to understand, and to chasten thyself before thy God, thy words were heard, and I am come for thy words. But the prince of the kingdom of Persia withstood me one and twenty days; but lo Michael, one of the chief princes, came to help me; and I remained there with the Prince of Persia" (Daniel 10:12–13). Daniel prevailed in prayer until his answer came. Prayer is the key that turns God's promises into reality.

Husbands and wives should strive to continuously live, walk, and remain under an open heaven. We are in constant need of breakthroughs, releases, and deliverances in many areas of our lives. We have only just begun to experience the manifestation of some of the releases we are in need of, as we learn to walk under an open heaven. There is so much to learn, to experience, and possess in the heavenly realm.

In this materialistic world we live in, man is constantly in search for heaven as man would define it–problem free, worry free, pain free, and full of joy and happiness. Can there be heaven on earth without the Creator of heaven and earth? To answer that question, the answer is no. Can there be an experience in the realm of the heavenly without the Creator? The answer is no.

Man is full of emptiness, and void without the Spirit of God abiding on the inside. The more economic serenity we gain, the more boredom we generate. The more worldly pleasure, the less satisfaction and contentment we have with life. We are like a restless sea, finding a little peace here and a little pleasure there, but nothing permanent and satisfying. And the search goes on! Men will kill, lie, cheat, steal, and war to satisfy their quest for power, pleasure, and wealth.

Heaven on earth elevates man to a realm in the heavens that ministers unto the total man, spirit, body, and soul. Because he has learned to live more abundantly and experience the joy of the Christ within, and not from the mundane external temporary joy, this leaves him still yearning for more happiness, joy, and peace.

Because man is a spirit, he lives in a body and possesses a soul, there exist a deep hunger to satisfy. The soul demands fellowship with

God. It demands worship, quietness, and meditation. The soul must feed upon the Word of God and apply the Word daily, or it will become weak and dwindle. In essence, it remains restless, confused, and discontent.

The inherit quest for excitement and pleasure has many people turning to drugs for pleasure, alcohol to drown the longings and cravings of the soul, and food to satisfy their hunger. In reality, the need is for a relationship and fellowship with God. The hunger is for the Word of God. Only God can completely satisfy our spirit, because the spirit was made for fellowship and communion with God. Without God, man can never be satisfied. It's assuring and comforting to know that "God fills all" our emptiness, and teaches the true meaning of what "Heaven On Earth" really means.

To experience heaven on earth requires surrender and sacrifice from us. It does not come without a price. We must first confess our spiritual poverty and need for a Savior and Lord of our lives. We must renounce our sins and turn by faith to His Son, Jesus Christ. When we confess our sins and become born again, He then puts a little Heaven down in our soul. Our lives change. Peace, happiness, and contentment have come into our heart for the first time. To experience a little of Heaven on earth, we must identify with He who has a message that makes men change their way of thinking. In learning to walk in, live, and follow Christ, we must know that experiencing Heaven on earth is a progressive truth that is ever unfolding in our lives.

Heaven on earth is a liberty in Christ Jesus. We have met Him, who is Truth, and He is making us free (Jn. 8:32). There is a continual operation of His liberating influence upon us. I love the God of Heaven more than I love Heaven. I love His presence more than His presents. We have been birthed into the heavenliness! Now we must continue or press on toward the goal to the heavenly prize to which God in Christ is calling us upward (Rom. 8:11; Phil. 3:10–14).

Heaven's mate is subject to the same challenges, trials, and tests as every couple living on this earth. We have learned through the Word of God and experience to think it's not strange concerning the fiery trials which are to try us, as though some strange thing happen unto us: but rejoice inasmuch as we are partakers of Christ sufferings, that, when His glory shall be revealed, we may be glad also with exceeding joy (1 Pet. 4:12–19). Through their love for God, and each other, they are learning to trust, depend, and look unto Jesus, the author and finisher of their faith. They have learned through experience, "and this is the victory that overcometh the world, even our faith (1 John 5:4).

Presumptuous Faith Marriage Matches

Prince Charming Riding On A White Horse!
The Movies Version Of Hollywood's Most Handsome Man/ Beautiful Woman/ Fantasy Island/
"Picture Perfect Person"
Waiting For Boaz- Wealth In His Chambers

And particularly those who walk after the flesh and indulge in the lust of polluting passion and scorn and despise authority. Presumptuous [and] daring (self-willed and self-loving creatures)! They scoff at and revile dignitaries (glorious ones) without trembling (2 Pet. 2:10 TAB).

But the soul that doeth ought Presumptuously, whether he be born in the land, or a stranger, the same reproacheth the Lord, and that soul shall be cut off from among his people (Num. 15:30 KJV).

So I spake unto you; and ye would not hear, but rebelled against the commandment of the Lord, and went Presumptuously up into the hill (Deut. 1:43 KJV).

And the man that will do Presumptuously and will not hearken unto the priest that stands to minister there before the Lord thy God or unto the judge, even that man shall die; and thou shall put away the evil from Israel (Deut. 17:12 KJV).

Then the King Ahasuerus answered and said unto Esther the queen, who is he, and where is he, that durst Presume in his heart to do so? (Est. 7:5 KJV)

Keep back thy servant from Presumptuous sins; let them not have dominion over me: then shall I be upright and I shall be innocent from the great transgression (Ps. 19:13 KJV).

And particularly those who walk after the flesh and indulge in the lust of polluting passion and scorn and despise authority. Presumptuous (and) daring (self-willed and self- loving creatures)! They scoff at and revile dignitaries (glorious ones) without trembling (2 Pet. 2:10 TAB).

Presumptuous Faith Love Match #1

And particularly those who walk after the flash and indulge in the lust of polluting passion and scorn and despise authority. Presumptuous (and) daring (self-willed and self-loving creatures). They scoff at and revile dignitaries (glorious ones) without trembling (2 Pet. 2:10 TAB).

Keep back your servant also from Presumptuous sins; let them not have dominion over me. Then shall I be blameless, and I shall be innocent and clear of great transgression (Ps. 19:13 TAB).

Sister Sue, spirit-filled believer, set her eyes on Brother Joe in the church. She *Presumed* that he was the mate God had chosen for her. She planned the entire wedding ceremony, purchased the wedding dress, invitations, and made preparation for the wedding day without the groom's knowledge. The day of the wedding, the family, believers, friends, and guests were invited to the wedding- to include the groom, who did not know that he was getting married, and that the bride was suppose to be his future wife. The groom did not know that this was his wedding day, and he was scheduled to show up for his wedding. The sister experienced great hurt, humiliation, financial loss, and disappointment as a result of failing to seek God's wisdom, directions, and confirmation in planning such an elaborate expensive wedding ceremony.

Presumptuous Faith Love Match #2

Sister Lou, from young adult to adulthood, cast her eyes on Brother Lee. She loved him from the moment she saw him and *Presumed* that he was her husband. She became completely engrossed with him, resulting in the birth of five children. This relationship impacted, changed her destiny, causing she and her children lives to become dysfunctional. She followed him early in her life, enlisted in the same branch of military, resulting in the birth of child after child for him. He married several women during her life of suffering in the relationship, and in the end he still did not marry her.

Eventually, on her dying bed, after Brother Lee had acknowledged Jesus as Saviour and Lord in his life, he sincerely went to visit her. She finally received her deliverance–on her dying bed after fifty years of unnecessary waiting and suffering and was empowered to release him at death. Years of painful, unnecessary sufferings, disappointments, and generational strongholds followed her and her family for years, leaving them in a state of dissension, confusion, division, and subjected to many satanic attacks and strongholds.

Presumptuous Faith Love Match #3

Sister Ann, spirit-filled believer, admired Brother Jones in the church. Magnifying her physical beauty, and appearance resulting in confused values; the attractive, young single mother, *Presumed* Brother Jones was the mate God had chosen for her and claimed Him as her mate. Brother Jones was totally unaware of her proposed marriage plans to him. She continued to faithfully attend church as scheduled; and planned an elaborate $10,000 wedding with Brother Jones, with him being totally unaware of his scheduled upcoming wedding date and marriage. He did not know the bride, had not asked her to marry him, and had not given her an engagement ring. Sister Ann rented an elaborate hotel meeting room, had it beautifully decorated, and prepared for the wedding day. Friends, family, and believers attended the planned ceremony, but the groom failed to show- he did not know he was getting married. The disappointment devastated her, and caused many spiritual and emotional set backs in her life. Presumptuous faith has caused many to experience depth of the valley experiences throughout the Body of Christ with the grace and mercy of God healing and restoring them.

In our walk with God, we all learn through various circumstances how to seek God and stand on His Word. These experiences were disappointing, and no doubt devastating in the lives of these believers, but God's Word has not changed. *Presumptuous* faith confessions are not scriptural, not in line with the will of God and are satanically led controlled. They are costly to our Christian journey and growth walk. He teaches us wisdom, knowledge, and understanding in all our experiences. In the book of James 1:5, the scripture declares, "If any of you lack wisdom, let him ask of God, which giveth to all men liberally, and upbraideth not, generous and gracious to all."

Many in the Body of Christ walk in *Presumptuous* faith, claiming mates, and similar steps of faith. In learning to walk by faith, man often overlooks the most powerful ingredient of any relationship and; that is love. God does not force man to love Him or us. He does not turn on love's flow. A small degree of discernment would enable one to discern that many have "missed the mark," or failed to discern the truth concerning their *Presumptuous* faith love match. There is no failure in God. God never makes a mistake. Mistakes happen when we fail to seek Him through prayer, and fail to get His instructions for the specific request we have made.

Mature Christians seek God's will and asks for His wisdom when facing a major decision. Believers must pray about all decisions–especially life decisions, such as "Whom I should marry? Should I marry this man? Is this the mate God has chosen for me?" Such decisions have serious consequences and must be answered through prayer. Seeking and knowing God's will does not happen solely in prayer. It also requires a commitment to know and obey His Word.

The scripture teaches that knowing God's will is the result of continuously conforming your thinking and behavior to God's Word over a lifetime. Our minds are renewed day- by- day through reading God's Word. Carnal ideas, attitudes, and prejudices are replaced by thoughts that conform to God's ways. This is a process that takes time, and there are no shortcuts. This transformation is never completed until death.

Christians who have ongoing fellowship with the Lord through His Word have learned to make decisions based on the Word of God and what he or she believes the Holy Spirit is leading them to do. Knowing God's will during major decision points is much easier if you are seeking His will daily through prayer, searching the scriptures, have fellowship in a local church, and have learned to meditate on the Word of God.

Presumptuous Faith Love Match #4

The Word of God is wisdom, knowledge, and revelation, enabling us to walk in faith with all confidence and assurance. The scriptures declare "none shall want their mate: for His mouth, it hath commanded and His spirit it hath gathered them" (Isa. 34:16). Women who are experiencing the "for every Queen Vashti there is an Esther Syndrome," and walking in *"Presumptuous Faith,"* must realize that Esther came from a genealogy rich in faith and obedience unto God. The preparation and training to assume Queen Vashti's position was a process. Handmaidens must learn to seek the wisdom of God in every step they take toward receiving Heaven's mate. There was a process involved with Esther knowing and realizing her spiritual priorities, and willing to offer up King Ahasuerus on the altar to remain in right standing with God. In essence, her position as queen was not more important than fulfilling her God ordained destiny, in which she proclaimed,

> "Go, gather together all the Jews that are present in Shushan, and fast ye for me, and neither eat nor drink for three days, night or day. I also and my maidens will fast likewise; and so will I go in unto the King, which is not according to the law: and if I perish, I perish"
> (Esther 4:16 KJV).

Esther knew her change from the state of singleness to marriage could only come through God. The title, power, and honor she would acquire were not greater than being used by God to meet the needs of her people. She submitted to spiritual preparation and mentoring under the leadership of Mordecai, her cousin, who adopted her and reared her as his own daughter. Her heart was humble and obedient unto the heavenly vision.

Presumptuous Faith Love Match #5

Countless handmaidens and daughters of Zion have *presumptuously* positioned themselves to wait for the spouse's death of the mate of their choice, in spite of their marriage to another. Waiting for Sarah's death syndrome is a sad and unnecessary path of suffering many singles have chosen.

The scripture has declared in Ecclesiastes 9:11, "I returned and saw under the sun, that the race is not to the swift, nor the battle to the strong, neither yet bread to the wise, nor yet riches to men of understanding, nor yet favour to men of skill, but time and chance happeneth to them all". Many handmaidens have failed to seek and wait upon God to direct them to the selection of their mate. One such Christian lady was the best friend of the pastor's wife. She fasted and prayed fifty days for a mate. Upon the death of her best friend's husband, she married her deceased best friend's husband and became the Pastor's wife. However, in the Sarah's death scenario, Abraham lived to be one hundred seventy five years of age.

After the death of Sarah, he married Keturah, who gave birth to six more children for Abraham. Although Keturah and Hagar (both Abraham's concubines) gave birth to children for Abraham, he gave all he had to Isaac, the child of the promise. He gave gifts to his other children and sent them to the East Country, away from Isaac, his son of promise. After the death of Abraham, Isaac and Ishmael buried their father in the cave of Machpelah. It was the field that he purchased from the Hittites. Relationships that are not according to the will and purpose of God bring challenges and unnecessary sufferings for the entire family (Gen 25:1–9).

Why Heaven's Mate?
The Fulfillment Of The Express Will Of God

> Seek ye out of the book of the Lord and read: no one of theses shall fail, none shall want her mate; for my mouth hath commanded, and his spirit it hath gathered them (Isa. 34:16 KJV).

Seek out of the book of the Lord and read: not one of these (details of prophesy) shall fail, none shall want and lack her mate (in fulfillment). For the mouth (of the Lord) has commanded, and His spirit has gathered them (Isa. 34:16 TAB).

Search from the book of the Lord, and read: Not one of these shall fail; Not one shall lack her mate. For My mouth has commanded it, and His spirit has gathered them (Isa. 34:16 NKJV).

Seek ye out of the book of the Lord and read: no one of theses shall fail, none shall want her mate: for my mouth it hath commanded and his spirit it hath gathered them (Isa. 34:16 SSB).

Thus saith the Lord, the Holy One of Israel, and his maker, Ask me of things to come concerning my sons, and concerning the work of my hands command ye Me (Isa. 45:11 KJV).

Thus saith the Lord, the Holy One of Israel, and its maker, would you question Me about things to come concerning My children, and concerning the work of My hands (would you) command Me (Isa. 45:11 TAB).

Heaven's mate is a mate born and created to fulfill God's purpose upon earth. They were called, chosen, and predestined before they were (Jer. 1:5) conceived in their mother's womb. Heaven's mate is the will or purpose God has ordained for a person, woman or man, before the foundation of the world. The scriptures confirm that it was the sovereign will of God that Abraham would be Sarah's husband, and she his wife. Isaac and Rebekah would marry. Jacob and Rachel would be united (he worked fourteen years), confirming that time is no hindrance to the power of love. Ruth and Boaz were in the foreknowledge and plan of God. It was written that Joseph and Mary would wed. Joseph was predestined and ordained by God to marry Mary, for she was the specially chosen mother of Jesus.

Heaven is in the realm of the spirit. Paul stated, God "has blessed us in the heavenly realm" (Eph. 1:3). He is not talking about a place, nor about the future. He is talking about a spiritual reality. Being seated in the heavenly realm (Eph. 2:6) is referring to a spiritual reality. These spiritual realities refer to our life and existence with Christ.

Marriage, family, children, home, and the total marriage unit is set in a woman's heart from childhood, from the moment she received her first doll and began to "play house." It has been said that "who to marry" is the second most important life affecting decision a person will make. This life altering decision has caused some happy and some very painful family consequences all over the world, including death.

Desiring to marry Heaven's Mate is an awesome request for he or she who loves Jesus, and desires to experience that Heavenly bliss in her relationship, marriage and home. When you love Jesus, have and is experiencing peace, joy and happiness within him- being united with someone who is like minded in the faith, of one mind, one spirit, you both learning to be led by and walk in harmony with His spirit, is beautiful and glorious. This is a manifestation of His Word which declares, "He gives us all things richly to enjoy. Heaven's mate relationships are not your typical "hap-hazard relationships." When the patriarchs of old met their wives, they were all busy, doing meaningful work on a daily basis. Ruth was so humble; she worked in the field gleaning behind the reapers. God knows what His chosen, His elect, needs to strengthen and empower them to "fulfill His purpose on earth."

In the world's Walt Disney story of Cinderella, the fairy tale story begins with a widowed gentleman who lived in a faraway kingdom. He had a lovely daughter named Ella. The gentleman was a kind and devoted father, and needed a mother for his daughter. He married again, choosing for his wife a woman who had two daughters, Anastasia and Drizella. The man soon died and the stepmother's true nature was revealed. She gave Ella old rags to wear and made her do all the housework. Soon, everyone called her Cinderella because she got covered in cinders cleaning the fireplace. But Cinderella had many friends: Bruno the dog, horse, and the mice.

In another part of the kingdom, the king was getting worried that his son wouldn't find a suitable bride. He decided to have a royal ball and to invite the kingdom, in order to encourage the prince to find a wife. When the invitations arrived, the step-mother read aloud, "Every girl in the kingdom is invited to a ball in honor of the Prince." Cinderella was excited! That meant she could go too! The stepmother agreed, but only if she finished all her chores and had suitable clothing to wear.

Cinderella had hoped to fix up her old party dress to wear to the ball. However, the stepmother and stepsisters kept her so busy, that when it was time to go, she wasn't ready. But the loyal mice had a surprise for her! They had managed to mend her dress for her themselves, and it looked beautiful. The step sisters shrieked when they saw Cinderella. "Those are my ribbons!" "That's my sash!" They soon tore her dress to pieces and left. Even Cinderella learned to develop an *intensified prayer life*. She realized she needed inner strength to endure the sufferings her step-mother and sisters were subjecting her unto. She went to her mother's grave where she had planted the branch. She wept so much that the tears fell down on it and watered it. *Three times a day Cinderella went and sat beneath it, wept, and prayed.* A little white bird always came on the tree, and if Cinderella expressed a wish, the bird threw down to her what she had wished for. Cinderella learned like many, that she had to pray through unto the breakthrough (Walt Disney Cinderella).

The essence of the story is, Cinderella ended up attending the royal ball, was the most beautiful woman at the ball, and had to leave at the appointed time, losing her glass slipper. The king's son picked it up. It was small, dainty, and a glass slipper. "The next morning, he went with it to his father and told him," no one shall be my wife but she whose foot this glass slipper fits. Then the two sisters were glad, for they had pretty feet. The eldest went with the glass slipper into her room and wanted to try it on, and her mother stood by. She could not get her big toe into it, and the shoe was too small for her. Then her mother gave her a knife and "told her to cut the toe off." When you are queen, you will have no more need to go on foot. The maiden cut the toe off, forced the foot into the shoe, swallowed the pain, and went out to the king's son. Then he took her on his horse as his bride and rode away with her. They were obliged to pass the grave, and there, on the hazel-tree, sat the two pigeons, which cried–

> *turn and peep, turn and peep,*
> *there's blood within the shoe,*
> *the shoe it is too small for her,*
> *the true bride waits for you.*

Then he looked at her foot and saw how the blood was trickling from it. He turned his horse around and took the false bride home again, and said, "She is not the one." The other sister was next to put the shoe on. Then this sister went into her chamber and got her toe safely into the shoe, but her heel was too large. So her mother gave her a knife and said, cut a bit off your heel, when you are queen you will have no more need to go on foot. The maiden cut a bit off her heel, forced her foot into the shoe, swallowed the pain, and went out to the king's son. He took her on his horse as his bride and rode away with her. But when they passed by the hazel-tree, the two pigeons sat on it and cried -

turn and peep, turn and peep,
there's blood within the shoe,
the shoe it is too small for her,
the true bride waits for you.

He looked down at her foot and saw how the blood was running out of her shoe, and how it had stained her white stocking red. Then he turned his horse and took the false bride home again. This also, "Is not the right one," said he. Have you no other daughter. No, said the mother, there is still a little stunted kitchen-wench, which my late husband left behind him, but "she cannot possibly be the bride." The king's son said she was to send her up to him, but the mother answered, "Oh, no, she is much too dirty. She cannot show herself." He absolutely insisted on it, and Cinderella had to be called. She first washed her hands and face clean, and then went and bowed down before the king's son, "who gave her the glass slipper." Then she seated herself on a stool, drew her foot out of the heavy wooden shoes, and put it into the glass slipper, which fit like a glove. When she rose up and the king's son looked at her face, he recognized the beautiful maiden who had danced with him and cried, "That is the true bride." The stepmother and the two sisters were horrified and became pale with rage. He took Cinderella on his horse and road away with her. As they passed by the hazel-tree, the two white doves cried -

turn and peep, turn and peep,
no blood is in the shoe,
the shoe is not too small for her,
the true bride rides with you.

When they had cried that, the two came flying down and placed themselves on Cinderella's shoulders, one on the right, the other on the left, and remained sitting there.

When the wedding with the king's son was to be celebrated, the two false sisters came and wanted to get into favor with Cinderella and share her good fortune. When the betrothed couple went to church, the elder was at the right side and the younger at the left, and the pigeons pecked out one eye from each of them. Afterwards, they came back, and then the pigeons pecked out the other eye from each of them. And thus, for their wickedness and falsehood, they were punished with blindness all their days.

Cinderella's glass slipper shoe was the *"perfect match"*. The shoe was her shoe. The prince knew she was his wife, and all the acts of desperation, manipulation, and panic could not stop what was ordained to be. The step-mother got desperate, led her daughters in desperation, and overlooked the stunted kitchen-wench, "who was the purpose for the royal ball."

Heaven's love matches are chosen by God, directly according to His will and purpose. Are you missing His best today? Are you going to return and seek the Lord's instructions?

> Thus saith the Lord, Stand in the ways, and see, and ask for the old paths, where is the good way, and walk therein, then walk in it, and you shall find rest for your souls. But they said, we will not walk therein
> (Jer 6:16 KJV)!

> And set your minds and keep them set on what is above (the higher things), not on the things that are on the earth
> (Col. 3:2 TAB).

> Trust in the Lord with all thine heart; and lean not unto thine own understanding. In all thy ways acknowledge Him, and He shall direct thy paths (Prov. 3:5–6 KJV).

> Learning to wait for Heaven's mate is a decision you won't regret. It is a life changing decision that can only bring peace, joy, and happiness in the Lord.

And So I Choose

I Choose Love . . .
No occasion justifies hatred–no in justice warrants bitterness.
I Choose Love . . .
Today I will love God and what God loves.
I Choose Joy . . .
I will invite my God to be the God of circumstance. I will refuse temptation to be cynical . . . the tool of the lazy thinker. I will refuse to see people as anything less than human beings, created by God. I will refuse to see any problem as anything less than an opportunity to see God.
I Choose Peace . . .
I will live forgiven. I will forgive so that I may live.
I Choose Patience . . .
I will overlook the inconveniences of the world, Rather than complaining that the wait is too long. I will thank God for a moment to pray, instead of clinching my fist at a new assignment, I will face them with joy and courage.
I Choose Kindness . . .
I will be kind to the poor, for they are alone. Kind to the rich, for they are afraid. And kind to the unkind, for such is how God has treated me.
I Choose Goodness . . .
I will go without a dollar before I take a dishonest one. I will see the good in others when it is hard to find. I will confess before I will accuse, I choose goodness.
I Choose Faithfulness . . .
Today I will keep my promises. My debtors will not regret their trust. My associates will not question my word. My wife will not question my love, and my children will never fear that their father will not come home.
I Choose Gentleness . . .
Nothing is won by force, I choose to be gentle. If I raise my voice, may it be only in praise. If I clench my fist, may it be only in prayer. If I make a demand, may it be only of myself.
I Choose Self-Control . . .
I am a spiritual being. After this body is dead, my spirit will soar, I refuse to let what will rot the eternal.

I Choose Self-Control . . .
Love, Joy, Peace, Patience, Kindness, Goodness.
Faithfulness, Gentleness, and Self-Control . . .
To these I commit my day. If I succeed, I will give thanks.
I will seek God's face. And then when this day is done, I will
place my head on my pillow and rest.

~

Author Unknown

Choosing Heaven's Love Match—fantasies/myths/fables

"I love her because she is tall, beautiful and well built." This is called looking at the physical qualities and not the character and integrity of the person.

"I love him because he has a good job, well educated, and has a bright future." This is called intellectual and financial convenience, without faith and confidence in the word foundation.

"I love her because she comes from a wealthy family." This is "Get Rich Quick Love", based on the financial status of the family and failure to trust the power of Christ within you.

"I love you because you are attractive." This is completely obvious and recognizable. Here, the mate selection process is based on physical qualities, not the character and attributes of God.

"I love you because you and I click, we enjoy the same interests, activities, and things." This is social love. Love based on the conformity of the loved one to the philosophy of the lover.

"I love you because it's the Christian thing to do." This is agape love- the Christ type of love. This is a divine type of love among Christian people. It is misunderstanding agape love during the mate selection process.

I love you because you are the father of my child." This is the perfect example of forced obligation to accept responsibility when there is obviously no love in the relationship. This is the physical bond of parents for their child.

"I love you because God has placed within me Agape love for you." This is the unconditional love of God all Christians are required to share with each other; not love for a mate.

Heaven's Mate Selection Process

The following examples are true-life experiences with healthy relationships and marriages based on the principle of Agape love during the mate selection process. These relationships are not based on outward appearance, but the inner person, who is created in the image of Christ Jesus.

Love The Lord

Christian, committed, dedicated, God fearing, destiny oriented, balanced Christian walk; growing in the character of Christ.

First Corinithian Thirteen Chapter Love

Christian, walking in First Corinthian Thirteen Chapter love of God; Character of Christ manifested with the Spirit of faithfulness; single mother of three, willing to live her life according to the scriptures.

Until Death Do Us Part

New disciple of Christ. Waiting for the baptism of the Holy Spirit; devoted to God; diligent in studying the scriptures; prayerful and Christ centered. Love children, family; young, healthy, physical fitted body.

Seeking The Right Mate

Christian, young, loves God, committed, dedicated, focused on completing his or her divine destiny, character of Christ in manifestation; loves family, children, cooking, caring, sharing and beautiful sense of humor.

Love / Committed / Spiritually-minded

Christian, Love God, mother of four; heart of love; understand the life of commitment, open minded to the Word of God and understand the challenges of life. Will make the right person the God kind of mate.

Waiting For The Right Mate

Allows the love of God to flow and have free course in his or her life and ministry. Friends and companions given to the Word and ways of God. Love the Lord, committed, dedicated, and taught to wait patiently upon the Lord. Given to the Word, wisdom and way of the Lord. Learning to wait patiently upon the Lord.

Obedience Unto God Is The Key

Chosen the true and only way. Passionately love the Lord and things of God. Taught, walking in and expects the Character of God to come forth in his or her mate. Given to the friends and lovers principle, richly enjoying all that God has given; know how, open, taught and trained to be the God kind of mate.

Preparation For Heaven's Mate

Let marriage be held in honor (esteemed worthy, precious, of great price, and especially dear) in all things. And thus let the marriage bed be undefiled (Heb. 13:4 TAB).
Again, he sent forth other servants, saying, tell them, which are bidden, Behold, I have prepared my dinner; my oxen and my fatlings are killed, and all things are ready. Come unto the marriage (Matt. 22:4 TAB).

Go ye therefore into the highways, and as many as ye shall find, bid to the marriage (Matt. 22:9 TAB).

And said, For this reason a man shall leave his father and mother, and shall be united firmly (joined inseparably) to his wife, and the two shall become one flesh (Matt. 19:5 TAB).

Husbands love your wives, even as Christ also loved the church and gave Himself up for it (Eph. 5:25 TAB).

Nevertheless let every one of you in particular so love his wife even as himself; and the wife see that she reverence her husband (Eph. 5:33 KJV).

Marriage is a beautiful threefold miracle God has ordained for man. It is a biological miracle by which two people actually become one flesh. It is a social miracle through which two families are grafted together. It is a spiritual miracle in that the marriage relationship pictures the union of Christ and his bride, the church.

No other human relationship is to supersede the bond between husband and wife. Marriage is a covenant commitment - a vow made to God and the partner, not only to love, but also to be faithful and to endure in this lifelong exclusive relationship.

God never intended for man to be alone (Gen. 2:18). The very bone from which woman was crafted came from man (Gen. 2:23). Woman was taken out of man, and then presented to man in order to complete him. God created the man and the woman in His image (Gen. 1:26) with physical and emotional needs that only another human being could meet (Gen.2: 18).

The world's principles and trends have confused the thinking and decision-making skills of many who desire to marry, and wait upon their mate according to God's principles. It has been said that "love is blind," and the blind can't lead the blind, less they both fall in a ditch. The revelation of God's Word declares that the "Entrance of thy Word giveth light, it giveth understanding unto the simple" (Ps. 119:130). The Word of God is a revealer of the motives and intents of the heart.

Beloved, don't let the pressures of society and family push you into marrying the wrong person. In His time, God makes all things beautiful (Ecc. 3:11). God has a set time for you to get married. You may feel you've made a mistake and you've missed God's best for you. God's timing is perfect. Faith in God turns hopeless circumstances around. The scriptures declare, "According to your faith, be it unto you" (Matt. 9:29). There is still hope. For every Queen Vashti, there is an Esther. God has divine selections and reselections. Learn to consecrate yourself and seek Him through fasting, prayer and studying His Word. Waiting upon Him with confidence and assurance enables believer to not only develop a deeper relationship with him and character, but to receive the petition he or she has requested of Him.

Refuse to choose your mate using your own wisdom. There is no failure in God. The scripture declares, he that believeth does not make haste (Isaiah 28:16).

The scripture declares when Job was stripped of all his glory and the crown taken from his head (Job 19:9), he positioned himself in faith. He said, "All the days of my appointed time, will I wait till my change come" (Job. 14:14). God alone changes the times and the seasons (Dan. 2:21). It is only God who will cause a permanent change that will change your status from the state of single to married. He is the one that will give you Heaven's Mate and will cause your joy to be full.

Divinely position yourself in faith through God's Word, and believe the scripture which declares, "None shall want her mate; for my mouth hath commanded, and His Spirit has gathered them (Isaiah 34:16)". Consecrating yourself, praying, meditating, and obeying Him will enable you to wait patiently upon God, and allow Him to give you an expected end- Heaven's mate" (Jer. 29:11).

When you believe, that at the right time God will reveal and release His will for you in marriage, only then will you avoid the spirit of worry, unbelief, doubt, and vain questioning. You will learn to enter into His rest and peace (2 Chr. 14:7). You will not be moved by the words, opinions, and thoughts of others. You will not be concerned about the looks of pity, defamation, and shame people thrust upon you.

Learning to build the foundation of your marriage on the foundation of Christ will endure the test of time, because it was perfect in its establishment. When you prayerfully and patiently wait upon the Lord for your mate, He will draw your God chosen mate to you (Isaiah 34:16).

The scriptures declare to be anxious for nothing; but in everything by prayer and supplication with thanksgiving, let your request be made known unto God (Phil. 4:6). Impulsiveness, over anxiousness, and hastiness into marriage causes many to be unprepared to conquer the challenges, trials, storms, and tests of life that come with making the transition from being single to married. Without developing a personal relationship with Jesus, and learning to grow up into Him in all things, confusion, misguided values, and lack of character leaves many singles weeping and crying at the altar.

The cry is, Lord I have missed it; my values are confused. I have been saved and attending church for years- and yet I don't know you. Your Word declares, "My thoughts are not your thoughts, neither are your ways my ways; For as the heavens are higher than the earth, so are my ways higher than your ways, and my thoughts than your thoughts (Isa. 55: 8–9).

The wrong principles and foundations in marriage, to include lust, sex before marriage, marrying for money, marrying to fulfill sexual needs, premature pregnancies, marrying because the man or the woman is handsome or beautiful, are all the wrong reasons for getting married.

Marriage Should Be Based On Four Principles:

Love- God has given you a deep and gentle love for the person. Love never fails. Your love will continue to grow as you both learn to relate sincerely and openly to each other; Your love for each other enables your marriage to grow and experience joy and happiness
(1 Cor. 13: 1–13).

God has given you the spirit of wisdom and revelation in the knowledge of His will and purpose for your mate
(Eph. 1:17).

God has guided and directed you in knowing His will concerning the mate He has chosen (Ps. 25:12).

God's Word has been confirmed by a threefold witness; You have received divine revelation through His Word; taken time to seek Him; heard His voice; and is confident and assured He is leading you to marry (Ps. 32:8).

Divinely Positioned To Receive Heaven's Mate
New Beginning! New Mindset! Fresh Start!

"Behold I make all things new" (Rev. 22:5 KJV)
"Behold I will do a new thing" (Is. 43:19 KJV)
"That you put on the new man" (Eph. 4:24 KJV)
"A new heart and a new spirit" (Ezek. 18:31 TAB)
"Renewed in the spirit of your mind" (Eph. 4:23 TAB)

Inventories are conducted daily in life, in one aspect or the other. However, in order for each one of us to learn to live life and "live it more abundantly" (John 10:10), experience the peace, joy, and happiness declared in God's Word, we must be honest with ourselves and with God. We must conduct a sincere self-inventory in the spirit of truth and sincerity according to God's Word. Are we honest with ourselves? Are we honest with each other? And are we honest with God? Are we inventorying ourselves according to the standards of others? Or, are we deeply involved in the "blame game," blaming our parents, poverty, race, everyone, everything, and anything? Look in the mirror, acknowledge the truth, and make a complete about face.

Yes, I admit, "It's time for change," "It's time for my turning point." "No more blame game!" "I have been parked too long: lingered too long; it's enough - the blame game cycle is over." "I am moving on–Heaven's blessings await me. I am ready for greater, better, awesome, and exceedingly wonderful things that await me as I arise and know that Jesus is real. He is alive, He lives and walks within me, and stands ready to bless as I yield and surrender unto Him.

We must find the turning point in our lives. There is a time and place for everything under Heaven (Eccl. 3:1). However, this only occur when we examine ourselves according to the Word of God; whether we are in the faith, or have fallen by the wayside; following the opinions, wisdom, and doctrines of man.

Is your turning point bound or locked up in that which profits not- the wisdom of man? Have you made that turning point decision to grab hold of faith and forget those things which are behind? Determine within yourself to reach, press forward to those things which are before, receiving and fulfilling His destiny in your life. There is no failure in love. *Love Never Fails.* God is love and He never fails. Receive heaven's showers in your life today.

Checklists/mishaps/overlooks

That Was Then—this Is Now Mentality
Destroying The Cycles Of Defeat And Discouragement

The thief cometh not, but for to steal, and to kill, and to destroy: I am come that they might have life and that they might have it more abundantly (John. 10:10 KJV).

He shall not fail nor be discouraged, till he have set judgment in the earth; and the isles shall wait for his law (Isa. 42:4 KJV).

For this purpose the Son of God was manifested, that he might destroy the works of the devil (1 John, 3:8 KJV).

Is there anything too hard for God (Gen. 18:14 KJV)?

The scripture refers to two types of wisdom. There is a worldly or natural wisdom, and a divine or spiritual wisdom. Worldly or natural wisdom is based on humanistic, casual reassuring. Divine or spiritual wisdom is based on the Word of God.

Countless men and women have missed meeting and receiving their mate because they focused totally on the current state or spiritual condition of the person. A man without the spirit or presence of God is miserable, unlovable, and lacks that sweet smelling savor, love, peace, and joy the indwelling presence the Holy Spirit gives. They have looked at the present state of the person and declared as Peter:

> On the morrow, as they went on their journey; and drew nigh unto the city, Peter went up upon the housetop to pray about the sixth hour.
>
> And he became very hungry, and would have eaten: but while they made ready, he fell into a trance,
>
> And saw heaven opened, and a certain vessel descending unto him, as it had been a great sheet knit at the four corners, and let down to the earth.
>
> Wherein were all manner of four-footed beasts of the earth, and wild beasts, and creeping things, and fowls of the air.
>
> And there came a voice to him, "Rise, Peter; kill and eat."
>
> But Peter said, "Not so, Lord; for I have never eaten any thing that is common or unclean."
>
> And the voice spoke unto him again the second time "What God hath cleansed, that call not thou common" (Acts 10:9–15 KJV).

Many are "dressed for success" as it is so easily stated, but perhaps the truth is; "dressed to deceive" or "dressed to kill." They have not put off concerning the old man, (outward) which is corrupt according to deceitful lusts; and put on the new man, which after God is created in righteousness and true holiness (Eph. 4:20–24). They have not been renewed in the spirit of their mind. The outward person's garments or clothes are still spotted with stains of sin. Everything is perfect–hairstyle, clothes, resume, brief case and all, but they are missing the main ingredient. Yes, one thing is missing. The heart remains the same. It has not been renewed. They have not acknowledged Jesus as Savior and Lord. They remain dressed in the old clothes (garments), and are void of the spirit of Christ in their heart.

Everyone is affected by life challenges and circumstances that often cause some to "hit rock bottom." Some become drug addicts, alcoholics, prostitutes, etc., but the rich grace, mercy, and power of God proves faith in His Word turns hopeless circumstances around. He takes what man has labeled X and makes it excel in the name of Jesus. For example, one such life was that of a prostitute, named Mary Magdalene.

She was a woman suffering from demonic possessions (seven). She met Jesus face-to-face, and that encounter changed her life. Jesus cast from Mary seven demonic spirits that had ruled and caused her to experience less than God's best for her life (Luke 8:2). After her healing experience, Mary became a devoted follower of Christ. Unflappable in her faithfulness, she was counted among the small group of women who, at her own expense, served Jesus and His disciples as they preached and ministered to the masses (Luke 8:2, 3).

Joseph, the beloved son of Jacob, was a second example. He was seventeen years old, and a young man in whom the spirit of God dwelled. He was sold for a servant, and cast into prison for thirteen years for an offense he did not commit. He shared a dream from God with his brothers who were all envious of him. The spirits of jealousy, envy, and hatred of his brothers provoked them to slay him, cast him into the pit, and lie, saying some evil beast had devoured him; to destroy the dream or vision God have given him (Gen. 37:20). Joseph was destined to prosper and succeed, but experienced the satanic hinderance of prosperity in his life because of the jealousy of his brethren.

> And Joseph dreamed a dream, and he told it to his brethren: and they hated him yet the more. And he said unto them, Hear, I pray you, this dream which I have dreamed. For behold, we were binding sheaves in the field, and lo, my sheaf arose, and also stood upright; and behold, your sheaves stood round about and made obeisance to my sheaf (Gen 37:5–7 KJV).

The spirit of God was so great upon Joseph life that everything he set his hand to, the Lord made all that he did to prosper (Gen 39:3). Jewels in disguise are in many pathways, but concealed because of life's circumstances. Are you high-minded, vain, and conceited? Do you despise small beginnings? Is your jewel passing you by, because you can't see your Heaven's Mate? Has man's professionally outlined checklists, opinions, wisdom and counseling caused your mate to pass you by? Are you following fantasies, *soap opera's myths,* how to marry a millionaire or have you fainted, given up or quit, because your picture perfect mate does not exist?

Heaven's mates are in all types of life circumstances. Today, many have and are experiencing life circumstances resembling Mary Magdalene, Joseph, Isaac, Abigail, Ruth, Rebecca, and many other patriarchs of old. In the book of Ecclesiastes 9:11, the scripture declares, "time and chance happeneth to us all." There is no such thing as good and bad luck in the sovereignty of God. In Mark 13:23, Jesus said "But take ye heed: behold I have foretold you all things." God makes all things beautiful in His time (Eccl. 3:11 KJV).

Heaven's mates know how to humble themselves, and received their divinely appointed mate. Have you learned how to humble yourself under the mighty hands of God? If not, consider your ways, wisdom, mindset, and experience renewal again unto repentance (Heb. 6:6). Your mindset must be changed. Be renewed in the spirit of your mind. Let that mind be in you which was also in Christ Jesus (Eph. 4:23).

Part Fifteen

Heaven's Love Matches

And Rebekah lifted up her eyes, and when she saw Isaac, she lighted off the camel.

For she had said unto the servant, what man is this that walketh in the field to meet us? And the servant had said, it is my master, therefore she took a veil, and covered herself (Gen. 24:64–65 KJV).

And the servant told Isaac all things he had done. And Isaac brought her into his mother's Sarah's tent, and took Rebekah, and she became his wife; and he loved her: and Isaac was comforted after his mother's death (Gen. 24:66–67 KJV).

And while he yet spake with them, Rachel came with her father's sheep: for she kept them.

And it came to pass, when Jacob saw Rachel the daughter of Laban, his mother's brother, and the sheep of Laban his mother's brother that Jacob went near, and rolled the stone from the well's mouth, and watered the flock of Laban, his mother's brother.

And Jacob kissed Rachel, and lifted up his voice and wept. And Jacob told Rachel that he was her father's brother and that he was Rebekah's son: and she ran and told her father (Gen. 29: 9–12 KJV).

Love

Love is a friendship that has caught fire.
It is quiet understanding, mutual
confidence, sharing and forgiving.
It is loyalty through good and bad.
It settles for less than perfection,
and makes allowances for human weakness.
Love is content with the present.
It hopes for the future and it doesn't brood over the past.
It's the day-in and day-out chronicle of irritations,
problems,
compromises, small disappointments, big victories,
and working toward common goals.
If you have love in your life,
it can make up for a great many things you lack.
If you don't have it, no matter what else there is,
it is not enough, so search for it,
Ask God for it, and share it!

☙

Author Unknown

Heaven's Love Matches

Meeting Heaven's Mate

Today's dating world is filled with professional techniques, strategies, myths, self-help books, and seminars on how to meet a man or woman, and develop a meaningful relationship. The scripture teaches that idle, desperate, and over anxious women create problems for themselves and everyone around them.

But understand this, that in the last days will come (set in) perilous times of great stress and trouble [hard to deal with and hard to bear].

For people will be lovers of self and {utterly} self centered, lovers of money and aroused by an inordinate {greedy} desire for wealth, proud and arrogant and contemptuous boasters. They will be abusive (blasphemous, scoffing), disobedient to parents, ungrateful, unholy and profane.

[They will be] without natural [human] affection (callous and inhuman), relentless (admitting of no truce or appeasement); [they will be] slanders (false accusers, troublemakers), intemperate and loose in morals and conduct, uncontrolled and fierce, haters of good.

[They will be] treacherous [betrayers], rash, [and] inflated with self- conceit. [They will be] lovers of sensual pleasures and vain amusements more than and rather than lovers of God.

For among them are those who worm their way into homes and captivate silly and weak- natured and spiritually dwarfed women, loaded down with [the burden of their] sins [and easily] swayed and led away by various evil desires and seductive impulses.

[These weak women will listen to anybody who will teach them]; they are forever inquiring and getting information, but are never able to arrive at a recognition and knowledge of the Truth (II Tim 3:1–7 TAB).

The world's statistics, to include the number of men incarcerated, drug addicts, divorcees, alcoholics and confessed homosexuals, are astounding for single men and women waiting for their mates. However, the scriptures instruct Christians to follow God's plans to seek their mate: Refuse to be governed and controlled by this world's statistics, but learn to trust in the wisdom of God (1 Cor. 2:5).

Seek ye out of the book of the Lord and read; no one of these shall fail, none shall want her mate; for my mouth it hath commanded, and His Spirit it hath gathered them (Isa. 34:16 KJV).

Meeting your mate is within the divine plan of God. Are you following God's plans for your life, or have you taken a detour? The scriptures declare "His thoughts are not our thoughts, His ways are not our ways, as the heavens are higher than the earth, so are His ways higher than ours ways, and His thoughts higher than our thoughts (Isaiah 55:8–9).

Dating and courtship have caused many to be sifted like wheat and miss heaven's best for their life. Satan has deceived many as a result of the vanity of their own mind and refusal to wait upon God. They can identify or relate to what the scripture refers to as "silly women laden with sin" (II Tim. 3:6). The lack of sound wisdom and feelings of desperation and depression have taken a grip on their minds and hearts, causing them to be led by their emotions rather than the Word of God. They have forgotten that they are born from above and not from beneath.

God fearing women do not compromise sound Christian teaching to receive satan's counterfeits. Otherwise, receiving Heaven's mate may seem like a modern day guessing game or twenty first century television show that mocks the sanctity of marriage.

- He looks like the mate I desire
- He's built like the mate I desire
- He's anointed, handsome, God fearing and I believe he's my mate
- He ministers God's Word under the anointing, sings, teach the Word and the Spirit of God is upon him
- He's from an anointed, God fearing family, given to the principles and guidelines of God's Word
- He has an anointed voice and ministers under the anointing and power of God.

When we are over anxious, excited, and restless, we can miss the mark (Heb 4:1). Specifically, we miss God's perfect will for our life because we are unwilling to wait upon Him to receive His will and purpose for our life.

The list of Heaven's Mate qualities and characteristics can become very extensive to those who are not willing to let God bring them to the level of perfection before they meet their mate. The interesting revelation for many is, if I want Heaven's Mate, God's Best; I must be willing to go from personal introduction, immersing in thought, work, Christian workshops, seminars and activities; and sincerely submit unto Him, His will, in workings and spiritual makeover.

The scripture declares "in all thy ways acknowledge him, and He shall direct thy paths" (Prov. 3:6). Be not wise in thine own eyes, fear the Lord, and depart from evil. I cannot receive His blessing other than through Him. I will miss it every time; because the lust of the flesh, the lust of the eyes, and the pride of life have blind my eyes. I am not ready for Heaven's Mate. I can't handle Heaven's Mate. My mind is too carnal (worldly). I have not humbled myself to His inworkings, and I see through a glass darkly; but then face-to-face: now I know in part; but then I shall know even as also I am known (1 Cor. 13:12).

For now we are looking in a mirror that gives only a dim (blurred) reflection (of reality as in a riddle or enigma), but then (when perfection comes) we shall see in reality and then face to face. Now I know in part (imperfectly), but then I shall know and understand fully and clearly, even in the same manner as I have been fully and clearly known and understood (by God) (1 Cor. 13:12 TAB).

When we sincerely seek God, He will teach us His ways, and lead us in a plain path (Psalms 27:11). There are no love matches like the matches made in Heaven. Heaven never makes a mistake. God's love never fails.

Here is a glance of a compiled list of healthy, well-rounded places of interest where people congregate for various periods of time:

- Church, Church Choir
- Christian Retreats/Workshops/Seminars
- Gospel Concerts/Extravaganzas
- Christian Conferences/Meetings
- Bookstores
- Theater, Opera
- The Park
- Walk A Dog
- Supermarket
- Art Galleries
- Health Clubs
- Library
- Colleges/Universities
- Shopping Malls

However, virtuous Christian women are women of destiny who have no time for restlessness or boredom. We have learned to surrender our will unto God, and refuse to give *place* to the devil (Eph. 4:27) through idleness, restlessness, or boredom. We are positioned to meet Heaven's mate in prayer and fellowship. We allow God to shape and mold us to be the mates He has predestined us to be.

The latest U.S. census reveals that there are over six billion people on earth. Between the ages of thirty-five and thirty-nine, there are 13,000,000 women for every 10,000,000 men. Between the ages of twenty-five and forty-nine, women outnumber men by 1,250,000. These figures don't reflect drug addicts, alcoholics, men locked up in jail, and the homosexual population (four million acknowledged, but 15 percent of total population show tendencies U.S. Census Bureau). None from these groups do us much good as love partners, so the reality is even worse than the statistics. Essentially, the world's statistics (U.S. Census Bureau) have stated that there are twenty-seven women to one man.

The scripture declares "And in that day, seven women shall take hold of one man, saying, we will eat our own bread and provide our own apparel; only let us be called by your name to take away our reproach (of being unmarried) (Isa. 4:1).

Through faith in God's Word, we know that as God told Elijah, "Yet I have left me seven thousand in Israel, all the knees which have not bowed unto Baal, and every mouth which hath not kissed him (I Kings 19:18). You must decide whose report will you believe? I choose to believe the report of the Lord. Destinies, purposes, missions, goals, and lifestyles are changing because the daughters of Zion are travailing in prayers. They are declaring "the best is yet to come."

When we travail in prayers, the sons and daughters of God will come forth (Gal. 4:19). The anointed Intercessors of God will with all prayer and supplications reverse the world's divorce statistics, for available singles and divorcees destroying generational curses in the Kingdom of God. Our sons and daughters will be delivered from drugs, alcohol, sexual perversions, prisons and all satanic strongholds holding them in captivity today. They will be set free from the strongholds of satan (Gal. 4:19). For the weapons of our warfare are not carnal, but mighty through God to the pulling down of strong holds (2 Cor. 10:4).

Christians are learning to live by faith and not by sight; growing from faith- to- faith, always bounding in the wisdom, knowledge and revelation of God. They are learning to walk like Abraham, who staggered not at the promises of God through unbelief, but called those things, which be are not as though they were, (Rom 4:17), and believed the Word of God. The report of the Lord for singles today is "none shall want their mate." Believing God at His Word means God has chosen a mate for me, and in whatsoever state my mate is currently experiencing and bounded up in; I have chosen to wait upon God for the manifestation and fulfillment of His Word. I will not to be moved by what I hear, what I see, the opinions and doctrines of man, this world's statistics, but only by the Word of God.

God changes the times and the seasons (Dan. 2:21). The power of prayer and committed Intercessors will pray without ceasing, believing God to turn the current divorce statistics and available Christian singles waiting for their mates. Prayer will restore God's principles and purpose to the institution of marriage, causing many families to restore the altar of prayer and supplication in the family, with many acknowledging Jesus as Savior and Lord of their lives. They will learn to walk by faith, and not by sight, determined to stand on God's Word with all wisdom, knowledge, and revelation of the hidden mystery of the gospel of Jesus Christ. They are learning to surrender their hearts and wills unto God, walking as vessels of honor to the glory and honor of God fulfilling His purpose and destiny on earth.

Many believers have chosen to follow and obey the God ordained fast, are positioned in prayer and fasting, (Isa. 58:5–13) standing on the Word; declaring "For this purpose, the son of God was manifested that He might destroy the works of the devil (1 John 3:8).

The Body of Christ is corporately following the scripture and declaring whatsoever ye shall bind on earth shall be bound in heaven, and whatsoever ye shall loose on earth shall be loosed in heaven (Matt. 18:18). They are corporately commanding satan to loose every satanic stronghold, imagination, and high thing that exalteth itself against the knowledge of God, and bringing into captivity every thought to the obedience of Christ (II Cor. 10:4–5). They are following, obeying and submitting to the fast He has chosen.

> Is it such a fast that I have chosen? A day for a man to afflict his soul? Is it to bow down his head as a bulrush, and to spread sackcloth and ashes under him? Wilt thou call this a fast, and an acceptable day to the Lord?
> (Isa. 58:5 KJV).

> If thou turn away thy foot from the Sabbath, from doing thy pleasure on my holy day; and call the Sabbath a delight, the holy of the Lord, honourable; and shalt

> honour him, not doing thine own ways, nor finding thine
> own pleasure, nor speaking thine own words
> (Isa. 58:13 KJV).

Meeting Heaven's Mate
Matched In Heaven

> Seek ye out of the book of the Lord, and read; no one of
> these shall fail, *none shall want her mate;* for my mouth
> it hath commanded, and his spirit it hath gathered them
> (Isa. 34:16 KJV).

Genesis is the book of beginnings. It records not only the beginning of the heaven and the earth, but also of all human institutions and relationships.

The scripture declares, "In the beginning, God created the heaven and the earth" (Gen. 1:1). Because He created the heaven and the earth, and is our source, counselor and wisdom,- He has proven through His word that He is our sufficiency, our all and all. He is wisdom, knowledge, and understanding. He is the great I Am. He is Jehovah-Jireh, our provider (Gen. 22:14).

We are admonished in the scriptures, "If any of you lack wisdom, let him ask of God, that giveth to all men liberally and upbraideth not; ask, and it shall be given him. But let him ask in faith, nothing wavering. For he that wavereth is like a wave of the sea, driven with the wind and tossed "(James 1:5–6)."

Man, in his natural intellect, has learned from the beginning to go around, above, and beyond, but never unto God to seek His wisdom concerning His will for their life. After all, He did create us. We are only earth, dust, and soil. The first scripture in the Bible declares He created the Heavens and the earth. His mind, hand, and wisdom created us. How awesomely made are we (Gen. 1:1).

In realizing how awesome God's creation is, we have peace and comfort in him. The wisdom, knowledge, and understanding to seek, trust and wait upon Him to meet and supply all our needs according to His riches in glory (Phil. 4: 19), and to direct us to Heaven's Mate–created and formed directly from the heart and mind of God. He is knowledge, and knows who your mate is. Can God miss it? Can He make a mistake?

Does He know who I am; what I desire and need, and what will enable me to experience fulfillment and completeness on this earth?

Yes He can! Yes He can! He was there in the original creation. We are all His "originals," His creation, and His design. Let us review the unveiling of several of Heaven's love matches in the scriptures.

Adam And Eve (Gen. 2:26–27 Kjv)

On the sixth day, God said, let us make man in our image, after our likeness; and let them have dominion over the fish of the sea, and over the fowl of the air, and over the cattle, and over all the earth, and over every creeping thing that creepeth upon the earth. So God created man in his own image, in the image of God created he him; male and female created he them (Gen. 1:26–27).

They were created to live in beauty and to replenish the earth. Then God blessed them there in the Garden of Eden. They were instructed to abstain from eating of the tree of knowledge of good and evil. For their disobedience, sin entered with the penalty of death. However, Jesus paid the price for our sins through the blood of the cross, thereby redeeming us from the curse of the law. In essence, we are living under a new and better covenant (Heb. 8:8), which is written on our hearts and not inscribed on stone tablets (Ex. 24:12). The new covenant includes conditions which are to be followed, with blessings for obedience, and curses for disobedience.

Adam and Eve were a couple matched in Heaven. God created them for each other. They were given divine instructions on how to enjoy Heaven on earth. He saw everything that He made, and behold, it was very good. Eve was not an afterthought or happenstance, but an indispensable part of God's Plan. Both Adam and Eve, made "in the image of God," stood as His representatives in the world to care for all He put under their dominion. Had Eve's ears not listened to the voice of the serpent, saying yea; circumstances would have been completely different for creation.

Listening to the wrong voices causes many women and men to miss Heaven's best and receive satan's counterfeit," allowing God's divinely appointed blessings and opportunities to pass them by. Being out of the will of God, in the wrong place, at the wrong time, will cause all of us to miss our God's ordained blessings.

Additionally, had Eve been vain, high minded, and puffed up in the vanity of her mind, she would have said, "Adam, I am not living in the Garden of Eden. I am sorry, I don't do gardens, can't you find another place for us to dwell?" Had she despised the day of small beginnings (Zech. 4:10), as many women and men do today, she would have missed Heaven's best for her life. God never makes a mistake. He is wisdom, knowledge, and understanding. We are prone to mistakes, failures, and defeats when we leave our gardens and despise small beginnings. Learn to thank God for your gardens in life.

By disobedience, man came to a personal and experimental knowledge of good and evil. Through that knowledge, conscience awoke. Expelled from Eden and placed under the second or Adamic covenant, man was responsible to do all known good, to abstain from all known evil, and to approach God through sacrifice.

Abraham And Sarah (Gen. 11:29 KJV)

Abraham and his descendants became distinctly the heirs of promise, (from the call of Abraham (Gen. 12:1) to the giving of the Mosaic Law (Exodus 19:8) living in the Fourth Dispensation; Promise–which was under the Abrahamic covenant an exclusively Israelite. (A dispensation is an era of time during which man is tested in respect to obedience to some definite revelation of God's will (Unger's Bible Dictionary). That covenant is wholly gracious and unconditional. The descendants of Abraham had but to abide in their own land to inherit their blessing. In Egypt, they lost their blessings, but not their covenant.

Abraham took as a wife Sarai (stands for "the mother of all of those who, by grace, are one with the true son of promise") whose name was later changed to the Greek form Sarah. She was indeed his sister (biblically permitted in the Old Testament - God's will during this dispensation), the daughter of his father, but not the daughter of his mother, and became his wife. Sarah was a beautiful and fair woman to look upon. When she and Abraham went to Egypt, the Egyptians beheld her beauty, and the princes commended her before Pharaoh; and she was taken into Pharaoh's house (Gen. 12:11–16). Two notable characteristics mark her life: beauty and barrenness. She undoubtedly had beauty, brilliance, and creativity, but the quality, which implants her in our memories and sets her apart is her unique submissiveness and devotion toward her husband Abraham.

Under trial, Abraham forsook his place of blessing, and made an ungodly decision by instructing Sarah to say she was his sister. He feared the Egyptians would kill him because of her beauty, but would keep her alive (Gen. 12:12). He was also entreated well for Sarah's sake; and acquired sheep, oxen, asses, camels, menservants, and maidservants for her sake (Gen. 12:16).

The Lord plagued Pharaoh and his house with great plagues because of Sarah. Pharaoh called Abraham and said, "What is this that thou hast done unto me? Why didst thou not tell me that she was thy wife? Why saidest thou, 'She is my sister?' So I might have taken her to me to wife; now therefore, behold thy wife, take her, and go thy way. And Pharaoh commanded his men concerning him; and they sent him away, and his wife, and all that he had (Gen. 12:17–20).

Heaven's mates are specially chosen by God to fulfill His specific purpose on earth. In the Old Testament as well as New, men were not allowed to disrespect God's divine order. They opened the door for the wrath of God to come upon them, their home, and all that belonged to them (Gen. 12:17). Men and women married to Heaven's mates are walking under a covenant with God and is protected by God's shield.

Abraham did not refuse to marry Sarah because she was barren. He did not abandon her because she was barren, but he was patient with her until the time God chose to open her womb (Gen. 21:1). He acknowledged the qualities God had invested in his wife. She shared not only her husband's challenges and heartaches, but also his dreams and blessings. She did not waiver. She stood by his side through good and bad decisions, adversities and blessings, in youth and in old age. She is a beautiful example of a woman who loved her husband unconditionally. God's will and purpose were so evident in Abraham's life that he fell upon his face (100 years old) and laughed (Gen. 17:17). Sarah also laughed within herself, being ninety years old when God revealed they would conceive a son. They both knew they were old and well stricken in age. What a walking miracle.

Heaven's blessings continued to flow upon Sarah and Abraham's lives, causing them to experience pleasure even when they were old. The Lord gave them both infallible proof that "there is nothing too hard for God" (Gen. 18:14). Isaac's birth was the manifestation of the Word of God.

Isaac And Rebecca (Gen. 24:1–67 Kjv)

Heaven's mates are conceived, ordained, and positioned for fulfillment of the purpose of God on earth. The book of Genesis is highly typical of how a king would make a marriage for his son (Matt. 25:10; John 2:9) and the unnamed servant who does not "speak of himself," but takes of the things of the bridegroom (Acts 13:4; 16:6,7; Rom. 8:11; 1 Thess. 4:14–16); Rebekah was the type of the church, the ecclesia, the "called out" virgin bride of Christ (Gen. 24:16; 2 Cor. 11:2; Eph. 5:25–32). Isaac was the type of bridegroom "who not having seen the bride," "loves through the testimony of the unnamed servant" (1 Pet. 1:8). Isaac was the type of the bridegroom who goes out to meet and receive his bride (Gen. 24:63; 1 Thess. 4:14–16).

> And Abraham was old, and well stricken in age; and the Lord had blessed Abraham in all things.

> And Abraham said unto his eldest servant of his house, that ruled over all that he had. Put, I pray thee, thy hand under my thigh.

> And I will make thee swear by the Lord, the God of heaven, and the God of the earth, that thou shalt not take a wife unto my son of the daughter of the Canaanites, among whom I dwell.

> But thou shalt go unto my country, and to my kindred, and take a wife unto my son Isaac.

> And the servant said unto him, Peradventure the woman will not be willing to follow me unto this land; must I needs bring thy son again unto the land from whence thou camest?

> And Abraham said unto him. Beware thou that thou bring not my son thither again.

> The Lord God of heaven, which took me from my father's house, and from the land of my kindred, and which spake unto me, and that sware unto me, saying unto thy seed

> will I give this land, he shall send his angel before thee,
> and thou shalt take a wife unto my son from thence.
>
> And if the woman will not be willing to follow thee, then
> thou shall be clear from this my oath, only bring not my
> son thither again.
>
> And the servant put his hand under the thigh of Abraham
> his master, and sware to him concerning the matter
> (Gen. 24:1–6 KJV).

Abraham was old and well stricken in age, and of course a wealthy man. He walked with God many years and learned to trust God. He knew the spirit of the Canaanites daughters among whom he dwelled would "not be the right mate" for his son. He had taught and nurtured his son in the admonition of the Lord. His son saw him live a life of faith and learned to trust God, "who quickeneth the dead and calleth those things that be not as though they were" (Rom. 4:17).

He stood in the gap, interceded on behalf of his son, and instructed his eldest servant to stand as "proxy" during the mate selection process for Isaac. He put his hand under his thigh, and imparted the anointing of God to follow him as he went to seek a bride for his son Isaac.

When parents, guardians, and believers are in right standing with God, whatsoever they ask in prayer, believing they receive, they shall receive in the name of Jesus (Matt. 21:22).

Abraham gave his servant specific instructions to follow, prayed, and trusted God to do the rest to fulfill His Word in his son's life.

He did not send his servant empty handed, but he sent him with a dowry.

> And he made his camels to kneel down without the city
> by a well of water at the time of evening, even the time
> that women go out to draw water.
>
> And he said, O Lord God of my master Abraham, I pray
> thee, send me good speed this day, and show kindness
> unto my master Abraham.
>
> And let it come to pass, that the damsel to whom I shall
> say, Let down thy pitcher, I pray thee, that I may drink;
> and she shall say, Drink, and I will give thy camels drink

also; let the same be she that thou hast appointed for thy servant Isaac; and thereby shall I know that thou hast showed kindness unto my master (Gen. 24:11–14 KJV).

> Behold, I stand here by the well of water; and the daughters of the men of the city come out to draw water (Gen. 24:11–28).

Rebekah has been described as a woman of faltering faith, chaste and beautiful (Gen. 24:16), courteous and helpful (v.8), industrious (v. 19,20), hospitable (v. 25), as well as responsive and trusting (v.58). Like Isaac's mother Sarah, Rebekah was very fair to look upon and a virgin. She went down to the well, filled her pitcher, and came up. Because Abraham had given his eldest servant instructions and prayed, the Spirit of God directed him in all he endeavored to do and made his journey prosperous. He was quickened and granted divine reassurance that "She was Isaac's wife." Remember God's Word, Spirit, and sovereignty reign in the lives of obedient men and women.

Then Laban and Bethuel answered and said, "The thing proceedeth from the Lord; we cannot speak unto thee bad or good" (Gen. 24:50 KJV).

To confirm the power and glory of a Heaven's mate selection, behold the scriptures describing the responses and reactions of Heavenly selections.

> And Isaac came from the way of the well Lahai-roi; for he dwelt in the South Country."

> And Isaac went out to meditate in the field at the eventide and he lifted up his eyes, and saw, and behold, the camels were coming.

> And Rebekah lifted up her eyes, and when she saw Isaac, she lighted off the camel.

> For she had said unto the servant, what man is this that walketh in the field to meet us? And the servant had said, It is my master; therefore she took a veil and covered herself.

> And the servant told Isaac all things that he had done.

> And Isaac brought her unto his mother Sarah's tent, and took Rebekah, and she became his wife; and he loved her; and Isaac was comforted after his mother's death (Gen. 24:62–67 KJV).

We don't read anywhere in the scriptures where Isaac or Rebekah were unhappy with the Heaven's mate selection process, or that their parents made a mistake, but they were happy. Their hearts, minds, and souls united. They were joyful, happy, and jubilant. They became as one in the spirit and experienced the joy of receiving Heaven's mate.

Also, Abraham did what many parents in the twenty first century should learn to do. He interceded unto God on behalf of his children for godly mates. He learned to destroy generational curses and satanic attacks through guarding his son with prayers according to the will of God for his life. Parents and Guardians must learn to trust God to lead and guide them in the path of the right mates and choices for their lives; and teach them to be selective, prayerful and discerning *in selecting divinely appointed mates.*

Jacob And Rachel (Gen. 27:38 Kjv)

Jacob was the younger of twin sons born to Isaac and Rebekah. Through cunning craftiness and manipulation, he stole his brother Esau's blessing and birthright. As his brother Esau said, "Is not he rightly named Jacob? For he hath supplanted me these two times; he took away my birthright, and, behold now he hath taken away my blessing." And he said to his father, "hast thou not reserved a blessing for me?" (Gen. 27:38)

In observing the release and receipt of the generational blessings in Abraham's family, we see that God blessed the men in Abraham's lineage with beautiful and fair women. The generational blessings passed down to the generations of Abraham's lineage. The scripture declares, "God is not a respecter of persons" (Acts 10:34). The same Heaven's mate selections and choices that were passed down from generation to generation-in Abraham's family can also be manifested in our families and lives today.

It behooves us to follow, walk with, serve, and obey our God. "No good thing will he withhold from them that walk uprightly" (Ps. 84:11). Heaven's husbands, wives, and mates are good things, and are absolute "blessings from the Lord."

> And Rebekah said to Isaac, I am weary of my life because of the daughters of Heth; If Jacob takes a wife of the daughters of Heth, such as these which are of the daughters of the land, what good shall my life do me
> (Gen. 27: 46 KJV)?

Rebekah loved her son Jacob, wanted the best for his life, and was determined to guard her son with prayers, supplications, and all watchfulness. She had observed the behavior of the daughters of Heth. The daughters' ancestors were the Hittites who the God of Heaven warned, and admonished the children of Israel not to marry (Gen. 27:46). We must learn how to stand in the gap and "fight the good fight of faith for our children."

> And Isaac called Jacob, and blessed him, and charged him and said unto him "Thou shall not take a wife of the daughters of Canaan.
>
> Arise, go to Padan-aron, to the house of Bethuel thy mother's father; and take thee a wife from thence of the daughters of Laban thy mother's brother
> (Gen. 28:1–2 KJV).

In obedience unto his parents, Jacob journeyed unto the east. Jacob, in running away from his brother Esau, ran into his blessings. Jacob was positioned to receive Heaven's mate and walked right into the blessings of God, despite Esau's anger and threat to kill him.

> And Jacob said unto them, my brethren whence be ye?
> And they said, of Haran are we.
>
> And he said unto them, know ye Laban the son of Nabor?
> And they said, we know him.
>
> And he said unto them, Is he well? And they said, He is well; and behold, Rachel his daughter cometh with the sheep. And while he yet spoke with them, Rachel came with her father's sheep; for she kept them.

And it came to pass, when Jacob saw Rachel, the daughter of Laban his mother's brother, and the sheep of Laban his mother's brother, that Jacob went near, and rolled the stone from the well's mouth, and watered the flock of Laban his mother's brother.

And Jacob kissed Rachel, and lifted up his voice and wept.

And Jacob told Rachel that he was her father's brother, and that he was Rebekah's son; and she ran and told her father (Gen. 29: 4–12 KJV).

The scriptures declare that Rachel was beautiful and well favored. Jacob loved and desired Rachel so much, he offered to serve seven years labor for her father Laban. The seven years he served for Rachel seemed unto him but a few days, for the love he had for her (Gen. 29:27).

In the fulfillment of Jacob days of serving for Rachel, Laban deceitfully gave Jacob his daughter Leah, and Zilpah his maid for a handmaid. Laban did not tell Jacob that the custom of their country was to give the firstborn, then the younger. He was instructed to fulfill the wedding feast week, and he would be given Rachel also for his service, which he shalt serve yet seven other years (Gen. 29:24–27).

Jacob loved Rachel from the time he laid eyes upon her. Serving an additional seven years was a small thing for Jacob. This was his Heaven's mate, and he was prepared to make the sacrifice to receive her as his wife. His love for Rachel reiterated the Word of God, which declares love "beareth all things" (1 Cor. 13:7). In man's quest for love, time, distance, or whatever the hindrance may be, does not stand in the way or stop the manifestation of that *fulfillment.*

Joseph And Mary (Matt. 1:19 Kjv)

There are many marriages, but none like Joseph and Mary's. This marriage was ordained and predestined to be Heaven's mate for Mary, who gave birth to Jesus, the Son of God. "Jesus was not begotten" of natural generation. Christ (Christ - anointed), the "Messiah" is the official name of our Lord, as Jesus is His human name (Luke. 1:31; 2:21). Jesus was anointed with the Holy Spirit, thus becoming officially "The Christ."

Now the birth of Jesus Christ was on this wise. When his mother Mary was espoused to Joseph, before they came together, she was found with child of the Holy Ghost.

Then Joseph her husband, being a just man, and not willing to make her a public example, was minded to put her away privately.

But while he thought on these things, behold, the angel of the Lord appeared unto him in a dream, saying, Joseph, thou son of David, fear not to take unto thee Mary thy wife; for that which is conceived in her is of the Holy Ghost.

And she shall bring forth a son, and thou shalt call his name Jesus; for he shall save his people from their sins.

Now all this was done, that it might be fulfilled which was spoken of the Lord by the prophet's saying,

Behold, a virgin shall be with child, and shall bring forth a son, and they shall call his name Emmanuel, which being interpreted is, God With Us.

Then Joseph being raised from sleep did as the angel of the Lord had bidden him, and took unto him his wife.

And knew her not till she had brought forth her firstborn son; and he called his name Jesus (Matt. 1:18–25 KJV).

The marriage of Joseph and Mary was so special and holy, that the angel Gabriel was sent from God unto a city of Galilee named Nazareth to announce the marriage and birth of Jesus (Lk. 1:26).

Mary was highly favored and specially chosen by God. The awesome concept of submitting her virgin body to the Holy Spirit and surrendering it as an instrument to be used unto the glory of God was misunderstood by many. However, Mary's trust in God and fulfilling her divine destiny of marriage to Joseph was the fulfillment of His purpose in their lives. Mary was on divine assignment. She joyfully submitted herself to fulfilling the assignment. The confirmation for fulfillment of such a divine assignment received special salutation and a word from the angel of the Lord.

> And the angel came in unto her, and said, Hail, thou that art highly favored, the Lord is with thee, blessed are thou among women.
>
> And when she saw him, she was troubled at his saying, and cast in her mind what manner of salutation this should be.
>
> And the angel said unto her, Fear not, Mary, for thou hast found favor with God.
>
> And, behold, thou shalt conceive in thy womb, and bring forth a son, and shalt call his name Jesus.
>
> He shalt be great, and shall be called the Son of the Highest; and the Lord God shall give unto him the throne of his Father David.
>
> And he shall reign over the house of Jacob forever; and of his kingdom there shall be no end. Then said Mary unto the angel, How shall this be, seeing I know not a man?
>
> And the angel answered and said unto her, The Holy Ghost shall come upon thee, and the power of the Highest shall overshadow thee; therefore also, that holy thing which shall be born of thee shall be called the Son of God (Luke. 1:28–35 KJV).

Heaven's mate receives the revelation and confirmation of their unions in many ways. Mary, the mother of Jesus Christ (Matt. 1:18), experienced an angelic visitation confirming God's purpose and destiny for her life and marriage. During a time of doubt and uncertainty about marrying Mary, Joseph decided to repudiate and dismiss her secretly. However, as he was thinking this over, an angelic visitation of the Lord appeared to him in a dream (Matt. 1:18–20), revealing unto him do not be afraid to take Mary as your wife, for that which is conceived in her is from the Holy Spirit. God has the power to release and stop all things, including marriages He has not ordained. This Heaven's mate marriage and all that was predestined, *had to be fulfilled.* She was called for such a time and holy purpose as this.

Twenty first century women and men can also receive their Heaven's mate. Learning to live a life of obedience, sacrifice, and commitment to God has a great recompense of reward. It is a reward not only for the couple, but the entire family. It positions the family for the blessings, honor, and glory of God in their lives. It positions the family to be vessels or men and women of honor, and not dishonor, birthed to fulfill God's mission, purpose and destiny on earth. What a mighty God we serve?

Mary was not only a virgin and virtuous woman, but she was an honored mother, and a wise woman of God. She learned to listen to and obey the voice of God. She was also able to keep great and wondrous things spoken unto herself, and ponder them in her heart (Lk. 2:19). Wise women learn when to speak and when not to; when to ponder great and wondrous things and when not to. She was called, chosen, and set aside by our Heavenly Father for such a time as that. Jesus had a wise mother.

Zacharias And Elizabeth (Luke 1:5-6 Kjv)

There was in the day of Herod, the king of Judea, a certain priest named Zacharias of the course of Abia: and his wife was of the daughters of Aaron, and her name was Elizabeth.

And they were both righteous before God, walking in all the commandments and ordinances of the Lord blameless (Luke 1:56 KJV).

Generational blessings flow in families destined by God to walk in righteousness.

Zacharias, whose name means the Lord remembers, was a priest belonging to the division of Abyah. It was one of the twenty-four shifts into which the Jewish priesthood had been divided by David (1 Chron. 24:10). Each shift was called on to serve at the temple, in Jerusalem, twice a year from Sabbath to Sabbath. There were so many priests at this time, that the privilege of burning incense in the Holy Place came only once in a lifetime, if at all.

Elizabeth, which means the oath of God, was also descended from the priestly family of Aaron. She and Zacharias were devout Jews, scrupulously careful in observing the Old Testament scriptures, both moral and ceremonial.

This couple had been taught the law and Word of God. The scriptures do not go into detail of their meeting, but it does states they had no children, which was considered to be a reproachful condition for any Jew. Doctor Luke notes that the cause of this was Elizabeth's barrenness. The problem was intensified by the fact that they were well advanced in years.

However, as a result of His destiny for their life, "He sent a divine revelation by the angel of God." An angel of the Lord appeared on the right side of the altar - the place of favor. Zacharias was terrified. None of his contemporaries had ever seen an angel. But the angel reassured him of wonderful news. A son would be born to Elizabeth, to be named John (the favor or grace of Jehovah). In addition to bringing joy and gladness to his parents, he would be a blessing to many.

The aged Zacharias was struck by the sheer impossibility of the promise. Both he and his wife were too old to become parents. Because Zacharias doubted the spoken Word, he lost his power to speak until the child was born (Lk.1: 20).

Heaven's mate experience the miracles, righteousness, and happiness of the Holy Spirit as he or she continues following and obeying Him. "For with God, nothing shall be impossible" (Luke. 1:37). This couple was old, and the glory of God, overtook their age, and empowered them to conceive a son named John The Baptist. John's mission would be to prepare the hearts of the people for the coming of the Lord, and proclaim salvation to His people through the forgiveness of their sins. John came to prepare the way before Jesus.

Boaz And Ruth (Ruth 2:3-14 Kjv)

And Naomi had a kinsman of her husband's, a mighty man of wealth of the family of Elimelech, and his name was Boaz. And Ruth the Moabite said unto Naomi, Let me now go to the field and glean ears of corn after him in whose sight I shall find grace. And she said unto her, Go, my daughter.

And she went, and came, and gleaned in the field after the reapers. And her hap was to light on a part of the field belonging to Boaz, who was of the kindred of Elimelech.

And, behold, Boaz came from Bethlehem, and said unto

the reapers, "The Lord be with you." And they answered him, The Lord bless thee.

Then said Boaz unto his servant that was set over the reapers, "Whose damsel is this?"

And the servant that was in charge of the reapers answered and said, "It is the Moabitish damsel that came back with Naomi out of the country of Moab. And she said, I pray you, let me glean and gather after the reapers among the sheaves: so she came, and has hath continued even from the morning until now, that she tarried a little in the house.

Then Boaz said to Ruth, Hearest thou not my daughter? Go not to glean in another field, neither go from hence, but abide here fast by my maidens. Let thine eyes be on the field that they do reap, and go after them: Have I not charged the young men that they not touch thee? and when thou are athirst, go to the vessels, and drink from what the young men have drawn.

Then she fell on her face, and bowed herself down to the ground, and said unto him "Why have I found grace in thine eyes that thou shouldest take knowledge of me, since I am a stranger?"

And Boaz answered and said to her, "it has been fully been shown me, all that thou hast done unto thy mother-in-law since the death of thine husband; and how thou hast left thy father and thy mother and the land of your nativity, and art come unto a people which thou knowest not heretofore. The Lord recompense thy work, and a full reward be given thee of the Lord God of Israel, under whose wing you have come to trust"
(Ruth 2: 2–12 KJV).

Ruth's example of *"Give Me Heaven's Mate"* is truly similar to the fairy tale *Cinderella* story. Her name, which is a contraction of the Hebrew reuth, comes from the root for "sight," meaning "something worth seeing." After the death of her husband, being a young wife, she cleaved unto her mother-in-law. Her vow to Naomi, her mother-in-law, stands as one of the most beautiful statements of commitment in history (Ruth 1:16, 17).

Ruth understood that moving to Bethlehem meant total renunciation of her heritage, and a lifetime of living as a foreigner. Her arrival to Bethlehem with Naomi marked the beginning of a new life for Ruth. She was a faithful young woman, and determined she would earn a living to take care of her mother-in-law. This commitment led her to work in the barley field, where she gleaned the edges left for the poor people. The sheaves of grain were collected and threshed with a heavy wooden hand tool. Then, with a large fork, the grain was lifted into the air to allow the wind to blow away the chaff. Many of the poor women flirted with the reapers and tried to steal grain, but Ruth soon gained a reputation for such honesty and integrity that Boaz commended her life.

Ruth was described as a faithful Moabite who saw "something special" in her mother-in law. She wanted what Naomi had. She wanted her God to become her God, and was determined to follow her whithersoever she went. She was seeking to get in the center of God's perfect will. She positioned herself to be in the right place, at the right time, doing the right thing. She was not going to look for Heaven's mate. "Men are hunters and do not desire to be hunted." They want to enjoy the pleasure of "hunting or finding their mate.

❦

"He who finds a wife, finds a good thing and obtaineth favor of the Lord" (Prov. 18:22 KJV).

❦

Interestingly enough, Ruth was positioned for Heaven's mate. She was not beyond working to support herself and her mother-in-law. Gleaning in the field was not an easy work assignment for Ruth. Those of us who are familiar with working in the field understand that she was dressed for fieldwork; head tied with hat, and prepared to endure the morning dew and hard labor of the field. However, this did not hinder the inner beauty of the indwelling Christ. Because she had, "called those things which be not as thou they were," calling favor on the meeting of she and Boaz. She experienced the manifestation of her decree, when she met Boaz, "She found favor in his eyes, and he took notice of her" (Ruth 2:5).

Boaz, the wealthiest man in the land, took notice of a poor young woman. He asked the question, "Who was that woman gleaning in the field–field clothing and all?" He commanded blessings upon her, and brought her from gleaning in the field, from "absolute poverty and deprivation," to "absolute wealth and riches." When God's will and purpose are being fulfilled against all odds; poverty, lack of education, obesity, or whatever the identified hindrance - nothing can stop it. "Whom God bless–no man curse" (Num. 22:12).

In order to receive Heaven's mate, Ruth needed counseling, coaching, and mentoring. Ruth did not tell Naomi she was old, had lived her life, and didn't have a clue about how to marry the wealthiest man in the land. She followed the wise counseling of her mother-in-law. Humble and teachable, Ruth earned the respect and eventually the love of Boaz, and became wife to the wealthiest man in the land.

Ahasuerus And Esther (Est. 2:8–9 KJV)

> So it came to pass, when the King's commandment and his decree was heard, and when many maidens were gathered together unto Shushan the palace, to the custody of Hegai, that Esther was brought also unto the King's house, to the custody of Hegai, keeper of the women.
>
> And the maiden pleased him, and she obtained kindness of him; and he speedily gave her things for purification, with such things as belonged to her, and seven maidens, which were meet to be given her, out of the King's house; and he preferred her, out of the King's house; and he preferred her and her maids unto the best place of the house of the women (Est. 2:8–9 KJV).

In the days of King Ahasuerus, he made a feast unto all the people that were present in Shushan, the palace. His wife Vashti made a feast for the women in the royal house, which belonged to King Ahasuerus. Vashti was commanded to come before the King with the royal crown to show the people and the princes her beauty, for she was fair to look on.

But Vashti refused to come at the king's commandment by his chamberlains. Her apparent disrespect, lack of reverence and honor provoked the king to wrath, and his anger burned within him.

The king said to the wise man who knew the times, "What shall we do unto the queen Vashti according to the law, because she hath refused the commandment of the king by the chamberlains" (Est. 1:12)?

The answer before the King and the princes was that Vashti hath not done wrong to the King only, but also to all the princes, and to all the people in the provinces of King Ahasuerus.

Vashti refused to honor the king and submit to the royal order of the king's house. Her decision to disobey the order of King Ahasuerus, assuming he would forgive her later, was a serious miscalculation. Her arrival was announced in front of the king's officials and guests, making her refusal equally public and humiliating in the presence of his subjects. The example of the queen was publicly announced, inciting all women to despise their husbands in their eyes. They stated that too much contempt and wrath would arise among the ladies of Persia and Media.

Vashti's disrespect, dishonor, and lack of submission and obedience unto the king caused her to forfeit her royal position. The king sent out a royal commandment, and had it written among the laws of the Persians and the Medes, that Vashti not be allowed to come anymore before King Ashasuerus, and that the king gave his royal estate unto another that was better than she.

The king sent letters unto all his provinces, and every province according to the writing thereof, that it should be published according to the language of every people.

God's principles and guidelines for relationships, marriages, and the home, establishes the foundation for developing and maintaining healthy Christian marriages, relationships, families and homes. Husbands and wives are required to provide examples for their children and the family in their Christian walk and lifestyle.

The scriptural standards and principles are the best guidelines for Christians to live, teach, and instruct their children and families.

When we examine ourselves according to the Word of God, healing, deliverance, growth, and spiritual maturity can be manifested in our lives and families.

There are many women today with the spirit and attitude of Vashti. She experienced a quick and rude awakening concerning her decision not to go before the king. If you truly and honestly love your spouse, you will seek ways to compliment him/her in all ways, will be determined to make your marriage work, and destroy with prayer, standing in faith, on the Word of God, and destroying all the works of the enemy working against your marriage, home and family. The scriptures declare that love is as strong as death. Only death can break the power of love. Vashti's behavior was inappropriate and disrespectful to her husband. Love apologizes, repents quickly, chooses to forgive, and make the necessary behavioral adjustments to correct the problem or circumstance.

God used the faithfulness of this ordinary woman to accomplish His extraordinary plans. She humbled herself, was faithful, and sincerely desired to follow God's plan for her life.

Twenty First Century Mates

Marriage and divorce rates among Christians have accelerated in the twenty first century. Divorce rates are astounding and leave much to the testimony of honoring the vow of marriage. A key question is "Who missed it?" "Who has missed it?" "Who is missing it now?" "Why are we missing the mark in this area of our lives?"

A typical phrase use in the world today is "that was then, this is now!" The scripture declares, "As Jesus is, so are we in this world" (1 John 4:17). He is the same, yesterday, today and forever more (Heb. 13:8). Examining ourselves according to God's Word provokes every one of us to seek the wisdom, knowledge, and revelation of God's Word concerning the problems and circumstances in our lives.

Thus saith the Lord, Stand ye in the ways, and see, and ask for the old paths, where is the good way, and walk therein, and ye shall find rest for your soul. But they said, We will not walk therein (Jer. 6:16 KJV).

The character of God, Christian morals, principles, and most importantly, the Word of God, have not changed. Are we prepared for growth and change? The foundation for the new birth, growth, and maturity in God's Word has not changed.

Forbearing with each other and longsuffering have become a byword of the past, catering to man's intellect, fantasies, vanities, and alienations.

In viewing the examples of the lives of Heaven's mate, it was evident that Jacob loved Rachel. Laban, in the spirit of deceit, changed the length of his waiting, to an additional seven, making it fourteen years. His apparent love for Rachel prevailed and persuaded him to pay the price for the love of his life. Consequently, he waited for the fulfillment of the second contractual agreement.

Fantasies, imagination, vanities, and the school of drama have perplexed man's mind to believe he is perfect, and must have nothing less, than the perfect mate. Remember, the title of this book is "Give Me Heaven's Mate," not "Give Me the Perfect Mate."

We are born as imperfect human beings. As the scripture declares, "Behold, I was shapen in inequity; and in sin did my mother conceive me" (Psalm 51: 5). We are imperfect human beings, and without Jesus, "The Perfector," we can never be made perfect. David, being a man after God's own heart, eloquently stated, "My God shall perfect all that concerneth me" (Psalms 138:8). He examined himself in line with the Word of God and realized there was a greater maturity, perfection, and manifestation of the character of God needed in his life.

In essence, "I love you and believe you are my Heaven's mate. Through prayer, His Word, we learn to surrender our will unto Him that we may stand perfect, complete in Him (Col. 4:12), and learn to grow up in Him in all things. From glory to glory He is changing us. From earthly things to heavenly things, He is changing us. There is a maturing process that must take place in all believers as we surrender unto Him in spirit and truth.

> See what (an incredible) quality of love the Father has given (shown, bestowed on) us, that we should (be permitted to) be named, called, and counted the children of God! And so we are! The reason that the world does not know (recognize, acknowledge) Him. Beloved, we are (even here and) now God's children; it is not yet disclosed (made clear) what we shall be (hereafter), but we know that when He comes and is manifested, we shall (as God's children) resemble and be like Him, for we shall see Him just as He (really) is. And every one who has his hope (resting) on Him cleanses (purifies) himself just as He is pure (- chaste, undefiled, guiltless)
> (1 Jn. 3:3–3- TAB).

"To live is to grow. To grow is to change! What beautiful and heavenly love for two Christians to grow up together in Him in all things. To change together in Him in all things! To develop together in Him in all things!

As believers, our growth is progressive. We don't remain a baby during our entire Christian walk. We don't remain a child during our Christian walk, but we must go on to maturity and adulthood in Christ Jesus.

God is doing something great in our life today that necessitates change.

In our Heaven's mate's relationship, saying and meaning "I am sorry" should never be a problem. We know that saying "I am sorry" is a key to maintaining a right spirit and attitude with God and each other.

> Therefore repent at once, instantly changing your attitude, and perform a right–about face in order that there may come epoch - making periods of spiritual revival and refreshment from the presence of the Lord and in order that He may send you off on a mission for Christ Jesus who has been appointed; this appointment being in the interest of your well-being; whom it is a necessity; in the nature of the case, for Heaven indeed to receive the fullness of the Godhead bodily, until times when all things will be restored to their pristine glory, things regarding which God spoke through the mouth of His holy prophets who lived in bygone times . . . And indeed, all the prophets since Samuel, and those who followed, one after another, as many as spoke, also announced these days" (Acts 3:19–21, 24-Wuest).

Heaven's mates learn not to go into relationships closed minded. They know that the greatest hindrance to any relationship is the way we think, especially when it is not the mind of Christ. The scripture declares to "Let this mind be in you, which was also in Christ Jesus" (Phil. 2:5)! The mind of Christ is His Word, the only answer and solution to our problems. Let us give ear and submit our minds to the living Word that is coming through God's ambassadors of this hour. We must stop thinking like men and start thinking like Sons of God (1 Cor 16:13).

Mate Selections To Avoid/watch

- Parent's Selection
- Mother's Selection
- Sister's Selection
- Teacher's Selection
- Friend's Selection
- Neighbor's Selection
- Pastor's Chosen Selection
- Satan's Counterfeits
- Lustful Selection
- Children's Selection
- Computerized Matches
- Blind Dates
- Supervisor's/ Employer's Selection
- Political Selection
- Ancestral Chosen Selection
- Carnally Minded Christian Selection

Knowing/obeying God's Voice

Christian believers, parents, and guardians must learn to believe and follow the Word of God. In Genesis 18:19, the scripture declares, "For I know him, that he will command his children and his household after him, and they shall keep the ways of the Lord, to do justice and judgment; that the Lord may bring upon Abraham that which he hath spoken. God has chosen Heaven's mates because He know that they will teach and instruct their children the right way. They will train them in the way of the Lord. This would ensure the fulfillment of the promise of God unto Abraham. If Abraham and his children had not walked in the ways of God, that would have been the end of the Abrahamic covenant. The scripture declares that God cannot bless those who do not follow him.

The pressures of society, friends, and family can push you into marrying the wrong person. Learn to position yourselves as Job, and decree, "All the days of my appointed time will I wait till my change come" (Job 14:14). He positioned himself to continue to trust God. Learn to be patient, wait upon God, and refuse to be over anxious for anything. Marriage is a lifetime commitment- until death do us part. Consequently, the necessity to learn to hear, follow, know, and obey the voice of God is of utmost importance. It has been said, "Love is blind and marriage is an eye opener." Once we are married, it is a lifetime commitment.

Part Sixteen

Satanic/Demonically Influenced Matches

And they went into Capernaum; and straightway on the Sabbath day he entered into the synagogue, and taught . . . And there was in their synagogue a man with an unclean spirit, and he cried out . . . And Jesus rebuked him saying, Hold thy peace, and come out of him (Mark 1: 21, 23, 35 KJV).

Finally, my brethren, be strong in the Lord, and in the power of his might. Put on the whole armour of God, that ye may be able to stand against the wiles of the devil. For we wrestle not against flesh and blood, but against principalities, against powers, against the rulers of the darkness of this world, against spiritual wickedness in high places (Eph 6: 10–12 KJV).

For though we walk in the flesh, we don not war after the flesh: (For the weapons of our warfare are not carnal, but mighty through God to the pulling down of strongholds) (2 Cor. 10: 3–4 KJV).

How can Christ and the Devil agree? What does a believer have in common with an unbeliever?

How can God's temple come to terms with pagan idols? For we are the temple of the living God! As God himself has said, "I will make my home with my people and live among them; I will be their God. And they shall be my people."

And so the Lord says, "You must leave them and separate yourselves from them. Have nothing to do wit what is unclean, And I will accept you.

I will be your father, and you shall be my sons and daughters, says the Lord Almighty" (2 Cor 6:14 TEV).

Satanic/demonically Influenced Matches
Mismated Matches/relationships

Jacob And Leah (Gen. 29: 17–27 Kjv)

Leah, the unwanted wife, is described as being "delicate" or "weak" eyes (Gen. 29:17), which could allude to poor eyesight or merely lack of sparkle. Through finesse, she became the wife of Jacob. Although Leah may have been a willing participant in this deception, she could have been merely an obedient daughter.

> Leah was tender eyed; but Rachel was beautiful and well favored.

> And Jacob loved Rachel; and said I will serve thee seven years for Rachel thy younger daughter.

> And Jacob served seven years for Rachel; and they seemed unto him but a few days, for the love he had for her.

> And Jacob said unto Laban, Give me my wife, for my days are fulfilled, that I may go in unto her.

> And Laban gathered together all the men of the place, and they made a feast.

> And it came to pass in the evening, that he took Leah, his daughter, and brought her to him; and he went in unto her.

> And Laban gave unto his daughter Leah, Zilpah his maid for a handmaid.

> And it came to pass, that in the morning, behold, it was Leah; and he said to Laban, What is this that thou hast

> done unto me? Did not I serve thee for Rachel? Wherefore then hast thou beguiled me?
>
> And Laban said, It must not be so done in our country, to give the younger before the firstborn.
>
> Fulfill her week, and we will give thee this also for the service, which thou shall serve with me yet seven other years (Gen. 29:17–27 KJV).

Jacob did not serve seven years for Leah, nor did he desire her as his wife. He asked Laban, what is this you have done unto me? Was it not for Rachel that I served you? Why then have you deceived me?

Relationships based on deception, manipulation and dishonesty are destined for failure and unnecessary sufferings from the beginning. Nevertheless, Leah loved Jacob, was devoted to him throughout their marriage, and personified what every woman in her situation experience–the crucial need to live primarily for God and His glory.

Leah began her marriage focusing on what she lacked and being miserable. Nevertheless, disappointments, rejections and circumstances caused her to change her heart and focus on her strengths and positive attributes. She learned how to praise the Lord in hard places, and the spirit of joy prepared her heart and body for the birth of her next son. It was not until the birth of her fourth son, Judah, did this unwanted wife learn to trust God saying, "Now I will praise the Lord" (Gen. 29:35).

Though she may have been unattractive in appearance, unloved, unwanted, and even despised, God saw in her an inner beauty that equipped her to carry out His plan (Gen. 29:31). She could not change Jacob, but she could change herself and recognize God's hand in her life (Gen. 29:13).

Living with the constant comparison to her unusually beautiful sister Rachel, Leah was not hidden from God's caring eyes. In his omniscience, God allowed her to conceive even though her sister's fertility was delayed. She had the honor of conceiving and mothering Jacob's oldest son, even though she wrongly assumed that conceiving would earn love from her husband (Gen. 29–32). She faced her second childbirth realistically, but apparent deep desire gnawed at her (v. 33). When she became pregnant the third time, she exclaimed, "Now this time my husband will become joined to me, revealing an intense longing for love" (v. 34).

Leah spent her life consistently trying to make Jacob love her. Countless women's days are spent following fantasies and vain imaginations. Human beings "cannot force any one to love them." The emotional impact of persons involved in unrequited love relationships in many circumstances eventually causes the victim to experience mental illness due to untamable emotions. Many children have been born as a result of the "Leah's Love Syndrome." However, Praise God for Jesus. "He is our healer, deliverer," and can not only deliver and mend every broken heart, but "erase the painful memory, hurt, and disappointment" resulting from this kind of relationship.

Thank God for Jesus Christ, who paid the price on Calvary that we may be free from bondage, illusions, and the negative effect destructive relationships can have upon us. Thank God for the healing, deliverance and power, of the blood of Jesus redeeming us from the curse of the law.

We must continue to seek Him for divine wisdom to lead and guide us in receiving healing, and deliverance from unhealthy, ungodly relationships. We must learn to depend upon Him to not only receive deliverance from the impact of destructive relationships, but to move on, go forward, and experience a new beginning in Him in all things. Learn to flee and dwell in the presence, arm, care, and protective love of Jesus, knowing that He is our comforter and careth for us.

Abraham And Hagar (Gen. 16: 1–13 Kjv)

Hagar was an Egyptian maidservant acquired by Sarah when she and Abraham, together with his nephew Lot, moved from Canaan to Egypt to escape a famine. In ancient Near Eastern households, the rank of personal maidservant to the master's wife reflected honor, obedience, and trustworthiness. However, the position stripped Hagar of all personal rights, making her totally subject to Sarah's every wish. Because Sarah was sterile, Hagar's surrogate maternity was perfectly legal, though a clear violation of God's law (Gen. 2:24) and evidence of a lack of faith on the part of Abraham and Sarah. Thus Hagar was rejected, but not abandoned.

> Now Sarai, Abram's wife, bare him no children: and she had a handmaid, an Egyptian, whose name was Hagar.

And Sarai said unto Abram, Behold now, the Lord has restrained me from bearing; I pray thee, go in unto my maid; it may be that I may obtain children by her. And Abram hearkened to the voice of Sarai.

And Sarai, Abram's wife took Hagar her maid the Egyptian, after Abram had dwelt ten years in the land of Canaan, and gave her to her husband Abram to be his wife.

And he went in unto Hagar, and she conceived; and when she saw that she had conceived, her mistress was despised in her eyes.

And Sarai said unto Abram, my wrong be upon thee. I have given my maid into thy bosom; and when she saw that she had conceived, I was despised in her eyes; the Lord judge between me and thee.

But Abram said unto Sarai, Behold thy maid is in thy hand; do to her as it pleaseth thee. And when Sarai dealt hardly with her, she fled from her face.

And the angel of the Lord found her by a fountain of water in the wilderness, by the fountain in the way to Shur.

And he said, Hagar, Sarai's maid, whence camest thou? And whither wilt thou go? And she said, I flee from the face of my mistress Sarai.

And the angel of the Lord said unto her, Return to thy mistress, and submit thyself under her hands.

And the angel of the Lord said unto her, I will multiply thy seed exceedingly, that it shall not be numbered for multitude.

And the angel of the Lord said unto her, Behold, thou art with child, and shalt bear a son, and shalt call his name Ishmael; because the Lord hath heard thy affliction.

And he will be a wild man; his hand will be against every man, and every man's hand against him; and he shall dwell in the presence of all his brethren.

And she called the name of the Lord that spake unto her, Thou God seest me for she said, Have I also here looked after him that seeth me (Gen. 16:1–13 KJV)?

Hagar's life speaks piercingly to the growing number of hurt, wounded, and dispossessed women. The care of God is not only requested but needed even more, for all women. God is "Jehovah Jireh," and He will provide for every woman or man as He provided for Hager. The angel of the Lord came to her rescue (Gen. 16:7; 21:17). He was involved with Hagar and her son in times of crisis and in the times in between (Gen. 21:20).

Throughout Hagar's life, she experienced estrangement and prejudice as a foreigner, hardship and abuse as a servant, grief and abandonment as an unwed pregnant woman, and hopeless despair on two occasions as she faced imminent death.

However, despite all these difficulties, Hagar responded to the God who addressed her. She did not receive compensation from Sarah and Abraham. Her life was never easy, but God did reward her. In the all-seeing God, Hagar found refuge and life.

Twenty first century women are blessed to live under a new covenant: a covenant where Jesus Christ has already paid the price for our sins and iniquities. Through learning to let Him reign as Savior and Lord of our lives, abiding in Him and letting His Word abide in us, He reverses and destroys all the works of the enemy, and makes what Satan meant for evil "turn for our good", prosperity, and success.

Samson And Delilah (Judges 16: 4–20 Kjv)

Seduction extends far beyond misconduct, although that is certainly included in its manifestation (Rev. 2:20). Seducers and imposters, who present evil as good, include those who have spoken "nonsense" and those who have presented falsehood as truth (Ezek. 13:10; 2 Tim. 3:13).

The seducer acts consciously and willfully to put another person in a position of vulnerability, with the ultimate intent to dominate completely or destroy. The ultimate seduction–whether in Samson's life, in the life of Israel, or in your life today–is to be led astray from God's presence, will, and power, and not even realize what is happening.

Samson and Delilah are among the most well known couples in the Bible. Samson is known for his strength; Delilah is known for her seductive manipulation.

God forewarned Samson's parents before his birth the type of woman he should marry (Judges 13:2; 3:5–16). Foreign, pagan wives were an absolute no-no for Samson.

Delilah, described as the teasing temptress, lived in a small village near Samson's hometown. She was possibly a Philistine, although her name is Senutie. She may have been a temple prostitute. She has been described as a teasing temptress. Samson had been visiting her frequently, and their relationship became known to the Philistine leaders. The Philistines wanted Samson so desperately; they went to Delilah with an offer she could not refuse.

Samson's family commitment, lifestyle, and own upbringing should have taught him to stay away from foreign women or entanglements, but the Word reflects evidence that he loved and became attached to Delilah.

Let us read and follow the impact his relationship and involvement with Delilah had upon not only his life, but his walk with God, family, and an entire nation.

> Then went Samson to Gaza, and saw there a harlot, and went in unto her.

> And it was told the Gazites, saying, Samson is come hither. And they compassed him in, and laid wait for him all night in the gate of the city, and were quiet all the night, saying, In the morning, when it is day, we shall kill him.

> And Samson lay till midnight, arose at midnight, and took the doors of the gate of the city, and the two posts, and went away with them, bar and all, and put them upon his shoulders, and carried them up to the top of an hill that is before Hebron.

> And it came to past afterwards, that he loved a woman in the valley of Sorek, whose name was Delilah.
>
> And the lords of the Philistines came up unto her, and said unto her, entice him, and see wherein his great strength lieth, and by what means we may prevail against him, that we may bind him to afflict him: and we will give thee every one of us eleven hundred pieces of silver (Judges 16:1–5 KJV).

Delilah was motivated by greed; selfishness and was perfectly willing to use all her seductiveness to make her a wealthy woman. Satan used Delilah in a great way to bring great destruction (Judges 16:15–17) in Samson's life. Her seduction was unrelenting as she "pestered and pressed" Samson daily (v. 16). She pressed him so greatly that his soul was vexed to death (v. 16). Her seduction was rooted in a lie that everything would be all right, even to the point of believing that the Lord is unconcerned about and approves of wrong behavior (v. 20).

The cycle of destructive relationships, wrong choices and selections had not yet grabbed a hold of Samson. The negatives forces of destruction were in place that would ultimately cost him his life. Unbridled passions of the heart have destroyed many women and men in the world and Kingdom of God.

The negative forces of disaster were in place; a morally weak man with uncontrollable sexual passions; a seductive temptress motivated by greed; a group of foreign leaders with unlimited funds, and the strong conviction that their national security, perhaps their national survival was at stake.

Satan used Delilah tremendously. Her methods were simple, and though it took time, they worked. She was playful, coquettish, provocative, alluring, and demanding. The fortune waiting Delilah was a great incentive to work twenty-four seven, to reveal where the strength of Samson's secret was. She was determined, and ultimately succeeded in prying Samson's secret from him. Perhaps Samson's pagan bride would have taught him "once is enough." I've been there, done that. "No more secrets revealed"; "God's secret in my life is sealed, locked forever."

Samson did the absolute no-no! He became too comfortable, relaxed, and overconfident during lustful passionate moments. He laid his head in the devil's lap and went to sleep. She lulled her lover to sleep after he told her all his heart, and had his hair cut off (that which

God had told his parents before his birth never to have done). With utter heartlessness, she watched as he struggled out of a deep sleep, thinking he would fend off his attackers as easily as before (Judges 16:20). He discovered, to his horror, that his strength was gone and that the spirit of God had departed from him. And where was Delilah? Counting her money and making plans for the next "set up and knock down".

Satan used Delilah, like many immoral women and men, to cause many men and women to fall from grace, lose honor, credibility, and right standing with God. Samson's relationship with Delilah caused him to lose everything- to include hitting rock bottom, his eyesight, honor, power, and left him grinding at the mill. He lost his anointing, (regardless of how anointed and powerful, man's lack of eyesight limits his level of accomplishments), his credibility (honor and glory), right standing with God, and ultimately his life. He lost all of this as a result of his lustful, attraction, and involvement with this immoral woman. Strangely to say, Samson–like many women and men–had no desire for Heaven's mate. Praying without ceasing is needed for men and women hooked on fulfilling their desires and pleasures with sinful, immoral people.

> And there was a certain man of Zorah, of the family of the Danites, whose name was Manoah; and his wife was barren, and bare not.
>
> And the angel of the Lord appeared unto the woman, and said unto her, Behold now; thou art barren, and bearest not; but thou shalt conceive, and bear a son.
>
> Now therefore beware, I pray thee, and drink neither wine nor strong drink, and eat not any unclean thing.
>
> For, lo, thou shalt conceive, and bear a son; and no razor shall come on his head; for the child shall be a Nazarite unto God from the womb and he shall begin to deliver Israel out of the hands of the Philistines
> (Judges 13:2–7 KJV).
>
> And the woman bare a son, and called his name Samson; and the child grew, and the Lord blessed him.

> And the spirit of the Lord began to move him at times in the camp of Dan between Zorah and Eshtaol (Judges 13:24–25 KJV).

Samson was the thirteenth judge to reign over Israel. The children of Israel had been delivered into the hands of the Philistines for forty years. They needed a deliverer. Not just any deliverer, but a deliverer especially chosen by God. Forty years of suffering under the hands of the Philistines created great burden on the children of Israel, and provoked them to cry out for deliverance.

Children born of ungodly, satanically influenced relationships, marriages, and friendships can bring years of division, dissension, discord, and confusion in families and marriages. These relationships create years of confusion, strife, and contentions to include fighting, imprisonment, and family deterioration that is passed from generation to generation.

Let us look at the destruction of the relationships of Samson, that not only eventually destroyed his life, but also hindered and stopped the deliverance of the children of Israel. His decision making process in selecting his mate was fulfillment of his uncontrollable fleshly desires and pleasures. He experienced absolute problems in selecting the right relationships and mates. The questions Samson's parents asked him, and what many parents should ask their sons and daughters are, "Is this the mate God has chosen?" "Do you want Heaven's mate? Why are you settling for satan's counterfeit? Wait upon the mate God's has chosen." Is there not a daughter of God that thou may take for a wife.

> And Samson went down to Timnath, and saw a woman in Timnath of the daughters of the Philistines.
>
> And he came up, and told his father and his mother, and said, I have seen a woman in Timnath of the daughters of the Philistines; now therefore, get her for me to wife.
>
> Then his father and his mother said unto him, Is there *never* a woman among the daughters of thy brethren, or among all my people, that thou goest to take a wife of the uncircumcised Philistines. And Samson said unto his father, Get her for me, for she pleaseth me well (Judges 14: 1–3 KJV).

> Then went Samson down, and his father and his mother, to Timnath, and came to the vineyards of Timnath and behold, a young lion roared against him.
>
> And the Spirit of the Lord came mightily upon him, and he rent him as he would have rent a kid, and he had nothing in *his hand;* but he told not his father or his mother what he had done.
>
> And he went down, and talked with the woman; and she pleased Samson well (Judges 14:5–7 KJV).

Samson's pagan bride from Timnath captured his affection with her beauty and charm, being highly infatuated with his strength and wit. They married hastily despite parental opposition. The marriage was doomed from the beginning because of competing loyalties, which pulled at the young couple.

Samson and the Timnath were definitely not Heaven's Match for many reasons:

Reason #1
Marriage to a foreign woman who was not committed to the God of Israel was strictly forbidden, because intermarriage was a definite factor in the destruction of a nation (Deut. 7:1–4; Judges 3:5–6).

Reason #2
They rushed into marriage based upon initial infatuation and physical attraction (Judges 14:2–3).

Reason #3
Neither had left their father or mother in order to give primary loyalty to the other (Gen. 2:24).

Reason #4
Neither one reached beyond self to be concerned about the best interest of the other (Eph. 5:33).

Reason #5
Neither had considered the ramifications of being linked to another

who did not have the same spiritual commitments (Amos 3:3).

Reason #6
Samson was not only an Israelite and committed to God, but he was also a Nazarite, thus set apart by God from the womb in a special way to deliver Israel out of the hand of the Philistines (Judges 13:4,5).

Reason #7
This marriage put Samson on the road to alienation and completely out of the will of God.

The life and ministry of Samson is an example of the divine revelation of the will, purpose, and destiny of God in fulfilling His sovereign will in a person's life.

The wife from Timnath, who had remained in her parent's home after her wedding was most concerned with her own self-preservation. Just as Samson, she was accustomed to getting her own way, if by no other means, through her tears and whining (Judges 14:2, 3, 16, 17). She used all her manipulative skills–including a week of tears–to meet the demands of her country men, knowing all the while that they planned evil against her husband. When Samson finally trusted her with his secret, she blatantly, and seemingly without remorse, betrayed him. She was under threat for her life and her family's, but in the end, perhaps because of her wrong choices, all their lives were lost (Judges 15:6).

Samson and the Timnath experienced many negative circumstances, with the end of that marriage resulting in his wife being given to his companion, whom he had used as a friend by her father. And her father said, "I verily thought that thou hadst utterly hated her; therefore I gave her to thy companion; is not her younger sister fairer than she? Take her I pray thee instead of her" (Judges 15:2).

David And Bathsheba (2 Sam. 11: 1–4 Kjv)

And it came to pass, after the year was expired at the time when kings go forth to battle, that David sent Joab, and his servant with him, and all Israel; and they destroyed the children of Ammon, and besieged Rabbah. But David tarried still at Jerusalem.

> And it came to pass in an evening tide that David arose from off his bed, and walked upon the roof of the king's house and from the roof he saw a woman washing herself, and the woman was very beautiful to look upon.
>
> And David sent and inquired after the woman. And one said, Is not this Bathsheba, the daughter of Eliam, the wife of Uriah the Hittite?
>
> And David sent messengers, and took her; and she came in unto him, and he lay with her; for she was purified from her uncleanness; and she returned unto her house (II Sam. 11:1–4 KJV).

This relationship was no doubt among the greatest tests in David's life. It was the result of his passionate lust for Bathsheba. The lust was conceived at a time when David was resting from battle. Instead of leading his army to battle, he chose to remain in the comfort of the palace. After resting in the heat of the day, he went out to enjoy the cool evening breezes on the roof, which functioned as a terrace of his house. From there his great temptation came. He refused to resist, but embraced it, and pursued the fulfillment of his passion that eventually cost him greatly.

The Word of God declares, he not only asked who she was, but sent for her and laid with her. The Bible states she was very beautiful to look upon. His passion for Bathsheba moved the man after God's own heart to commit a sin against God. This act of unbridled passion and lust caused the sword to never depart from his house (II Sam. 12:10).

> Now therefore the sword shall never depart from thine house; because thou hast despised me, and hast taken the wife of Uriah the Hittite to be thy wife.
>
> Thus saith the Lord, Behold, I will raise up evil against thee out of thine own house, and I will take thy wives before thine own eyes, and give them unto thy neighbor, and he shall lie with thy wives in the sight of this sun.
>
> For thou didst it secretly; but I will do this thing before all Israel, and before the sun.

> And David said unto Nathan, I have sinned against the Lord. And Nathan said unto David, The Lord also hath put away thy sin; thou shalt not die.
>
> Howbeit, because by this deed thou hast given great occasion to the enemies of the Lord to blaspheme, the child also that is born unto thee shall surely die (II Sam. 12:10–14 KJV).

Upon being told by Bathsheba that she was pregnant, David brought Uriah, her husband, home from battle, hoping he would enjoy intimacy with Bathsheba, and thereby perceive himself as the father of the unborn child. When this plan went wrong, David arranged for Uriah's death on the battlefield, then sent his messengers and brought Bathsheba to his palace.

> And it came to pass in the morning, that David wrote a letter to Joab, and sent it by the hand of Uriah.
>
> And he wrote in the letter, saying, Set ye Uriah in the forefront of the hottest battle, and retire ye from him, that he may be smitten and die (II Sam. 11: 14–16 KJV).

This decision of David greatly displeased the Lord, and caused the wrath of God to come upon him. Passions of the heart without prayer, fasting, the Word of God, and a great determination to live in the fear of God causes man to make terrible decisions.

Though perhaps she could have rejected the King's initial overtures, by this point she obviously had no choice in the matter. The Word of God enables us to make right decisions in every area of our life. It enables us to know the mind of God, and determine whether a particular thing is God's choice for us. In Psalms 25:12, the scriptures declare, what man is he that feareth the Lord? Him shall He teach in the way he shall choose. We are responsible for the choices and decisions we make. We must learn to be still in the presence of the Lord and let Him speak unto us in a way we understand. His will always align with His Word.

David's decision caused his house, sons, and daughters to live under the cloud of the sword. Husbands and wives, guardians, and family members can bring generational curses and the wrath of God upon their family through evil lust, passion, and unacceptable works of the flesh.

The decisions we make before, after, and during the course of the marriage and relationship have great impact on our lives and all involved in the family lineage. We are instructed in His Word to acknowledge Him in all our ways and he shall direct our path (Prov. 3:6). Decisions and choices have great consequences.

David And Michal (1 Sam. 18:12 Kjv)

And David said unto Saul, who am I? and what is my life, or my father's family in Israel, that I should be son-in-law to the king?

But it came to pass at the time when Merab Saul's daughter should have been given to David, that she was given unto Adriel the Meholathite to wife.

And Michal, Saul's daughter, loved David; and they told Saul, and the thing pleased him.

And Saul said, I will give him her, that she may be a snare to him; and that the hand of the Philistines may be against him. Wherefore Saul said to David, Thou shalt this day be my son- in- law in the one of the twain.

And Saul commanded his servants, saying commune with David secretly, and say, Behold, the king hath delight in the thee, and all his servants love thee:

And Saul servants spake those words in the ears of David, and David said, seemth it to you a light thing to be a king's son-in-law, seeing that I am a poor man, and lightly esteemed?

And Saul saw and knew that the Lord was with David, and that Michal, Saul's daughter loved him.

And Saul was yet the more afraid of David; and Saul became David's enemy continually
(I Sam. 18:18–19; 20–21; 28 KJV).

The scriptures declare when Saul saw that the Lord was with David, and that he behaved himself very wisely, he was afraid of him (1 Sam. 18:12,14). Michal was the younger daughter of Saul. She was called a scornful wife and was in love with David.

She was a political appointment wife, appointed specifically to be a snare to lure David to his death (II Sam. 18:12). (We all should be watchful of satanic snares manifested in the form of marriage). David accepted her love to better his position before Saul (I Sam. 18:26).

Interestingly enough, the Lord used Jonathan, Saul's son as a friend and encouragement in David's transition into kingship. The close bond of friendship between he and David is described in the phrase "the soul of Jonathan was knit to the soul of David." They developed a true friendship covenant, where neither sword would come against each other until death. Michal, who also loved David, was used as a shield. She knew the call, purpose, and destiny in David's life, and would not allow Saul's jealousy to hinder the fulfillment of God's manifestation in David's life and ministry.

Michal schemed, in order to save David when Saul sent soldiers to his house to kill him. Consequently, by helping David to escape, she lost him. Later, Michal was given away by her father to another man.

There is no record of David's concern for Michal, or of any attempt on his part to contact her during the years of their separation. However, fourteen years later and seven years after the death of Saul, David was still not king of Israel. As a condition of a treaty with Abner, David demanded the return of Michal in order to stabilize his position over the kingdom. Again, Michal was used for political advantage. Her brother, Ishbosheth, took Michal from her husband, Paltiel, and reunited her to David.

When Michal was reunited with David, because he loved God greatly and "danced before the Lord with all his might," she accused him of not acting like a king when the ark was returned to Jerusalem (II Sam. 6:16). Her scorn for her husband, who happened to be God's chosen king, resulted in the loss of her ability to bear children, the ultimate curse for any Hebrew woman (II Sam. 6:23).

> Then David returned to bless his household. And Michal the daughter of Saul came out to meet David, and said, How glorious was the King of Israel today, who uncovered himself today in the eyes of the handmaids

of his servants, as one of the vain fellows shamelessly uncovereth himself.

And David said unto Michal, It was before the Lord, which chose me before thy father, and before all his house, to appoint me ruler over the people of the Lord, over Israel; therefore will I play before the Lord.

And I will yet be more vile than thus, and will be base in mine own sight; and of the maidservants which thou hast spoken of, of them shall I be held in honour.

Therefore Michal the daughter of Saul had no child unto the day of her death (II Sam. 6:20–23 KJV).

Michal, like many women married to men and women after God's own heart, had to learn that there is no joy or pleasure that exceeds the love, joy, and relationship he or she has with God. They were created for such a purpose, destiny and relationship like unto this. It should be a blessing and ultimate pleasure to be allowed of God to share their lives, ministries, and all the manifestation and splendor of God revealed during the course of their journey.

Perhaps David, when he glanced on Bathsheba, never in his life had experienced such a feeling of passionate desire for a woman. Because of political appointed relationships, true love, his ultimate desires and pleasures were unfulfilled. Consequently, to Abigail, David said, "I . . . respected your person," and because of her wisdom and character he desired her to be his wife (1 Sam. 25:35). She illustrates for wives today vital principles of restraint and proper priorities, as well as the determination to make the best of a difficult situation.

However, David, like all persons today desiring Heaven's mate, had to learn to wait upon God with all prayers and supplications, believing that His timing is perfect.

Felix And Drusilla (Acts 24:24 Kjv)

And after certain days, when Felix came with his wife Drusilla, which was a Jewess, he sent for Paul, and heard him concerning the faith in Christ (Acts 24:24 KJV).

Drusilla was the youngest daughter of Herod Agrippa I, by his wife Cypros and the young sister of Bernice Herod II. She was early promised in marriage to Epiphanies, son of Antiochus, but the match was broken off because of his refusal to conform to the Jewish religion.

She has been described as a woman of rare beauty–beauty that corrupted her and led to her moral decadence. She married King Azizus of Emessa when she was only fourteen years old. A year or so after her marriage, Felix, the Roman governor of Judea, persuaded Drusilla to leave Azizus and to marry him illegally.

She came from the family lineage of Herod the Great, who murdered Jewish baby boys in his effort to destroy the newborn Jesus, the promised Messiah. Mentioned only once in Scripture, Drusilla was present when the imprisoned apostle Paul gave his defense of the gospel before Felix. She heard first hand the good news of Jesus Christ. Drusilla did not respond to Paul's message. The apostle's words so frightened Felix that, to please the Jews, the governor returned Paul to his confinement under house arrest.

Drusilla lived a shameless, wasted life. She was described in Proverbs 6:24–28. She was a woman of rare beauty- beauty that corrupted her and led to her moral decadence.

> For the commandment is a lamp; and the law is light; and reproofs of instruction are the way of life:
>
> To keep thee from the evil woman, from the flattery of the tongue of a strange woman.
>
> Lust not after her beauty in thine heart; neither let her take thee with her eyelids.
>
> For by a means of a whorish woman a man is brought to a piece of bread; and the adulteress will hunt for the precious life.
>
> Can a man take fire in his bosom, and his clothes not be burned?
>
> Can one go upon hot coals, and his feet not be burned (Prov. 6:23–28 Scoffield Study Bible)?

Her life and marriage were destined for life's mishaps. As a beautiful young teenager, the exploitation of her beauty and youth appealed to wicked and ungodly men, whose only interest was physical satisfaction and pleasure. Her lack of growth, maturity, and experience in life further corroded her decision-making skills and moral character. However, during her lifetime she was exposed to the Gospel of Christ and given an opportunity to make a drastic change in her life. She had an opportunity to receive Jesus as Savior and Lord of her life through the ministry of Paul, an apostle of Jesus.

Drusilla died a horrible, violent death before her forty-first birthday. While she and her only child, Agrippa, were in Pompeii, Mount Vesuvius erupted, burying under burning lava, Pompeii and Herculaneum, as well as Drusilla and her son.

Herod Antipas And Herodias (Mk. 6: 17–22 Kjv)

For Herod himself had sent forth and laid hold upon John and bound him in prison for Herodias sake, his brother Philip's wife: for he had married her.

For John had said unto Herod, it is not lawful for thee to have thy brother's wife.

Therefore Herodias had a quarrel against him, and would have killed him, but she could not.

For Herod feared John, knowing that he was a just man and an holy, and observed him; and when he had heard him, he did many things, and heard him gladly.

And when a convenient day was come, that Herod on his birthday made a supper to his lords, high captains, and chief estates of Galilee;

And when the daughter of the said Herodias came in, and danced, and pleased Herod and them that sat with him, the king said unto the damsel, Ask of me whatsoever thou wilt, and I will give it thee (Mk 6:17–22 KJV).

Herodias, who lived in Tiberias, the capital city built by her husband on the southwest shore of the Sea of Galilee, was a woman out of control. Crafty, ambitious, greedy, and politically astute, Herodias would stop at nothing to attain what she wanted.

When Herod Antipas, the brother of Philip and the stepbrother of Herodias' father Aristobulus, visited Philip, he and Herodias were immediately attracted to one another. Herod Antipas was a far more powerful man then Phillip. Herodias saw her chance for more power, a better position, and an increase in wealth. She insisted Herod divorce his wife; she divorced her husband and they married. This incestuous marriage was very offensive to the Jews.

In many marriages, couples complement each other. The strengths of one are so overwhelming, it motivates the other to strive for excellence; likeness, the weaknesses of the other are so negatively visible, it causes great impediments for the other person. Herodias is said to have definitely brought out the worst in Herod. Sadly to say, this happens in many marriages, often leading to separation and divorce.

"Bringing out the worst in a mate" was evident in the beheading of the fearless preacher, John the Baptist, the only one who dared to reprove this unscrupulous couple. Herodias hated John the Baptist because he did not hesitate publicly to call her alliance with Herod sin. She wanted to sentence John to death (Mark 6:19), but Herod was awed and fascinated by John. He liked to hear him speak, even though John confronted him with the truth, and he feared the reaction of the people if this popular preacher was harmed.

Herodias's resentment festered like a sore. Her opportunity for revenge finally came on Herod's birthday. The military and political leaders came to help him celebrate at a great feast in his palace at Machaerus. Herodias's sensuous teenaged daughter, Salome, danced so alluringly that Herod offered the girl anything she wanted up to half his kingdom. Her mother was ready with what she wanted, and it was not half a kingdom. Herodias knew that her husband was an unprincipled, cruel man. He was also boisterous and proud, and the embarrassment of backing down on his offer to Salome in front of all these people would be a humiliation he could not tolerate. Sometimes a woman's manipulation can outdo all the political maneuvers and power available to men.

Herodias, like many ungodly mothers, not only exploited her daughter, but entangled her daughter Salome in her obsession. Salome not only asked for John's head, but she also demanded it "immediately" on a platter. Obsessions of hate not only take over a person's life but usually infect others as well. Herodias led her young daughter into sin as an accomplice in the murder of a godly preacher. Her husband and daughter were tools in the hand of Herodias, who planned and orchestrated the tragic crime.

In 1 Samuel 3, the Word of the Lord came to the child Samuel, who ministered unto the Lord before Eli. And the Word of the Lord was precious in those days. There was no open vision.

> And the child Samuel ministered unto the Lord before Eli,
>
> And the word of the Lord was precious in those days, there was no open vision.
>
> And it came to pass at that time, when Eli was laid down in his place, and his eyes began to wax dim, that he could not see;
>
> And ere the lamp of God went out in the temple of the Lord, where the ark of God was, and Samuel was laid down to sleep.
>
> That the Lord called Samuel; and he answered. Here am I.
>
> And he ran unto Eli; and said, Here am I; for thou calledst me. And he saideth, I called not; lie down again. And he and went lay down.
>
> And the Lord called yet again, Samuel. And Samuel arose and went to Eli, and said, Here am I; for thou didst call me. He answered, I calleth not, my son; lie down again.
>
> Now Samuel did not yet know the Lord, neither was the Word of the Lord yet revealed unto him.
>
> And the Lord called again the third time. And he arose and went to Eli, and said, Here am I; for thou didst call me. And Eli perceived that the Lord has called the child (1 Sam 3:1–17 KJV).

In essence, Samuel was raised as Jehovah's prophet in

Eli's house. Eli's sons were full of iniquity. They made themselves vile and he restrained them not (1 Sam. 3:13).

Now the sons of Eli were sons of Belial; they knew not the Lord.

And the priest's custom with the people was that, when any man offered sacrifice, the priest's servant came, while the flesh was in seething, with a flesh hook of three teeth in his hand;

And he struck it into the pan, or kettle, or caldron, or pot; all that the flesh hook brought up the priest took for himself. So they did in Shiloh unto all the Israelites that came thither.

Also before they burnt the fat, the priest's servant came, and said to the man that sacrificed, Give flesh to roast for the priest; for he will not have sodden flesh of thee, but raw.

And if any man said unto him, Let them not fail to burn the fat presently, and then take as much as thy soul desireth; then he would answer him, Nay; but thou shalt give it me now; and if not, I will take it by force.

Wherefore the sin of the young men was very great before the Lord; for men abhorred the offering of the Lord (I Sam. 2:12–17 KJV).

John the Baptist and the child Samuel spoke the Word of God with all sincerity and truth. They proclaimed the Word of God, and stood up, and reproved unscrupulous behavior.

Married couples, parents, guardians, and all who would live holy and righteous lives must not only live, but must speak righteousness and declare things that are right (Isa. 45:19). They must proclaim truth unto their love ones and all He sends their way for a word of wisdom, knowledge, and revelation concerning the will of God for their lives.

Part Seventeen

SATANIC/DEMONICALLY INFLUENCED STRONGHOLDS/HINDRANCES

For the weapons of our warfare are not carnal, but mighty through God to the pulling down of strongholds (2 Cor. 10:4 TAB). I (the Lord) have cut off nations; their battlements and corner towers are desolate and in ruins. I laid their streets waste so that none passes over them; their cities are destroyed so that there is no men, there is no inhabitant (Zep. 3:6 TAB).

In conclusion, be strong in the Lord (be empowered though your union, with Him); draw your strength from Him (that strength which His boundless might provides).

Put on God's whole armor (the armor of a heavy-armed solider which God supplies), that you may be able successfully to stand up against (all) the strategies and the deceits of the devil.

For we are not wrestling with flesh and blood (contending only with physical opponents), but against the despotisms, against the powers, against (the master spirits who are) the world rulers of this present darkness, against the spirit forces of wickedness in the heavenly (supernatural) sphere (Eph. 6:10–12 TAB).

Therefore put on God's complete armor, that you may be able to resist and stand your ground on the evil day (of danger), and, having done all (the crisis demands), to stand (firmly in your place). Stand therefore (hold your ground), having tightened the belt of truth around your lions and having put on the breastplate of integrity and of moral rectitude and right standing with God. And having shod your feet in preparation (to face the enemy with the firm- footed stability, the promptness, and the readiness produced by the good news) of the Gospel of peace. Lift up over all the (covering) shield of saving faith, upon which you can quench all the flaming missiles of the wicked (one). And take the helmet of salvation and the sword that the Spirit wields, which is the Word of God (Eph 6:10–17 TAB).

Discerning Satanically Influenced Marital Enticements

And it came to pass on the seventh day that they said unto Samson's wife, Entice thy husband, that he may declare unto us the riddle, lest we burn thee and thy father's house with fire: ye have called us to take that we have? Is it not so?

And Samson's wife wept before him, and said, Thou dost but hate me and loves me not: thou has put forth a riddle unto the children of my people, and hast not told me. And he said unto her, Behold, I have not told it my father nor my mother, and shall I tell it thee?

And she wept before him the seven days, while their feast lasted: and it came to pass on the seventh day, that he told her, because she lay sore upon him: and she told the riddle to the children of her people (Judges 14:15–17 KJV).

And my heart hath been secretly enticed, or my mouth hath kissed my hand (Job 31:27 KJV).

And this I say, least any man should beguile you with enticing words (Col. 2:4 KJV).

Finally, my brethren, be strong in the Lord, and in the power of His might. Put on the whole armor of God, that ye may be able to stand against the wiles of the devil. For we wrestle not against flesh and blood, but against principalities, against powers, against the rulers of darkness of this world, against spiritual wickedness in high places (Eph. 6:10–12 KJV).

For though we walk in the flesh, we do not war after the flesh: For the weapons of our warfare are not carnal, but mighty through God to the pulling down of strongholds) (II Cor. 10:3, 4 KJV).

Weddings are much more than beautiful gowns, crowds of people, and expensive decorations. A wedding is a time of commitment. It should include worship and giving thanks unto God, as well as celebrating the wonderful blessing God has given you in a spouse. However, many couples fail to recognize the necessity to pray before the engagement, during the engagement, before the wedding and after the ceremony.

Believers must continue to realize that during the marriage preparation process, demon spirits are present. It is their responsibility to deal with them directly in spiritual warfare. During the engagement, which is seen as the time of deepening intimacy when a couple has the freedom to make sure that marriage is the step they want to take that, Satan's tactics are to put pressure on each person. He uses our emotions, thoughts, and our physical bodies to get us distracted. In times of waiting and preparation, believers feel pressured one way or the other. However, God's Word provides a solution for panic, over anxiousness, and victory over demonic pressure. That Word is spiritual warfare. Believers must take authority over demonic spirits and destroy them. We must learn the practical ways to conduct spiritual warfare. We must put away carnal weapons and take up spiritual weapons.

There are many satanically influenced forces that seek to destroy marriages before the union is consummated. We are describing satanically influenced marriage trespassers whose main job is to stop the marriage. These include activities by friends and family, as well as demonically influenced associates.

Because the battle is very personal, and the enemy is a spiritual one, the weapons are spiritual. Discerning the evil spirits behind the activities, the Holy Spirit will reveal every evil trespasser assigned by the enemy to stop the marriage. Praying in the name of Jesus will release the spirit of power and victory over marital conflict, confronting and destroying all activities of the enemy in love.

Discerning Satanic Marital Strategies?

Problems can be a negative weapon in a marriage–dividing hearts and destroying unity–or they can be a positive, causing recommitment and renewal. Disagreements between spouses appear a number of times in scriptures. Solomon's poetic description of the misunderstandings with his new bride demonstrates a difference of feelings, awkward communication, and poor timing in learning to live together in love. Abraham and Sarah quarreled over her childlessness, (Gen. 16:5) as did Jacob and Rachel (Gen. 30:1,2). Job's wife disagreed with his response to his illness (Job 2:9, 10). The prophet Malachi denounced the priests who had broken and mended their wedding vows (Mal. 2:14–15).

Disagreements are common, but the scripture also provides guidance. Both Paul and Peter give clues to the prevention and settlement of domestic clashes. To the discordant couples in Corinth, Paul wrote, "God has called us to peace" (1 Cor. 7:15). That is the ultimate objective. Peter advised wives experiencing strained relations with unbelieving husbands to win them through a gentle and quiet spirit (1 Pet. 3:1–4).

Human nature has not changed. Competition and contention leads only to harsh consequences. Love, on the other hand, "bears . . . believe . . . hopes . . . endure all things" (1 Cor. 13:7). Jesus taught us to remove the plank in our own eyes before we try to get rid of the speck of dust in the eyes of others (Matt. 7:3–5).

Mercy is a vital part of relaxing tensions. A patient, forgiving spirit eases confrontations (Mic. 6:8). Sensitivity in timing also recaptures warm affection. We should not let problems fester into bitterness. The Word of God cautions us to address anger before the sun goes down (Eph. 4:26). Peace is the ultimate goal.

Most importantly, we must choose to forgive. Calmness settles over us as we allow Christ to control our hearts. He modeled forgiveness (1 Pet. 2:23), and He alone can give us strength to bury revenge and to restore harmony in relationships. Believers are called to be peacemakers (Matt. 5:9).

Discerning Marriage Trespassers

Believers should always consider indwelling demons or undesirable trespassers. A trespasser is one who unlawfully and stealthily encroaches upon the territory of another. Trespassers can continue their unlawful practice until they are confronted and challenged on the basis of one's legal rights. Jesus has purchased the believer with His own blood, and has made him a steward over his own life. The devil has no legal right to him; it is up to him to defend his rights. No devil can remain when the Christian seriously desires him to go! "Resist the devil and he will flee from you" (James 4:7).

> When the unclean spirit is gone out of a man, he walketh through dry places, seeking rest, and findeth none. Then he saith, I will return into My House from whence I came out (Matt. 12:43, 44 KJV).

The first step in overcoming problems, whether they are physical, emotional, or spiritual, is to admit you are in need, and desire a change. Jesus asked the man who had been laying by the Bethesda pool for thirty-eight years a very important question. Do you want to be made well (John 5:1–15)? In other words, do you care enough about your problem to do something about it–even if it requires on your part some action, sacrifice, or even suffering?

It has been said, "love is blind." So many people, even believers, are blinded by the presence of satanic spirits; they fail to utilize discernment, one of nine gifts of the Holy Spirit (1 Cor. 2:10). The second method of knowing the presence of evil spirits is detection. Detection is simply observing what spirits are doing to a person. We can learn to detect evil spirits by observing what they are doing to a person. Some of the most common symptoms of indwelling demons are as follows:

Emotional Problems

> Disturbances in the emotions, which persist or recur. Some of the most common disturbances are resentment, hatred, anger, fear, rejection (feeling unwanted and unloved), self-pity, jealousy, depression, worry, inferiority and insecurity.

Mental Problems

> Disturbances in the mind or thought life, such as mental torment, procrastination, indecision, compromise, confusion, doubt, rationalization, and loss of memory.

Speech Problems

Outbursts or uncontrolled use of the *tongue*. These include lying, cursing, blasphemy, criticism, mockery, railing and gossip.

Sex Problems

Recurring unclean thoughts and acts regarding *sex*. These include fantasy sex experiences, masturbation, lust, perversions, homosexuality, fornication, adultery, incest, provocativeness and harlotry.

Addictions

The most common addictions are nicotine, alcohol, drugs, medicines, caffeine, and food.

Physical Infirmities

Many diseases and physical afflictions are due to spirits of infirmity. (See: Luke 13:11). When a demon of infirmity is cast out, there is often the need to pray for a healing of whatever damage has resulted. Thus, there is a close relationship between deliverance and healing.

Religious Error

Involvement to any degree in religious error can open the door for demons. Objects and literature from sources of religious error have been known to attract demons into houses. (1) False religions, e.g. Eastern religions, pagan religions, philosophies, and mind sciences. Note: This includes such popular interests as yoga exercises and karate, which cannot be divorced from heathen worship. (2) Christian Cults, e.g. Mormonism, Jehovah's Witnesses, Christian Science, Rosicrucianism, Theosophy, Unity, and many more. Such cults deny or confuse the necessity of Christ's blood as the way of atonement for sin and salvation. Cults also include some lodges, societies, and social agencies, which use religion (scripture and even God) as a foundation, but omit the blood atonement of Jesus Christ. All such cults may be classified as "bloodless religions"–"having a form of godliness, but denying the power thereof" (II Tim. 3:5).

(3) Occult and Spiritism, e.g. séances, witchcraft, magic, ouija boards, levitation, palmistry, handwriting analysis, automatic handwriting, esp, hypnosis, horoscopes, astrology, divination, etc. note: Any method of seeking supernatural knowledge, wisdom, guidance, and power apart from God is forbidden! (Deut. 18:9–15)
(4) False doctrine. Doctrinal errors promoted by deceiving and seducing spirits (I Tim. 4:1). Such doctrines are designed to attack both the humanity and deity of Jesus Christ. It also denies the inspiration of scripture to distract Christians from the move of the Spirit, and to cause disunity in the Body of Christ. Finally, it causes confusion in the Church, obsession with doctrine, a compulsion to propagate, such puff up with a sense of superiority, and fosters emphasis upon fleshly activities as a gateway to the spiritual, as in asceticism and vegetarianism.

Delays/lateness In Marriage

"Seek ye out of the book of the Lord, and read; no one of these shall fail, none shall want her mate; for my mouth it hath commanded, and his spirit it hath gathered them" (Isaiah 34:16 KJV).

And being fully persuaded that what he had promised, he was able to perform (Rom. 4:21 KJV).

For the Lord God will help me; therefore shall I not be confounded; therefore have I set my face like a flint, and I know that I shall not be ashamed (Isa. 50:7 KJV).

"According to your faith be it unto you" (Matt. 9:29 KJV).

"Is there anything too hard for the Lord?" (Gen. 18:14 KJV).

The state of being single is an unhappy and lonely state for many singles. For many ages thirty and over, desperation, loneliness, and panic have overwhelmed them; and is provoking them to settle for satan's counterfeit, rather than waiting for Heaven's best.
St. Francis de Salesi observed that the single person who mar-

ries later faces the challenge of preserving a heart capable of love as opposed to a heart quite worn out, spoiled, and weary with love.

The scriptures declare, "According to your faith be it unto you" (Matt. 9:29). The choice of lifestyles for singles is a permanent state for some, and a temporary state for others. There are some Christians who choose celibacy, which is an opportunity to imitate Christ in a unique way during their earthly pilgrimage. It becomes a lifelong vow so that they might fully and completely give themselves to the Lord and His church (1 Cor. 7:32–34). It can be a call to love Christ wholeheartedly, just as Christ loves the church (Eph. 5:29), and to be holy both in body and in spirit (1 Cor. 7:34). However, the scriptures refer to three types of eunuchs:

- Some eunuchs were so born from their mother's womb.
- Some eunuchs were made eunuchs of men.
- Some eunuchs made themselves eunuchs for the kingdom of heaven's sake. He that is able to receive it, let him receive it (Matt. 19:12 KJV).

Singles can make a choice through faith, believing that "Faith turns hopeless circumstances around," and "there is nothing too hard for God." Indeed, marriage is a gift from God- positioning each person to take a stand in faith, believe the Word of God, and receive and enjoy all things He has given us richly to enjoy (1 Tim 6:17).

Singles can position themselves to wait upon God. Job positioned himself, and confessed through faith "all the days of his appointed time would he wait till his change come" (Job 14:14). Believers who are determined through faith to wait upon God, realize that being unequally yoked (marrying the wrong person), not marrying (realize they are not called to live a life of celibacy), are not options, but a failure to believe God at His Word. Waiting upon the mate God has chosen is the position and choice that has to be made through faith and trust in His Word to receive your divinely appointed mate.

Prayerfully and patiently waiting upon the Lord for "the mate He has chosen" positions you to wait upon the Lord, and for Him to magnetize the mate He has chosen for you (Isaiah 34:16).

The wisdom of His Word teaches that building the foundation of marriage on divine principles and guidelines will "stand the test of time", and conquer the storms of life. Hurrying into marriage provokes you to hurry, hastily and regret your choice later. Wrong foundations to include lust, sex before marriage, marrying for money, or marrying because of the man or woman, physical appearance are wrong reasons for getting married.

Marriage Should Be Based On Four Principles:

Love- God has given you a deep and gentle love for the person. Love never fails. Your love will continue to grow as you both learn to relate sincerely and openly to each other; Your love for each other enables your marriage to grow and experience joy and happiness
(1 Cor. 13: 1–13).

God has given you the spirit of wisdom and revelation in the knowledge of His will and purpose for your mate
(Eph. 1:17).

God has guided and directed you in knowing His will concerning the mate He has chosen (Ps. 25:12).

God's Word has been confirmed by a threefold witness; You have received divine revelation through His Word; taken time to seek Him; heard His voice; and is confident and assured He is leading you to marry (Ps. 32:8).

Singles should refuse to allow the pressures of society, family, friends, and associates to push them into marrying the wrong person. There is a season and a time for every matter or purpose under the heaven (Ecc. 3:11). God has a set time for you to get married. You may feel you've made a mistake and missed God's best for you. Know that God has not forgotten or abandon you. He neither sleeps nor slumbers (Ps. 121: 3–4).

Faith in God's Word "turns hopeless circumstances around." For every Queen Vashti, there is an Esther. God has His own divine replacement. Don't choose a replacement on your own. The Bible teaches he that believeth does not make haste (Isa. 28:16). If you believe His Word, and is confident, at the right time God will reveal and grant you His will for you in marriage. As you set your face as a flint toward God's Word and promises; renounce unbelief, doubt, and worrying; you will enter into His rest and peace. Victory is yours in the name of Jesus. You will not be moved by the words, opinions and unscriptural comments of others. You will not be bothered by the reproach, shame, and looks of pity they throw your way.

Job realized that in his place of testing and need for deliverance, only the hand of God was able to heal, deliver, and restore all that the enemy has stolen and taken away. He took a stand in faith and proclaimed; "all the days of my appointed time will I wait till my change come." (Job 14:14). It is only God who will cause a permanent change in your lifestyle from single to married. He is the one that will give you a spouse who will cause your joy to be full.

In marriage, remember two hearts are grafted together, making them dependent upon one another for life! Marriage that is built on the right foundation will stand the test of time and conquer the storms of life. Learn to wait patiently upon God for your mate. Don't be in a hurry or hasty.

No Time

I knelt to pray but not for long
I had too much to do.
Must hurry off and get to work
For bills would soon be due.
And as I said a hurried prayer
Jumped up from off my knee.
My Christian duty now was done
My soul could be at ease.
Although the day I had no time
To speak a word of cheer.
No time to speak of Christ to friend
They'd laugh at me I feared.
N o time–no time too much to do
That was my constant cry.
No time to give to those in need
At last it was time to die.
And when before the Lord I came
I stood with downcast eyes.

Within His hand He held a book
It was the BOOK OF LIFE.
He looked in the book and said,
"Your name I can not find.
I once was going to write it down
But never found the time."

≈

Author Unknown

Take Time

Take Time to Think,
it is the source of power.
Take Time to Read,
it is the secret of staying young.
Take Time to be Quiet,
it is the moment to seek God.
Take Time to be Aware,
it is the opportunity to help others.
Take Time to Love and Be Loved,
it is God's greatest gift.
Take Time to Laugh,
it is the music of the soul.
Take Time to be Friendly,
it is the road to happiness.
Take Time to Dream,
it is what the future is made of.
Take Time to Pray
it is the greatest power on earth.
There is a time everything
and a season for every activity under heaven.

≈

Ecclesiastes 3:1

Part Eighteen
WAITING FOR HEAVEN'S MATE

Rest in the Lord, and wait patiently for Him: fret not thyself because of him who prospereth in his way, because of the men who bringeth wicked devices to pass (Ps. 37:7 KJV).

But they that wait upon the Lord shall renew their strength; they shall mount up with wings as eagles; they shall run, and not be weary; and they shall walk, and not faint (Isa. 40:31 KJV).

Truly my soul waiteth upon God, from him cometh my salvation (Ps. 62:1 KJV).

My soul, wait thou only upon God and silently submit to Him; for my hope and expectation are from Him (Ps. 62:1,5 TAB).

The Lord is good unto them that wait for him, to the soul that seeketh him.

It is good that a man should both hope and quietly wait for the salvation of the Lord (Lam. 3:25,26 KJV).

I waited patiently for the Lord; and he inclined unto me, and heard my cry (Ps. 40:1 KJV).

Lead me in thy truth, and teach me: for thou art the God of my salvation; on thee do I wait all the day (Ps. 25:5 KJV).

Therefore turn thou to thy God: Keep mercy and judgment, and wait on thy God continually (Hos. 12:6 KJV).

Wait

Desperately, helplessly, longingly, I cried:
Quietly, patiently, lovingly God replied.
I pled and I wept for a clue to my fate,
And the Master so gently said, "Child, you must wait."

"Wait? You say, wait!" my indignant reply.
"Lord, I need answers, I need to know why!
Is your hand shortened? Or have you not heard?
By faith, I have asked, and am claiming your Word.

My future and all to which I can relate
hangs in the balance, and YOU tell me to WAIT?
I'm needing a 'yes,' go ahead and sign,
or even a 'no' to which I can resign.

And Lord, You promised that if we believe
we need but ask, and we shall receive.
And Lord, I've been asking, and this is my cry:
I'm weary of asking! I need a reply!

Then quietly, softly, I learned of my fate
As my Master replied once again, "You must wait."
So I slumped in my chair, defeated and taught
and grumbling to God, "So, I'm waiting . . . for what?"

He seemed, then, to kneel, and His eyes wept with mine,
And he tenderly said, "I could give you a sign.
I could shake the heavens, and darken the sun.
I could raise the dead, and cause mountains to run.

"All you seek, I could give, and pleased you would be.
You would have what you want–But, you wouldn't know Me.

You'd not know the depth of My love for each saint;
You'd not know the power that I give to the faint;
You'd not learn to see through the clouds of despair;
You'd not learn to trust just by knowing I'm there;

"You'd not know the joy of resting in Me
When darkness and silence were all you could see.

"You'd never experience that fullness of love
As the peace of My Spirit descends like a dove;
You'd know that I give and I save . . . (for a start),
But you'd not know the depth of the beat of My heart.

"The glow of My comfort late into the night,
The faith that I give when you walk without sight,
The depth that's beyond getting just what you asked
Of the infinite God, who makes what you have LAST.

"You'd never know, should your pain quickly flee,
What it means that "My grace is sufficient for Thee."
Yes, your dreams for your loved one overnight would come true,
But, Oh, the loss! If I lost what I'm doing in you!

"So, be silent, My Child, and in time you will see
That the greatest of gifts is to get to know Me.
And though oft' My answers seem terribly late,
My most precious answer is still, WAIT."

❧

Author Unknown

Waiting For Heavens Mate
Waiting On The Lord: Pathway To Victory

He said to them, Is it well with him? And they said, He is doing well; and behold, here comes his daughter Rachel with (his) sheep!

He said, The sun is still high; it is a long time yet before the flocks need be gathered (in their folds). (Why not) water the sheep and return them to their pasture?

But they said, We cannot until all the flocks are gathered

together; then (the shepherds) roll the stone from the well's mouth and we water the sheep.

While he was still talking with them, Rachel came with her father's sheep, for she shepherded them.

When Jacob saw Rachel daughter of Laban, his mother's brother, and the sheep of Laban his uncle, Jacob went near and rolled the stone from the well's mouth and watered the flock of his uncle Laban.

Then Jacob kissed Rachel and he wept aloud.

Jacob told Rachel he was her father's relative, Rebekah's son; and she ran and told her father.

When Laban heard of the arrival of Jacob his sister's son, he ran to meet him, and embraced and kissed him and brought him to his house. And (Jacob) told Laban all these things.

Then Laban said to him, Surely you are my bone and my flesh. And (Jacob) stayed with him a month.

Then Laban said to Jacob, just because you are my relative, should you work for me for nothing? Tell me, what shall your wages be?

Now Laban had two daughters; the name of the elder was Leah and the name of the younger was Rachel.

Leah's eyes were weak and dull looking, but Rachel was beautiful and attractive.

And Jacob loved Rachel; so he said, I will work for you for seven years for Rachel your younger daughter.

And Laban said, It is better that I give her to you than to another man. Stay and live with me.

And Jacob served seven years for Rachel; and they

seemed to him but a few days because of the love he had for her.

Finally, Jacob said to Laban, Give me my wife, for my time is completed, so that may I take her to me.

And Laban gathered together all the men of the place and made a feast (with drinking).

But when night came, he took Leah his daughter and brought her to (Jacob), who had intercourse with her.

And Laban gave Zilpah his maid to his daughter Leah to be her maid.

But in the morning (Jacob saw his wife, and) behold, it was Leah! And he said to Laban. What is this you have done to me? Did I not work for you (all those seven years) for Rachel? Why then have you deceived and cheated and thrown me down (like this)?

And Laban said, It is not permitted in our country to give the younger (in marriage) before the elder.

Finish the (wedding feast) week (for Leah); then we will give you (Rachel) also, and you shall work for me yet seven more years in return.

So Jacob complied and fulfilled (Leah's) week; then (Laban) gave him Rachel his daughter as his wife.

(And Laban gave Bilhah his maid to Rachel his daughter to be her maid).

And Jacob lived with Rachel also as his wife, and he loved Rachel more than Leah and served (Laban) another seven years (for her) (Gen 29: 6–30 TAB).

The word wait means to remain in readiness or expectation. In scripture, the word wait normally suggests the anxious, yet confident, expectation by God's people that the Lord will intervene on their behalf.

Such waiting may be for answers to prayer (Ps. 25:5), for the coming of the Holy Spirit (Acts 1:4), for salvation (Gen 49:18), or especially as the title of the chapter; Waiting for Heaven's Mate. Waiting therefore, is the working out of hope (Thomas Nelson's Illustrated Bible Dictionary).

We are living in a "now" generation. I desire to marry now. Give me my mate now. I am ready for Heaven's Mate now. Impulsiveness, hastiness and instant decisions does not come without a price. Many are living with the results or consequences of yesterday's decisions.

It is comforting for every single Christian waiting on their mate to remember who you are waiting on! Why you are waiting, and what are you waiting for? The Lord knows your desire. He hears and will answer your prayer. Learning to exercise patience or wait upon God means . . . the trying of your faith worketh patience. You must learn to let patience have her perfect work, that ye may be perfect and entire wanting nothing (James 1:3–4).

There is countless Christian who is praying, working, and has left God out of their plans. They have made plans and forgot to seek Him. Many have taken it to the extreme; claimed their mate, planned the wedding, purchased or layawayed their wedding gown and said; "Lord it's all in order; I am ready now for marriage now. Release the bridegroom.

These presumptions faith actions alone reveals you are not ready for Heaven's Mate. There are many revelations and unveilings of God's will in our lives He does not allow us to touch. He works in a mysterious way, in His wonders to perform. You may be the perfect candidate for His extreme makeover. Perhaps you are not ready for Heaven's mate now, and would not only stifle or hinder his destiny or purpose in the marriage, ministry, and life of His chosen, but will be responsible for completely aborting His work in their life.

The waiting process is divinely ordained. There are many Christians who have the wrong attitude and mindset about marriage. The current sixty percent divorce rate in Christian marriages validates this principle. We have planned elaborate weddings, to include invitations, honeymoons with all the makings of a prosperous successful marriage, but forgot the source- the blueprints for the union. Consequently, we forgot that "marriage still takes three." We left the Foundation- Creator out of our marriage, relationship and family.

Learning to willingly submit to divine preparation is a necessity for all Christian singles. We serve a God that cannot lie. In Isaiah 34:16, the scripture declares to "seek ye out of the book of the Lord, and read:

no one of these shall fail, none shall want her mate: for my mouth it hath commanded, and his spirit it hath gathered them." He watcheth over His Word to perform it; and His Word shall not return unto him void (Isaiah 55:11).

His destiny and purpose concerning our lives will surely come to pass. He is the one who instituted the union of marriage and performed the first wedding ceremony in Genesis chapter two. He has a mate for every man or woman. Are you willing to trust Him with your destiny? Are you willing to submit to His principles and guidelines? Are you willing to remain in His waiting room for preparation and perfection?

Esther is one of the daughters of God, who had neither father nor mother. She was not only fair and beautiful, but humbly submitted to divine preparation under the spiritual mentoring of Mordecai. She positioned herself to the pathway for victory from the obscurity of poverty and lack, to royalty, and to the king's palace.

> Now in Shushan the palace there was a certain Jew, whose name was Mordecai, the son of Jair, the son of Shimei, the son of Kish, a Benjamite;
>
> Who had been carried away from Jerusalem with the captivity which had been carried away with Jeconiah, king of Judah, whom Nebuchadnezzar the king of Babylon had carried away.
>
> And he brought up Hadassah, that is, Esther, his uncle's daughter: for she had neither father nor mother, and the maid was fair and beautiful; whom Mordecai, when her father and mother were dead, took for his own daughter.
>
> So it came to pass, when the king's commandment and his decree was heard, and when many maidens were gathered together unto Shushan the palace, to the custody of Hegai, that Esther was brought also unto the king's house, to the custody of Hegai, keeper of the women.
>
> And the maiden pleased him, and she obtained kindness of him; and he speedily gave her her things for purification, with such things as belonged to her, and seven maidens, which were meet to be given her, out of the king's house:

and he preferred her and her maids unto the best place of the house of the women.

Esther had not shewed her people nor her kindred: for Mordecai had charged her that she should not shew it.

And Mordecai walked every day before the court of the women's house, to know how Esther did, and what should become of her.

Now when every maid's turn was come to go in to king Ahasuerus, after that she had been twelve months, according to the manner of the women, (for so were the days of their purifications accomplished, to wit, six months with oil of myrrh, and six months with sweet odours, and with other things for the purifying of the women;)

Then thus came every maiden unto the king; whatsoever she desired was given her to go with her out of the house of the women unto the king's house.

In the evening she went, and on the morrow she returned into the second house of the women, to the custody of Shaashgaz, the king's chamberian, which kept the concubines: she came in unto the king no more, except the king delighted in her, and that she were called by name.

Now when the turn of Esther, the daughter of Abihail the uncle of Mordecai, who had taken her for his daughter, was come to go in unto the king, she required nothing but what Hegai the king's chamberlain, the keeper of the women, appointed. And Esther obtained favour in the sight of all them that looked upon her.

So Esther was taken unto king Ahasuerus into his house royal in the tenth month, which is the month Tebeth, in the seventh year of his reign.

And the king loved Esther above all the women, and she obtained grace and favour in his sight more than all the

> virgins; so that he set royal crown upon her head, and made her queen instead of Vashti.
>
> Then the king made a great feast unto all his princes and his servants, even Esther's feast; and he made a release to the provinces, and gave gifts, according to the state of the king (Esther 2: 8–18 KJV).

Esther's makeover is a testimony and example for all Christian daughters who have, and are deviated from the eternal path, and are not asking where is the good, old way, nor seeking to walk in it to find rest for your souls. But are proclaiming, we will not walk in it (Jer 6:16). You are rejecting the wisdom of mature Christian women and men who will wisely teach and train you to be sane and sober minded (temperate, disciplined) and love your husband and your children (Titus 2: 3–4). You are rejecting the counsel of the divinely assigned Naomi's, Mordecai's, Elizabeth and Mary's in the twenty first century.

> Bid the older women similarly to be reverent and devout in their deportment as becomes those engaged in sacred service, not slanderers or slaves to drink. They are to give good counsel and be teachers of what is right and noble,
>
> So that they will wisely train the young women to be sane and sober of mind (temperate, disciplined) and to love their husbands and their children,
>
> To be self-controlled, chaste, homemakers, good-natured (kindhearted), adapting and subordinating themselves to their husbands, that the word of God may not be exposed to reproach (blasphemed or discredited).
>
> In a similar way, urge the younger men to be self-restrained and to behave prudently (taking life seriously).
>
> And show your own self in all respects to be a pattern and model of good deeds and works, teaching what is unadulterated, showing gravity (having the strictest regard for truth and purity of motive), with dignity and seriousness.

And let your instruction be sound and fit and wise and wholesome, vigorous and irrefutable and above censure, so that the opponent may be put to shame, finding nothing discrediting or evil to say about us.

(Tell) bond servants to be submissive to their masters, to be pleasing and give satisfaction in every way. (Warn them) not to talk back or contradict,

Nor to steal by taking things of small value, but to prove themselves truly loyal and entirely reliable and faithful throughout, so that in everything they may be an ornament and do credit to the teaching (which is) from and about God our Savior.

For the grace of God (His unmerited favor and blessing) has come forward (appeared) for the deliverance form sin and the eternal salvation for all mankind.

It has trained us to reject and renounce all ungodliness (irreligion) and worldly (passionate) desires, to live discreet (temperate, self- controlled), upright, devout (spiritually whole) lives in the present world,

Awaiting and looking for the (fulfillment, the realization of our) blessed hope, even the glorious appearing of our great God and Savior Christ Jesus (the Messiah, the Anointed one),

Who gave Himself on our behalf that He might redeem us (purchase our freedom) from all iniquity and purify for Himself a people (to be peculiarly His own, people who are) eager and enthusiastic about (living a life that is good and filled with) beneficial deeds.

Tell (them all) these things. Urge (advise, encourage, warn) and rebuke with full authority. Let no one despise or disregard or think little of you (conduct yourself and your teaching so as to command respect) (Titus 2:3–15 TAB).

Esther's received her divine makeover before she was presented to the king. The beauty preparations further complimented her fair and beautiful appearance. Unlike the world's twenty first century makeovers that cater to the flesh, Esther submitted to her spiritual makeover early in her life. She positioned herself to receive a victorious transition from a single lifestyle unto married.

There are many beautiful extreme makeovers today. However, fleshly beautification is the center of each makeover; focusing on the outward man, which perishes, enhancing the beautification and perfection of the flesh; and not the inward man which is renewed day-by-day (2 Cor. 4:16).

As a displaced, orphaned Jewess, Mordecai, an older relative, reared Esther in the admonition of the Lord. Whether at his bidding, by force of evil officials, or by her own choice, she had entered the beauty contest and won. Now Mordecai's sources informed Esther that the Jewish people were scheduled for extinction by the wicked Haman, a self-promoter who had elevated himself to vice-regent, second only to the monarch, King Ahasuerus.

Faced with a desperate challenge to survival, Esther pondered Mordecai's question: "Who knows whether you have come to the kingdom for such a time as this?" (Esther 4:14).

> No place of privilege can ever exempt a person from responsibility to respond to God's call.

> Although a situation may look hopeless, God is never helpless.

> A God- given opportunity is an individual's received privilege.

The question that remained in Esther's heart, maybe the question of many sons and daughter's of God today: "who knows whether you have come to the kingdom for such a time as this" (Esther 4:10)? The revelation and unveiling of the necessity to return, follow, and fulfill His destiny in our life is the divine call for Heaven's mate. We are called to reverse and destroy the statistics of failed marriages and high divorce rates, to the manifestation of healthy, successful Christ- centered marriages and families.

The second example of waiting for Heaven's Mate we will discuss is; "Jacob's love for Rachel- his Heaven's mate." The scriptural example of his love for Rachel, whose name means "ewe", was caring for her father's sheep when she met Jacob. After what seems to have been love at first sight,

(Gen 29:11, 12) Jacob promised Rachel's father, Laban, that he would work seven years to earn the right to marry the beautiful shepherdess (Gen 29:20).

The wedding ceremony proceeded according to local tradition, allowing the men to celebrate while keeping the bride out of sight until he entered the darkened tent.

Only after it was too late did Jacob realize that Laban had deceived him. He had actually married Laban's older daughter, Leah, whom he did not love.

Jacob's love for Rachel was so strong and powerful that he told Laban he would work seven more years for her, and they seemed to him but a few days, because of the love he had for her (Gen 29:20). In reality the waiting process for his Heaven's mate was fourteen years. The power of his love for her made the waiting process worth waiting for- joy and happiness. How much more happy and joyous we are, when we are enjoying and dwelling in His presence; in a constant flow of knowing that it's in Him we move, live and have our being. He is our joy unspeakable.

The scripture declares Jesus, the author and finisher of our faith, who for the joy that was set before him, endured the cross, despising the shame, and is set down at the right hand of the throne of God (Heb. 12:2). Jacob's love for Rachel, his Heaven's mate was so strong, he served fourteen years for her, and it seemed to him but a few days. Although obtaining the prize for each was different, each endured the cross- one resulting in many sons and daughters birthed into the kingdom; the other, the receiving of his heaven's mate.

There are many advantage of waiting upon Heaven's mate. Spiritual discipline is essential for waiting and receiving Christian growth and development.

- Results from obedience and faith which produces abundant blessings (Heb. 12:11)
- Enables believers to seek to become more disciplined in order to grow spiritually
- Enables believers to mature in Christ and know God's will
- Is an attitude of commitment
- An activity in holiness
- Essential to deliverance from the power of sin and disobedience to God's will

Specific Spiritual Disciplines

- Personal training in Bible study
- Prayer
- Worship
- Fellowship
- Service
- Witnessing

Without spiritual discipline, believers cannot develop a steadfast spiritual walk with Christ, grow in faith, or receive the heavenly rewards awaiting those who diligently walk in the spirit, apply and practice His Word. A conscientious, creative pursuit of the aforementioned spiritual disciplines should continue through out a believer's life (Heb 6:11, 12).

Part Nineteen

FINANCE AND MARRIAGE

The earth is the Lord's, and the fullness thereof; the world, and they that dwell in therein (Ps 24:1 KJV).

He that tilleth his land shall be satisfied with bread: but he that followeth vain persons is void of understand (Prov. 12:11 KJV).

I love them that love me, and those that seek me early shall find me.

Riches and honor are with me; yea durable riches and righteousness.

My fruit is better than gold, yea, than fine gold; and My revenue than choice silver.

I lead in the way of righteousness, in the midst of the paths of judgment:

That I may cause those that love Me to inherit substance; and I will fill their treasures (Prov. 8:17–21 KJV).

Upon the first day of every week, let every one of you by him in store, as God hath prospered him, that there be no gatherings when I come (1 Cor 16:2 KJV).

Finance And Marriage

For the love of money is the root of all evil: which while some coveted after, they have erred from the faith, and pierced themselves through with many sorrows (1 Tim. 6:10 KJV).

> Will a man rob God? Yet ye have robbed me. But ye say, wherein have we robbed thee? In tithes and offerings.
>
> Ye are cursed with a curse: for ye have robbed me, even this whole nation.
>
> Bring ye all the tithes into the storehouse, that there may be meat in mine house, and prove me now herewith, saith the Lord of hosts, if I will not open you the windows of heavens, and pour you out a blessing, that there shall not be room enough to receive it (Mal. 3: 8–10 KJV).

The scripture declares, "money answereth all things" (Ecc. 10:19). Money is a defense (Ecc. 7:12). Every couple should develop a sound financial understanding before entering into the union of marriage, learning how to communicate effectively based on kingdom principles. Many marriages relationships are not working harmoniously and scripturally as a result of financial problems. Financial problems create strife, and many conflicts in the home.

Many husbands and wives are married, but maintain separate accounts. One pays three bills, the other pays two bills, and the savings remain empty. The impact of the lack of money in a marriage is devastating. It causes much pain and sorrow, and consequently ends in divorce for a lot of couples. Managing money wisely not only demonstrates that the couple "is not walking and living under the curse of the law, but have been redeemed from curse of poverty" (Gal. 3:13). Wise financial-management requires commitment and sacrifice form both partners. It cannot be accomplished without the power of agreement between both partners (Amos 3:3).

The scripture declares, the thief cometh not, but for to steal, and to kill, and to destroy: I am come that they might have life, and that they might have it more abundantly (John 10:10).

Financial mismanagement, pressures, and the stress of household lack create the spirits of strife, division, discord and dissension in many marriages. It also escalates to broken relationships and in some cases, eventually divorces. Learning to communicate openly and honestly about financial concerns prior to marriage empowers the couple to develop sound financial understanding, and equip them to destroy the works of the devil. The blessing of obedience (Deut 28: 1–14) positions married couples to experience financial prosperity in their marriage. Equally, the curses of disobedience, position couples to experience financial defeat and failure in their marriage and home (Deut. 28: 15–64).

The scripture declares "and this is the victory that overcometh the world, even our faith" (1 John 5:4). God's original plan for his man, Adam, was that he be a wealthy man and never have to experience poverty. However, Adam sold out to the devil, and the devil became the god of this world (2 Cor. 4:4). Believers must learn to trust and follow God, who has all power in heaven and on earth, exceeding all the works of the devil. In learning to experience life more abundantly, we must learn to abide in Him, let His Word abide in us, and work together with Him in all things.

༄

But my God shall supply all your need according to his riches in glory by Christ Jesus (Phil. 4:19 KJV).

༄

We are taught scripturally, "all our expectation is from God" (Ps. 62:5). As we look unto Him, the author and finisher of our faith, He shall supply all our needs. God is the greatest supplier there is. He is a bountiful supplier. The silver and gold are the Lord's, the earth, and the fullness thereof.

The greatest hindrances to receiving financial increase in our marriage are strife, offenses, failure to pay tithes and offerings, and being impatient. Deception and a lack of knowledge are also a great hindrance in receiving from God. Knowledge is power, and where the Word of the king is, there is power (Ecc. 8:4). It is glorious and wonderful to behold couples tapping into the unsearchable riches of God, learning and experiencing the faithfulness of God in every aspect of our lives. They learn to believe the scripture which declares, "He is faithful that has promised, and He is not a man that He should lie" (Heb 10:23; Num. 23:19).

Believers must learn to walk in the Word in all things. The scripture declares, "according to your faith, be it unto you" (Matt 9:29). We must choose to believe the scriptures, learn to stand, and act upon His word in our day-to-day living. His Word is totally ineffective, invaluable and of no effect unto us, if we choose not to believe the report of the Lord's- His Word.

Part Twenty
DESTROYING CYCLES OF DEFEAT

As it is written, Behold, I lay in Sion a stumblingstone and rock of offence: and whosoever believeth on him shall not be ashamed (Rom 9:33 KJV).

And the God of peace shall bruise Satan under your feet shortly. The grace of our Lord Jesus Christ be with you. Amen (Rom 16:20 KJV)

What shall we then say to these things? If God be for us, who can be against us?

He that spared not his own Son, but delivered him up for us all, how shall he not with him also freely give us all things?

Who shall lay any thing to the charge of God's elect? It is God that justifieth.

Who is he that condemneth? It is Christ that died, yea rather, that is risen again, who is even at the right hand of God, who also maketh intercession for us.

Who shall separate us from the love of Christ? shall tribulation, or distress, or persecution, or famine, or nakedness, or peril, or sword?

As it is written, For thy sake we are killed all the day long; we are accounted as sheep for the slaughter.

Nay, in all these things we are more than conquerors through him that loved us (Rom 8:31–37 KJV).

And have no fellowship with the unfruitful works of darkness, but rather reprove them (Eph 5:11 KJV).

Who hath delivered us from the power of darkness, and hath translated us into the kingdom of his dear Son:

In whom we have redemption through his blood, even the forgiveness of sins:

Who is the image of the invisible God, the firstborn of every creature: (Col 1:13–15 KJV)

Blotting out the handwriting of ordinances that was against us, which was contrary to us, and took it out of the way, nailing it to his cross;

And having spoiled principalities and powers, he made a shew of them openly, triumphing over them in it (Col 2:14–15 KJV).

Wherefore, sirs, be of good cheer: for I believe God, that it shall be even as it was told me (Acts 27:25 KJV)

Surely there is no enchantment against Jacob, neither is there any divination against Israel: according to this time it shall be said of Jacob and of Israel, What hath God wrought (Num 23:23 KJV)!

And he shall pass through Judah; he shall overflow and go over, he shall reach even to the neck; and the stretching out of his wings shall fill the breadth of thy land, O Immanuel.

Associate yourselves, O ye people, and ye shall be broken in pieces; and give ear, all ye of far countries: gird yourselves, and ye shall be broken in pieces; gird yourselves, and ye shall be broken in pieces.

> Take counsel together, and it shall come to nought; speak the word, and it shall not stand: for God is with us (Isa 8:8–10 KJV).

Severing Unhealthy Soul Ties

> What? Know you not that he which is joined to an harlot, is one body? For two, saith he, shall be one flesh (1 Cor. 6:16 KJV).

> And they that are Christ's have crucified the flesh with the affections and lusts (Gal. 5:24 KJV).

> From henceforth let no man trouble me: for I bear in my body the marks of the Lord Jesus (Gal 6:17 KJV).

A soul tie can be defined as an obsessive affection for a person, which is often strengthened by sexual intercourse or blood covenant. When there are soul ties, one's actions are controlled and subject to those of the other person. An unholy union is formed with this person, and is consecrated so that the two share mind, purpose, and life. One is living for the other person.

Soul ties can be between a man and a woman, a mother and a son (this is called Olympus Complex), or a boyfriend and girlfriend. Therefore, when a man or woman is being manipulated in the name of love, this bond has to be broken because the scripture declares this is witchcraft.

The first revelation of a "soul tie" in the scripture is found in Genesis 2:21–24.

> And the Lord caused a deep sleep upon Adam, and he slept; he took one of his ribs and closed up the flesh instead thereof. And the rib, which the Lord God had taken from man, made he a woman, and brought her to the man. And Adam said "This is now bone of my bone and flesh of my flesh; she shall be called woman, because she was taken out of man. Therefore shall a man leave his father and mother, and shall cleave unto his wife, and they shall be one flesh (Gen. 2:21–24 KJV).

The scriptures reveal that from the beginning, God's will has been that the soul ties men and women have with their parents should be broken prior to marriage. This is because when a meddlesome parent, still emotionally controls one partner, it causes marriage destruction. Consequently, we see the scripture admonition to destroy or cut the soul tie.

The bonding of soul ties often takes time, specifically in the area of friendships. Man is a spirit. He lives in a body and possesses a soul. Man's soul consists of his mind, emotions, and will. A soul involves the joining of minds, views, and ideas, as well as the emotional unions in the feeling realm. Soul ties can range from being laid back and fairly loose to quite intense and overpowering.

Because we are living in a world full of cultural diversity with creative manipulative ways, man has put too much confidence in the flesh as it relates to his soul. Lack of discernment, vanity, greed, and all unprofitable works of the flesh causes unhealthy and damaging relationships. Parents, do you know who your son or daughter is dating? Young man, young woman, do you know who you are dating? Married man, adulterer or adulteress, do you know you are risking your home, marriage, and family? For your adversary, the devil, walketh about as a roaring lion, seeking whom he may devour (1 Peter 5:8). Learning to be temperate, sober of mind, and cautious at all times will enable man or woman to develop balanced, healthy relationships.

The scripture reveals that the thief cometh not, but for to steal, kill, and destroy. But He has come that we might have life, and have it more abundantly (John 10; 10). Demons are evil personalities. They are spirit beings. They are the enemies of God and man. Their objectives in human beings are to tempt, deceive, accuse, condemn, pressure, defile, oppose, control, steal, afflict, kill and destroy. Unhealthy relationships and attachments to ungodly people adversely affect the lives of many, and cause great destruction in marriages.

A soul tie is a "channel." Because demonic spirits can transfer so easily through soul ties, it is essential to identify and destroy the soul ties that are ungodly, controlling, or emotionally binding.

Soul Ties In Unhealthy Relationships

Do not be unequally yoked with unbelievers (do not make mismated alliances with them or come under a different yoke with them, inconsistent with your faith). For what partnership have right living and right standing with God with iniquity and lawlessness? Or how can light have fellowship with darkness?

What harmony can there be between Christ and Belial (the devil)? Or what has a believer in common with an unbeliever?

What agreement (can there be between) a temple of God and idols? For we are the temple of the living God; even as God said, I will dwell in and with and among them and will walk in and with and among them, and I will be their God, and they shall be My people.

So, come out from among (unbelievers), and separate (sever) yourselves from them, says the Lord, and touch not (any) unclean thing; then I will receive you kindly and treat you with favor (2 Cor. 6:14–17 TAB),

Can two walk together, except they be agreed (Amos 3:3)?

Although love is one of the greatest forces or weapons on this earth, the scripture admonishes us to be wise and discerning in our relationships. The love of God distinguishes between the person's true self and the negative behavior or works of the flesh. Such discerning enables one close to the person to love the person and not get distracted by the challenges of an unstable personality. Persons within relationships without prayer, fasting, staying in God's presence, and standing on His word will be unable to maintain their walk with God. Unhealthy soul ties can become a destructive force in the life of the believer.

It is a necessity when relating to such persons to let love, or the Holy Spirit, be transferred from you rather than an unclean spirit from them.

Believers, if you are already romantically tied to an unbeliever, God has provided a way of escape (II Peter. 2:18). Cut or destroy the soul tie in the name of Jesus! It can and must be done. Submit yourself unto the Lord and pray under the anointing to sever the bond of emotional attachment. During the healing process, determine that every thought, word, and action will reflect the very nature of Christ. Abide in

Christ that the fruit of the spirit might come forth in abundance. Demon spirits are enemies of the fruit of the Spirit. Faith and trust in God are the greatest weapons against the devil's lies.

> Above all, taking the shield of faith, wherewith ye shall be able to quench all the fiery darts of the wicked (Eph. 6:16 KJV).

> And take the helmet of salvation, and the sword of the Spirit, which is the Word of God.

> Praying always with all prayer and supplication in the Spirit, and watching thereunto with all perseverance and supplication for all saints; (Eph. 6:16–18 KJV).

> Learn to walk in daily obedience. Do not settle for anything less!

Severing Unhealthy Sexual Soul Ties

And Dinah, the daughter of Leah, which she bare unto Jacob, went out to see the daughters of the land. And when Shechem, the son of Hamor the Hivite, prince of the country, saw her, he took her, and lay with her, and defiled her. And his soul clave to Dinah, the daughter of Jacob, and he loved the damsel, and spake kindly unto the damsel (Gen. 34:1–3 KJV)

> Then went Samson to Gaza, and saw there an harlot, and went in unto her (Judges 16:1 KJV).

> And it came to pass afterward, that he loved a woman in the valley of Sorek, whose name was Delilah (Judges 16:4 KJV).

> But King Solomon loved many strange women, together with the daughter of Pharaoh, women of the Moabites, Ammonites, Edomites, Zidonians, and Hittites;

> Of the nations concerning which the LORD said unto the

children of Israel, Ye shall not go in to them, neither shall they come in unto you: for surely they will turn away your heart after their gods: Solomon clave unto these in love (1 Kings 11: 1–2 KJV).

Know ye not that your bodies are the members of Christ? Shall I then take the members of Christ, and make them the members of a harlot? God forbid. What? Know ye not that he which is joined to a harlot is one body? For two, saith he, shall be one flesh (I Cor. 6:15–16 KJV).

Interestingly enough, God's plan for a man and woman is unlike the worlds. First, He would lead them to bond in the area of spirit. After getting to know one another, a bonding of the mind and emotions would occur. Then, after solemn vows of commitment in marriage, bonding of the body would be possible.

The world insists on doing things its way. The first thing to bond is the body, through sexual indulgences of diverse measures. Then, due to strong physical attraction, a couple gets married (many are not doing that anymore). They then become acquainted with one another in their soul, mind, and emotions. This is when they begin to realize that they are incompatible and are unable to sever that fleshly or sexual bond.

The woman realizes that her attractive husband was abusive and had violent tendencies. The man observes that the beautiful woman he married is filled with insecurity.

The world's ways are totally backwards. The way of the Lord is not. Therefore, there is only one way for Christians to go. The way of the Lord is straight and narrow. When you are seeking Heaven's mate, you learn to establish the priorities of the Lord over the issues of a relationship. The scripture declares, "but seek ye first the kingdom of God, and His righteousness, and all these things shall be added unto you" (Matt. 6:33).

Symptoms Of Ungodly Soul Ties

- Obsessive preoccupation with another, to the neglect of the things of the Lord.
- Tendencies to be domineering and controlling in a relationship.

- Tendencies to be passive and apathetic in a relationship (easily manipulated).
- Inability to truly forgive from the heart.
- Another person's voice playing over and over in the mind like a tape-recorder.
- Inability to bring a relationship under the godly order and control of the Holy Spirit.
- Patterns of anger, blame and accusations in a relationship.
- Fear of "being real with" or speaking truth to another (intimidation and fear of man).
- Psychic or occult phenomena within a relationship.

Steps To Breaking Ungodly Soul Ties

Confess any and all ungodly ties to the Lord.

Repent from your heart for violating God's ordained boundaries in your relationships.

Make a solemn commitment to the Lord to break off any relationship that is not pure or righteous in His eyes.

Become accountable to others to help you keep that commitment. Until you do that, any prayers for freedom are in vain. Continue fasting, praying, and meditation upon the Word of God. Learn to dwell in God's presence in praise and worship. However, God is not mocked. Reinforce your requests to the Lord with commitment to obey.

Before praying, do whatever is necessary for the anointing of the Holy Spirit to come.

This is so important. Pray, wait, forgive, or worship. Once His presence and anointing is present, then proceed with the soul tie destroying prayer. It's the anointing that destroys the yoke. The ties won't break with a simple prayer from the mind. The anointed power of the Holy Spirit must be present to be effective.

Heavenly Covering

And the Lord shall deliver me from every evil work, and will preserve me unto His heavenly kingdom: in who be glory for ever and ever Amen (2 Tim. 4:18 KJV).

Blessed be the God and Father of our Lord Jesus Christ, who hath blessed us with all spiritual blessings in heavenly places in Christ (Eph. 1:3 KJV).

And hath raised us up together, and made us sit together in heavenly places in Christ Jesus (Eph. 2:6 KJV).

To the intent that now unto the principalities and powers in heavenly places might be known by the church the manifold wisdom of God (Eph. 3:10 KJV).

And as we have borne the image of the earthly, we shall also bear the image of the heavenly (I Cor. 15:49 KJV).

    The scriptures declare that God has blessed us all with spiritual blessings in heavenly places. We are partakers of His heavenly blessings. He is a sword and shield. He will give us grace and glory, "and no good thing will He withhold from them that walk upright" (Prov. 3:27).
    The heavenly covering acknowledges that Jesus Christ is Lord. He rules and reigns in the hearts and lives of His chosen. He imparts righteousness, peace, and joy to our spirit, mind, and body. The scrip-

tures declare that the kingdom of God is within us. What does that mean? Wherever we find the lordship of Jesus Christ actively operating, there is the kingdom–peace, joy and righteousness in the Holy Ghost. The essence of all this is that, these benefits are ours and they are ours now. The mentality of many proclaims that this life is a wilderness, and that one of these days after we die we shall find happiness. This way of thinking is totally unknowledgeable of the Word of God. The Kingdom of God is within us; enabling us to live and experience the mountain top life as we abide in Him and let His word abide in us (John 15:5).

> But our God is in the Heavens. He hath done whatsoever He hath pleased. And He hath raised us up together with Him and made us sit down together (giving us "joint seating with Him) in the heavenly sphere (by virtue of our being) in Christ Jesus (the Messiah, the Anointed One). (Not in your own strength) for it is God who is all the while effectually at work in you (energizing and creating in you the power and desire), both to will and to work for His good pleasure and satisfaction and delight (Ps. 115:3; Eph. 2–6; Phil. 2:13 TAB).

Heaven has been described as a place prepared for believers (John 14:1–3), one without sorrow, darkness, or any kind of sin (Rev. 21:1–7). In heaven we will be like Christ, yet we will be able to recognize one another (I John 3:2). The most important thing however, is the presence of God. We will be forever with Him.

The earth is the Lord's and the fullness thereof. God has everything in the palm of His almighty hand. He is sovereign. Jesus is Lord. Jesus is king! He knows everything that is happening, not only in the world system, but in your life and mine. This is the day that He has made. Let us rejoice and be glad in it.

We must give ourselves unto the Word of God, which is the will of God. God has given us His Word, that we might know His principles, the mind, thoughts, and ways of God (Isa. 58:8 KJV).

Part Twenty-One

Destroying Strongholds/ Hindrances Believeing And Receceiving Your Mate

Return to the stronghold (of security and prosperity), you prisoners of hope; even today do I declare that I will restore double your former prosperity to you (Zech 9:12 TAB).

The LORD is good, a strong hold in the day of trouble; and he knoweth them that trust in him (Nah.1: 7 KJV).

He brought me up also out of an horrible pit, out of the miry clay, and set my feet upon a rock, and established my goings (Ps. 40:2 KJV).

Thou hast broken down all his hedges; thou hast brought his strong holds to ruin (Ps. 89: 40 KJV).

He stretched out his hand over the sea, he shook the kingdoms: the LORD hath given a commandment against the merchant city, to destroy the strong holds thereof (Is. 23: 11 KJV).

And I will cut off the cities of thy land, and throw down all thy strong holds (Mic. 5:11 KJV):

All thy strong holds shall be like fig trees with the firstripe figs: if they be shaken, they shall even fall into the mouth of the eater (Nah. 3:12 KJV).

For the weapons of our warfare are not physical (weapons of flesh and blood), but they are mighty before God for the overthrow and destruction of strongholds (2 Cor. 10:4 TAB).

Destroying Marriage Strongholds / Hindrances In Believing God For And Receiving Your Mate

He that committeth sin is of the devil; for the devil sinneth from the beginning. For this purpose the Son of God was manifested, that he might destroy the works of the devil (1 John 3:8 KJV).

Or else how can one enter into a strong man's house, and spoil his goods, except he first bind the strong man? and then he will spoil his house (Matt. 12: 29 KJV).

And I say also unto thee, That thou art Peter, and upon this rock I will build my church; and the gates of hell shall not prevail against it.

And I will give unto thee the keys of the kingdom of heaven: and whatsoever thou shalt bind on earth shall be bound in heaven: and whatsoever thou shalt loose on earth shall be loosed in heaven (Matt 16: 18, 19 KJV).

For the weapons of our warfare are not carnal, but mighty through God to the pulling down of strong holds

Casting down imaginations, and every high thing that exalteth itself against the knowledge of God, and bringing into captivity every thought to the obedience of Christ (2 Cor. 10: 4–5 KJV).

Singles believing God for their mate must come to understanding that evil strongholds and hindering spirits have no sense of fairness. They will never hesitate to take advantage of times of weakness in a person's life. There are many serious questions to ask yourself in relation to believing God for your mate. Specifically, when was the last time you exercised the gift of discernment in relation to believing God for your mate?

Have you examined yourself, whether you are in the faith (2 Cor. 13:5)? Exercising the gift of the Spirit will require you to take personal initiative. Selecting and marrying a mate is the second most important decision you will make in your my life. You must take time to seek the Lord through prayer, His word to examine your life, walk with God, and develop priorities, focus and ministry (if there is one) in your life. Lord, am I ready for marriage? Do I need further preparation and deliverance before marriage? Do I have blind spots? Are there strongholds and hindrances that I am totally unaware of?

In our personal walk with God we must take full responsibility for our life and the decision me make before, after, and during our marriage. Personal initiative should be taken before marriage to enable each personal to not only acknowledge Jesus as Savior and Lord, but to receive the baptism of the Holy Spirit, with power to develop their prayer life, become rooted and grounded in the faith, and grow up into the fullness of Him in all things.

When both mates have matured to a certain level spiritually, they can grow from faith to faith, victory to victory, always abounding in the wisdom, knowledge, understanding, and revelation of our Savior and Lord Jesus Christ.

They strengthen, encourage, motivate, support and learn to keep each other lifted in prayer and supplication daily. If they both are empty, they cannot minister unto each other. You cannot give what you don't have. It's a blessing when couples have matured spiritually and know how to minister to each other during good and bad times.

Christian singles should learn to wait upon the deliverance and healing processing of God before hastily or impulsively running into marriage. Your question or questions unto God should be: Lord is this the mate you have chosen for me? If you discern that God has not finished His processing with your mate; prayerfully, confidently, and wisely learn to wait upon the completion of His divine processing. This is vitally important in the marriage relationship and fulfillment of His divine destiny in your life.

The scripture declares every wise woman buildeth her house, but the foolish plucketh it down with her hands (Prov. 14:1). In today's world, there are many pre- fabucated houses that can be built in one day (ready to be assembled), the building material is already assembled and packaged. However, our heavenly Father has no spiritually cloned mates for His chosen, elect and heirs of the royalty of God. The salvation process is progressive. He has laid the foundation to our walk with Him, and provided the right growing substance to grow up in Him in all things. Give Him time to process you and your mate.

Give each other time to grow, mature, and develop a stronger, deeper relationship with Him. Yield and surrender unto Him and allow him to enable the both of you, to not only love and minister unto each other, but enjoy your personal walk with Him, your marriage and ministry. He has given us all things richly to enjoy. Learn to richly enjoy your divine portion He has given us richly to enjoy.

> Therefore, let us go on and get past the elementary stage in the teachings and doctrine of Christ (the Messiah), advancing steadily toward the completeness and perfection that belong to spiritual maturity. Let us not again be laying the foundation of repentance and abandonment of dead works (dead formalism) and of the faith (by which you turned) to God,
>
> With teachings about purifying, the laying on of hands, the resurrection from the dead, and eternal judgment and punishment. (These are all matters of which you should have been fully aware long, long ago.)
>
> If indeed God permits, we will (now) proceed (to advanced teaching) (Heb. 6: 1–3 TAB).

If you desire to enjoy a loving, healthy, marriage, you both must be perfected (matured) in him. Has a solid foundation been laid in your life? Has it been laid in your mate's life? The foundation has to be laid and laid well in your life (Matt. 7: 24–27; Luke 6: 46–49). The greatest challenge for many singles is, they are not using the right building permits (Heb 6:3) and materials on their Christian journey (1 Cor. 3: 12–13). They are using the world's building materials (wood, stubble and hay); and failing to use the eternal building materials that will withstand the test of time (gold, silver, precious stones).

> For we are fellow workmen (joint promoters, laborers together) with and for God; you are God's garden and vineyard and field under cultivation, (you are) God's building.
>
> According to the grace (the special endowment for my task) of God bestowed on me, like a skillful architect and master builder I laid (the) foundation, and now another

(man) is building upon it. But let each (man) be careful how he builds upon it,

For no other foundation can anyone lay than that which is (already) lay, which is Jesus Christ (the Messiah, the Anointed one).

But if anyone builds upon the Foundation, whether it be with gold, silver, precious stones, wood, hay, straw,

The work of each (one) will become (plainly, openly) known (shown for what it is); for the day (of Christ) will disclose and declare it, because it will be revealed with fire, and the fire will test and critically appraise the character and worth of the work each person has done.

If the work which any person has built on this Foundation (any product of his efforts whatever) survives (this test), he will get his reward.

But if any person's work is burned up (under the test), he will suffer the loss (of it all, losing his reward), though he himself will be saved, but only as (one who has passed) through fire.

Do you not discern and understand that you (the whole church at Corinth) are God's temple (His sanctuary), and that God's Spirit has His permanent dwelling in you (to be at home in you, collectively as a church and also individually)?

If anyone does hurt to God's temple or corrupts it (with false doctrines) or destroys it, God will do hurt to him and bring him to the corruption of death and destroy him. For the temple of God is holy (sacred to Him) and that (temple) you (the believing church and its individual believers) are (1 Cor. 3: 9–17 TAB).

The scripture declares, if any man build upon this foundation gold, silver, and precious stones, his work shall be made manifest: for the day shall declare it, because it shall be revealed by fire; and the fire shall try every man's work of what sort it is.

Life's circumstances manifested in relationships, marriages, misunderstandings and daily crisis's, requires us to learn to endure the test of time, destroy the works of the enemy, and walk in overcoming faith. The scripture declares "and this is the victory that overcometh the world, even our faith" (1 John 5:4).

In the twenty first century, "new carts" are very prevalent (1 Chron. 13: 7). The twenty first century new carts have led many of the sons and daughters out of the will and purpose of God in choosing their mate. When King David realized he had carried the Ark of the Lord wrong, he returned unto the law and carried the Ark as Moses commanded; according to the Word of God. Singles, married couples, divorcees and families must know that God has not changed His plans concerning marriage and the family. It remains the same. Singles must lay a solid foundation by removing the strongholds and hindrances between them and the principles of the Word of God.

Singles must learn to deeply seek the revelation of His Word and purpose in their lives. After the foundation has been laid, you should be taught His Word, line upon line, precept upon precept, here a little and there a little. He will give you His building permit. God is building a house, and has commissioned a team of architects to make sure "the house of the king is brought to completion" (Ps. 127: 1 KJV).

> Then the kingdom of heaven shall be likened to ten virgins who took their lamps and went to meet the bridegroom.
>
> Five of them were foolish (thoughtless, without forethought) and five were wise (sensible, intelligent, and prudent).
>
> For when the foolish took their lamps, they did not take any (extra) oil with them;
>
> But the wise took flasks of oil along with them (also) with their lamps.
>
> While the bridegroom lingered and was slow in coming, they all began nodding their heads, and they fell asleep.

But at midnight there was a shout, Behold, the bridegroom! Go out to meet him!

Then all those virgins got up and put their own lamps in order.

And the foolish said to the wise, Give us some of your oil, for our lamps are going out.

But the wise replied, There will not be enough for us and for you; go instead to the dealers and buy for yourselves.

But while they were going away to buy, the bridegroom came, and those who were prepared went in with him to the marriage feast; and the door was shut.

Later the other virgins also came and said, Lord, Lord, open (the door) to us!

But He replied, I solemnly declare to you, I do not know you (I am not acquainted with you).

Watch therefore (give strict attention and be cautious and active), for you know neither the day nor the hour when the Son of Man will come (Matt 25: 1–13 TAB).

The parable of the ten virgins further illustrates the need for singles to marry Heaven's mate. The five foolish (thoughtless, without fore thought) and five wise (sensible, intelligent, and prudent) indicates the spiritual state of many singles today. The five foolish took their lamps and did not take any extra oil within their vessel. It is His spirit that sparks and ignites the oil. It is His spirit that explodes and becomes a chain reaction to divide the light from the darkness. It is His spirit within that has been ignited and shall consume and destroy the negative darkness.

Single Christians, you are His lamps, you are His vessels. He is the oil, the fire, and the spark. He is the substance of life, and when you become one with Him, the light breaks forth and consumes the darkness. This fire- lights, and generates heat to dispel the coldness of the body, soul and spirit of His chosen. The heat becomes as a cutting torch to circumcise the hardness of the heart and fleshly mind.

Daily He works within us to cause light to overtake and destroy all darkness. He dwells within us to pour out, and to minister unto each other. The Holy oil within the lamps is His substance, and His life.

There is a necessity for singles to keep their lamps trimmed and oil burning; keep your vessels filled with His spirit, His word, prayer and supplications. From vessel to vessel the oil is poured, sparking to light, and it's burning within waiting vessels; believing Him for their chosen mates.

When you continuously submit to the dealings, and processing's of His preparation, no greater love, peace, happiness and joy can be experienced by you or your mate. You both have submitted unto His preparation, and are now released to marry each other, ministering (pouring out) unto each other through the awesome anointing He has released through both of you.

Part Twenty-Two
Prayer And Supplication

Confess your faults one to another and pray one for another; that ye may be healed. The effectual fervent prayer of a righteous man availeth much (James 5:16 KJV).

And when they were come in, they went up into an upper room where abode both Peter, and James, and John, and Andrew, Philip, and Thomas, Bartholomew, and Matthew, James the son of Alphaeus, and Simon Zelotes, and Judas the brother of James (Acts 1:13–14 KJV).

These all continued with one accord in prayer and supplication, with the women, and Mary the mother of Jesus, and with his brethren (Acts 1:14).

Peter therefore was kept in prison; but prayer was made without ceasing of the church unto God for him (Acts 12:5 KJV).

And on the Sabbath we went out of the city by a river side, where prayer was wont to be made; and we sat down, and spake unto the women, which resorted thither (Acts 16:13 KJV).

And it came to pass, that, as he was praying in a certain place, when he ceased, one of his disciples said unto him, Lord, teach us to pray, as John taught his disciples.

And he said unto them, When ye pray, say, Our Father which art in heaven, hallowed be thy name. Thy kingdom come. Thy will be done, as in heaven, so in earth.

Give us day by day, our daily bread.
And forgive us our sins: for we also forgive every one that is indebted to us. And lead us not into temptation, but deliver us from evil (Luke 11:1–4 KJV).

And when he had sent the multitudes away, he went up into a mountain apart to pray: and when the evening was come, he was there alone (Matt. 14:23 KJV).

Neither pray I for these alone, but for them also which shall believe on me through their word.

That they all may be one, as thou, Father, art in me, and I in thee, that they also may be one in us; that the world may believe that thou hast sent me.

And the glory which thou gavest me I have given them, that they be one, even as we are one
(John 17:20–22 KJV).

Friendship Poem

I shot an arrow into the air
It fell to the earth, I knew not where;
For, so swiftly it flew, the sight
Could not follow it in its flight.
I breathed a song into the air,
It fell to earth, I knew not where;
For who has sight so keen and strong,
That it can follow the flight of song?
Long, long afterward, in an oak
I found the arrow, still unbroken;
And the song, from beginning to end,
I found again in the heart of a friend.

H.W. Longfellow

The Power Of Prayer

> If my people, who are called by My name, shall humble themselves, pray, seek, crave, and require of necessity, My face and turn from their wicked ways, then will I hear from heaven, forgive their sin, and heal their land.
>
> Now my eyes will be open and my ears attentive to prayer offered in this place (2 Chr. 7:14–15 TAB).

One of the greatest hindrances to twenty first century believers is the lack of prayer and supplication. There are countless books available on prayer, and many are very good, however, you must submit unto Him in sincere prayers and supplications to receive your expected breakthrough. They provide the revelation, insight, and theory; you activate their instructions through the practice of being a doer of the Word. You must change your posture in prayer from prayerlessness to prayerfulness. In essence, you must develop and grow in your prayer life. You must learn to "pray without ceasing."

Many believers desire to spend time with God in prayer. However, many ask, and receive not, because they ask amiss, they ask with wrong purpose and selfish motives. Their intention when they receive their desired release is to spend it in sensual pleasures and forget their focus (James 4:3). Spiritual discipline is necessary to make prayer a priority in our lives. Sincere believers who are striving to live this life in spirit and truth are fully persuaded that "sincere prayer unto God is one of the keys to living and enjoying a victorious life through Christ Jesus" (Ps. 66:18–19; Phil. 1:10).

The scripture speaks repeatedly of the importance of prayer. Paul instructs us to be careful for nothing; but in every thing, by prayer and supplication with thanksgiving, let your requests be made known unto God (Phil. 4:6). Believers are to make all their requests know unto God, praying without ceasing. David promised the Lord, "evening and morning and at noon I will pray" (Ps. 55:17). Jesus prayed for extended periods of time, especially when making important decisions (Luke. 6:12).

Learning to discipline ourselves in prayer, encourages, strengthens, and comforts every believer experiencing diverse tests, trials, and challenges. Prayer becomes not only a major aspect of the believer's attitude, but a continual dialogue with the Lord.

Marriage and family are the cornerstones of society and the church. It is a necessity that an "altar of prayer" is established in every home and family. All believers should have a place of solitude for prayer and supplication unto the Lord. Learning to take time to be still and hear from God is a necessity. This is a spiritual discipline needed for families learning to live a victorious life in the twenty first century. Families, unmarried singles, divorcees, and all believers experiencing delays in waiting for their mate must make prayer a number one priority in their personal life.

Prayer is an opportunity God gives His children to become intimately acquainted with Him. As a conversation with God, prayer enables the believer to build a personal relationship with the Lord. Prayer is an expression of a believer's dependence on God, and an affirmation of God's promise to the redeemed.

The primary purpose of prayer is to seek God's will (1 John 5:14). Jesus told His disciples in His model prayer, to ask according to the will of God (Matt. 6:10). When believers talk to the Father, each request for help and desire for guidance should be asked in the name of Jesus.

Prayer provides an opportunity for adoration, praise, thanksgiving, confession of sin, and requests for self and others. There are many formats for prayer; however, prayer is as unique as each person. Prayer is an awesome privilege and occasion offered unto all believers, and is available unto all who need and desire to tap into the divine stream of His power and anointing. The three purposes manifested during the time of prayer are: 1) learning to express oneself honestly and sincerely unto the Lord, (2) learning to listen to His reply, (often in the form of revelation, insight and His Word), and (3) participating in fulfilling His purposes on earth.

Many believers, in making prayer a priority, use a devotional book to write out a prayer list. We should learn to share our commitment to prayer with others, both to encourage them and to hold ourselves accountable for praying regularly.

Prayer For Heaven's Mates For Your Children

Do not be unequally yoked with unbelievers (do not make mismated alliances with them or come under a different yoke with them, inconsistent with your faith). For what

> partnership have right living and right standing with God with iniquity and lawlessness? Or how can light have fellowship with darkness (2 Cor. 6:14 TAB)?

> Wives, be subject (be submissive and adapt yourselves) to your own husbands as (a service) to the Lord. For the husband is head of the wife as Christ is the head of the church; Himself the Saviour of (His) body (Eph. 5:22–23 TAB).

> For I know him that he will command his children and his household after him, and they shall keep the way of the Lord, to do justice and judgment; that the Lord may bring upon Abraham that which he hath spoken of him (Gen. 18:19 TAB).

The scripture declares the necessity for parents and their children to marry godly husbands and wives. Christian parents have learned the necessity of marrying godly spouses through the Word of God, and experientially. Parents who are prayerful and knowledgeable concerning the scriptures are cognizant of the impact of marriage to an unbeliever.

Abraham's command to his son not to marry outside the chosen people was the first revelation in the Old Testament. He recognized that God's promise to build a nation would be fulfilled by Isaac. He did not ask Isaac to return to Haran, because this would undo Abraham's first obligation to separate himself and come to the Land of Promise.

> When the Lord your God brings you into the land which you are entering to possess and has plucked away many nations before you, the Hittites, the Girgashites, the Amorites, the Canaanites, the Perizzites, the Hivites, and the Jebusites, seven nations greater and mightier than you. And when the Lord your God gives them over to you and you smite them, then you must utterly destroy them. You shall make no covenant with them, or show mercy to them.

> You shall not make marriages with them: your daughter you shall not give to his son nor shall you take his daughter for your son.

> For they will turn away your sons from following Me, that they may serve other gods; so will the anger of the Lord be kindled against you and He will destroy you quickly (Deut. 7:1–4 TAB).

Abraham knew his son's marriage to a Canaanite wife would turn away his son from following God, and emphasized the importance of his son's set-apart character, for use in the ministry.

He was honored with a godly wife who loved him greatly. She was pictured as chaste, beautiful, courteous, helpful, and industrious, as well as responsive and trusting.

Isaac, Abraham's son, recognized the importance of godly marriages in the family. He positioned himself as Abraham in requesting through prayer, the provision of a godly mate for his son Jacob. Rebekah was vexed and grieved with the daughters of Heth, and became weary with her life as a result of their behavior.

Then Rebekah said to Isaac, I am weary of my life because of the daughters of Heth (these wives of Esau)! If Jacob takes a wife of the daughters of Heth such as these Hittite girls around here, what good will my life be to me (Gen. 27:46 TAB)?

Marriage to an unbeliever has caused strife, division and discord in many Christian families. Parents, knowing and discerning the will of God for their family, have learned to pray during the growth and developmental stages of their children's lives. They have learned to ask God to lead and guide the right mates in the lives of their children.

The mates your children marry play a significant role in the destiny of the family. The scripture reveals God knew Abraham would teach and train his children in the principles of God (Gen. 18:19). The Abrahamic covenant had to be fulfilled through his seed, God's blessings rested upon his seed, the chosen, Isaac. To ensure the fulfillment of the promise, Abraham sent Eleazar to his country to secure a wife for his son. He knew marriage to an unbeliever was outside of the will of God. God's Word has not changed in the twenty first century. It remains the same.

Prayer Points

Confessions

Isa. 34:16: Seek ye out of the book of the Lord, and read: no one of these shall fail, none shall want her mate: for my mouth it hath commanded, and his spirit it hath gathered them.

Matt. 7:7: Ask and it shall be given you; seek and ye shall find; knock and it shall be opened unto you.

Isa. 54:13: And all thy children shall be taught of the Lord; and great shall be the peace of thy children.

Isa. 54:17: No weapon that is formed against thee shall prosper; and every tongue that shall rise against thee in judgment thou shalt condemn. This is the heritage of the servants of the Lord, and their righteousness is of me, saith the Lord.

Josh. 24:15: And if it seem evil unto you to serve the Lord, choose you this day whom ye will serve; whether the gods which your fathers served that were on the other side of the flood, or the gods of the Amorites, in whose land ye dwell; but as for me and my house, we will serve the Lord.

Isa. 49:25: But thus saith the Lord, Even the captives of the mighty shall be taken away, and the prey of the terrible shall be delivered; for I will contend with him that contendeth with thee, and I will save thy children.

Praise And Worship

1. Thank God because he alone is the perfect matchmaker.

2. Lord, release the man/woman who has been preordained as my daughter/son's husband/wife.

3. Lord, cause it to happen that the divine match will come soon.

4. Lord, let it be a person who loves you wholeheartedly.

5. Lord, establish their home in accordance with the scriptures (Eph.5: 20–28).

6. Lord, let all satanic hindrances keeping them from meeting be dissolved in the name of Jesus.

7. Lord, send forth your warring angels to battle on their behalf.

8. Lord, I believe you have created the right mate for my son/ daughter. Bring it to pass, in Jesus name.

9. I stand it in the gap and call him/her out of obscurity into my son/ daughter life in the name of Jesus.

10. I reject the provision of counterfeit spouse by the enemy, in the name of Jesus.

11. I cut off the flow of any inherited marital problems into the life of my children, in the name of Jesus.

12. Let patience reign in the life of . . . (mention the name of your son/ daughter) until the right person comes, in the name of Jesus.

13. Lord, in the name of Jesus, just as Abraham sent his servant to find his son, Isaac, a wife, send the Holy Spirit to bring my son/ daughter's future wife/husband to him/her.

14. Thank the Lord for the answer.

Intercessory Prayer Points

Pray for Heaven's Mate in each of the twenty-four hours-
"Heaven's Mate" Isaiah 34:16;
"Christ Centered Marriages" (Genesis 18:19).

Midnight–1:00 am	An "Open Heaven" (Isa 64:1–65:1)
1:00 - 2:00 am	An Outpouring of the Spirit of Prayer (Zech 12:10)
2:00 - 3:00 am	Boldness for Witness
3:00 - 4:00 am	Reconciliation - Unity
4:00 - 5:00 am	Desire for Believers/ Families to Pray for Heaven Mates in the Lives of their children/grandchildren and family

5:00	-	6:00 am	The mind of Christ/mind to please God
6:00	-	7:00 am	Integrity and character in fulfilling the will of God
7:00	-	800 am	Salvation and reclaiming of unmarried/married in the family backsliders (Spirit of Conviction)
8:00	-	9:00 am	Families and marriages; men/women; change in the Spiritual conscious of unmarried/married couples in the family; same sex marriages
9:00	-	10:00 am	Fresh Anointing for Intercessors and Family Leaders in the family; new zeal for Prayer and Supplication in the Family
10:00	-	11:00 am	Spiritual hunger - more of God Word/ principles in the Family
11:00	-	Noon	Children - early salvation and special protection
Noon	-	1:00 pm	Family Outreach - good works; transformed marriages/lives in the family
1:00	-	2:00 pm	Spirit of Worship - Thanksgiving to God in the Family
2:00	-	3:00 pm	Great Authority in the Word of God
3:00	-	4:00 pm	Children–A desire for God and aspiration of holiness in their lives.
4:00	-	5:00 pm	Filled and re-filled with the Holy Spirit
5:00	-	6:00 pm	Prosperity for families in Obeying God in Spirit and Truth
6:00	-	7:00 pm	Favor with God and Man
7:00	-	8:00 pm	Spiritual Revival in families/ marriages and relationships
8:00	-	9:00 pm	Humility-a broken and contrite spirit in families, couples and children

9:00	-	10:00 pm	Deliverance of Captivities-drugs and alcohol–demonic relationships and cults
10:00	-	11:00 pm	Family Leaders will be turned by God towards righteousness, mercy, or compassion ministries
11:00	-	Midnight	The spirit of peace, joy and righteousness in the family

The effectual fervent prayer of a righteous man availeth much (James 5:17 TAB).

Our Faith

Our faith in God is easy when the
Waters 'round are stilled,
When the voyage undertaken finds
Our dreams and hopes fulfilled.
But holding on to God is hard,
When wrestling with our doubt,
And when the storms are fiercest,
And our boat is tossed about.
It's then our faith is shaken,
When the Master's sound asleep,
Not knowing we are sinking, and
The waters 'round are deep.
We wonder then how He, Who's Lord
Of all the land and sea,
Could seem to be so unaware
Of our catastrophe.
It's when our faith seems weakest,
God will calm the sea and soul
And when we are most broken that
He'll touch, and make us whole
~
Author Unknown

Prayer For Heaven Mates Marriages
(Delayed / Postponed / Deferred)

For the vision is yet for an appointed time and it hastens to the end (fulfillment); it will not deceive or disappoint. Though it tarry, wait (earnestly) for it, because it will surely come, it will not be behindhand on its appointed day (Hab. 2:3 TAB).

If a man dies, shall he live again? All the days of my warfare and service I will wait, till my change and release shall come (Job 14:14 TAB).

Seek ye out of the book of the Lord, and read, no one of these shall fail, none shall want her mate; for my mouth it hath commanded, and his spirit it hath gathered them (Isa. 34:16 TAB).

But if that servant is wicked and says to himself, My master is delayed and is going to be gone a long time (Matt. 24:48 TAB).

So when they came here together, I did not delay, but on the morrow took my place on the judgment seat and ordered that the man be brought before me (Acts 25:17 TAB).

There are many singles who have grown weary during the process of waiting for their mates. Single women who have "passed the flower of age" (1 Cor. 7:36) have allowed the enemy to discourage, deceive, and challenge them in the faith. The Spirit of God led an angel to Sarah at the age of ninety. At this age, medical science declares it is humanly impossible for a woman to conceive and bring forth a child, but the Lord "opened Sarah's womb." The Lord visited Sarah as he said, and fulfilled his promise (Gen. 21:1–2). Sarah was a walking miracle in her generation, whose life showed the evidence of God's fulfilling His Word. God has not changed His Word or purpose. Your miracle has not passed you by. Choose to believe the report of the Lord.

The scripture declares, "that the just shall live by faith and in His righteousness" (Hab 2:4).

The world's statistics of singles available for marriage are devastating for those lacking faith in the Word of God. Singles, unmarried groups, cyber-surfs, and computer dating services cannot replace prayer, faith and confidence in God's Word. When Job declared, "All the days of his appointed time would he wait till his change come" (Job 14:14), he positioned himself to wait upon God for his deliverance. He refused to give up, and chose to, trust God to turn his captivity. The scripture declares "and the Lord turned the captivity of Job, when he prayed for his friends: also the Lord gave him twice as much as he had before (Job 42:10).

He realized he couldn't trust in the wisdom of his wife or friends; they spoke the wisdom of their thoughts and minds, and not the wisdom of God. It is a necessity during the waiting process to "trust not in the wisdom of man, but in the power of God" (1 Cor. 2:5). The state of being single or unmarried will change as you learn to wait upon God, and believe that "His Word shall not return unto him void, but shall accomplish that which He please, and shall prosper in the thing whereunto He send it" (Isa. 55:11).

We serve a God that cannot lie. His Word, will, and purpose concerning your life will come to pass as you learn to wait upon him. The scripture declares, *"none shall want their mate"* (Isa. 34:16). *He has a mate for everyone who will take a stand in faith and trust in Him to bring this manifestation to pass.*

The scripture declares, "I have fought the good (worthy, honorable, and noble) fight, I have finished the race, I have kept (firmly held) the faith" (2 Tim. 4:7). If you have been waiting a long time, for your mate, continue to stand in faith, with your loins girded with truth." Your Heavenly Father has not "forsaken you, for lo, He" will not in any way fail you, nor give up, or leave you without support. He will not in any degree leave you helpless or forsake you (Heb. 13:5).

It's very important during this time of praying and waiting upon God to develop a deep, love relationship with the Lord. Believe the scripture that declares, "He changeth the times and the seasons" (Dan 2:21). Learn to wait only upon God, for your expectation is from Him (Ps. 62:5).

Prayer Points

Confessions

Luke 18: 27: And he said, the things which are impossible with men are possible with God.

Matt. 17:20: And Jesus said unto them. Because of your belief; for verily I say unto you, If ye have faith as a grain of mustard seed, ye shall say unto the mountain, Remove hence to yonder place, and it shall remove, and nothing shall be impossible unto you.

Matt. 19: 26: But Jesus beheld them, and said unto them, with men this is impossible; but with God all things are possible.

Mark 10: 27: And Jesus looking upon them saith, With men it is impossible, but not with God: for with God all things are possible.

Hebrews 11:6: But without faith it is impossible to please him: for he that cometh to God must believe that he is, and that he is a rewarder of them that diligently seek him.

Luke 1:37: For with God nothing shall be impossible.

Phil. 2:9-10: Wherefore God also hath highly exalted him, and given him a name which is above every name that at the name of Jesus every knee should bow, of things in heaven, and things in earth, and things under the earth.

Rev. 12:11: And they overcame him by the blood of the Lamb, and by the word of their testimony, and they loved not their lives unto the death.

Praise And Worship

1. Thank the Lord because your miracle has come.

2. Ask the Lord to forgive any sin that would hinder answers to your prayers.

3. Lord, make known to me the secrets of my inner life.

4. Let every imagination of the enemy against my marital life be rendered impotent.

5. Let every force attracting the wrong people to me be destroyed.

6. I destroy every covenant of delayed marriage.

7. I destroy every hindrance created against my settling down in marriage.

8. I command all forces of evil manipulating, delaying, or hindering my marriage to be completely destroyed.

9. Let all the enemies of Jesus Christ operating against my life be exposed.

10. I sever myself from any satanic linkage and any strange power.

11. Let the angel of the living God roll away the stone blocking my marital breakthrough.

12. Lord, turn away all that will jilt, disappoint, or fail me.

13. Thank you God for the victory.

> The effectual, fervent prayers of a righteous man availeth much (James 4:1–6).

Prayer To Reconcile And Restore Your Marriage

For this cause shall a man leave his father and mother, and cleave to his wife; and they twain shall be one flesh: so then they are no more twain, but one flesh. What therefore God has joined together, let not man put asunder (Mk. 10:7–9 KJV).

Set me as a seal upon your heart, like a seal upon thine arm; for love is as strong as death; jealousy is as hard and cruel as the Sheol (the place of the dead). It flashes of fire, a most vehement flame (the very flame of the Lord)! Many waters cannot quench love, neither can floods drown it. If a man would offer all the goods of his house for love, he would be utterly scorned and despised (Song. 8:6–7 TAB).

> Two are better than one, because they have a good reward for their labour. For if they fall, the one will lift up his fellow: but woe to him that is alone when he falleth; for he hath not another to help him up. Again, if two lie together, then they have heat: but how can one be warm alone? And if one prevails against him, two shall withstand him; and a threefold cord is not quickly broken (Ecc. 4:9–12 KJV).

The scripture instructs us to "pray without ceasing" (Acts 12:5). When married couples keep the altar of prayer saturated, the enemy cannot come in. Prayer is the key to strengthen and sustain the family.

United prayers unleash the power of God for specific prayer petitions and requests. The scripture declares, "one shall chase a thousand and two ten thousand" (Deut. 32:30). One of the symbols of marriage is a triangle. The triangle is outlined with God centered at the top, symbolic of the head, and the husband and wife at the bottom. There is a line joining the woman to God, and a line joining the man to God, signifying their relationship with God. There is also a line joining the man and woman. The threefold cord is not quickly broken. Married couples must diligently strive to maintain their relationship and walk in harmony with God's Word.

Life is a continuous growth process. We grow up into Him in all things. Marriage does not stifle our growth, but stimulates our overall growth and development. When two imperfect human beings are joined together in marriage, they compliment each other, and are perfected by the Word of God in all things.

Married life is a continuous growth process, enabling couples to share love, peace, fruit of the spirit, and all the blessings of God in their lives. Misunderstandings, petty differences, disagreements, trials, tests, and tribulations shall come, thereby reinforcing the necessity to keep the family altar saturated with prayer. There is tremendous power in prayer, empowering couples to pray through unto the breakthrough, and to pray without ceasing.

The Song of Solomon stated it very beautifully when he wrote, "set me as a seal upon thine heart, like a seal upon your arm; for love is as strong as death" (Song 8:6). Love is the most powerful weapon available to restore and reconcile a marriage. Love covereth a multitude of sins (Prov. 10:12). The scripture declares, "Love never fails" (1 Cor.

13:18). Love is the core of the desire to make your marriage work.

Love is as strong as death. Only death can break the power of love.

Many waters cannot quench love, neither can the floods drown it: if a man would give all the substance of his house for love, it would be contemned (Song 8:6).

Neither can the floods of problems or crisis overwhelm love. No fires or storms can destroy true love. Love is a gift from God, and is shed abroad into our heart by the Holy Ghost, which is given unto us (Rom. 5:5).

Prayer Points

Confessions

Isa. 57:18: I have seen his ways and will heal him. I will lead him also, and restore comforts unto him and to his mourners.

Matt. 12:13: Then saith he to the man, stretch forth thine hand. And he stretched forth: and it was restored whole, like as the other.

Joel 12:25: And I will restore to you the years that the locust hath eaten: the cankerworm, and the caterpillar, and the palmerworm, my great army which I sent among you.

Col. 1:20: And having made peace through the blood of his cross, by him to reconcile all things unto himself; by him, I say, whether they be things in earth, or things in heaven.

Gen. 18:14: Is anything too hard for the Lord? At the time appointed I will return unto thee, according to the time of life, and Sarah shall have a son.

Matt. 17:20: And Jesus said unto them, Because of your unbelief, for verily I say unto you, if you have faith as a grain of mustard seed, ye shall say unto this mountain, remove hence to yonder place, and it shall remove: and nothing shall be impossible unto you.

Luke. 1:37: For with God, nothing shall be impossible.

Praise And Worship

1. Thank God for reconciling and restoring your marriage.

2. Ask the Lord to forgive you or whoever may be involved in the marriage breakup.

3. I command my marriage to be restored in the name of Jesus.

4. Lord Jesus, heal every wound and scar created by the enemy in my marriage.

5. Let all satanic forces contributing to destroying my marriage be destroyed.

6. Let God arise and the enemies of my marriage be scattered.

7. Let all the love, affection, and glory that has departed from my marriage be restored.

8. Let the anointing to prosper fall upon my marriage, relationships, health, home, even as my soul prosper.

9. Lord, let divine understanding enter into our relationship in the name of Jesus.

10. Let the blood of Jesus erase all past unprofitable memories of my marital relationship.

11. I retrieve my marriage from the altar of satanic destruction, in the name of Jesus.

12. Let every power preventing me as a wife from accepting the headship of my husband be destroyed in the name of Jesus.

13. Let every power preventing me as a husband from living as a true head be destroyed in the name of Jesus.

14. Pray in the Spirit daily.

15. Thank God for answered prayer.

Prayer For The Unmarried Believer

Be very careful, then, how you live–not as unwise but as wise, making the most of every opportunity, because the days are evil. Therefore do not be foolish, but understand what the Lord's will is (Eph. 5:15–17 NIV).

Nevertheless, to avoid fornication, let every man have his own wife; and let every woman have her own husband (1 Cor. 7:2 KJV).

But if they have not self-control (restraint of their passions), they should marry. For it is better to marry than to be aflame (with passion and tortured continually with ungratified desire) (1 Cor. 7:9 TAB).

Shun youthful lusts and flee from them, and aim at and pursue righteousness (all that is virtuous and good, right living conformity to the will of God in thought, word, and deed); (and aim at and pursue faith, love, [and] peace) (harmony and concord with others) in fellowship with all (Christians), who call upon the Lord out of a pure heart (2 Tim. 2:22 TAB).

That ye may be blameless and harmless, the sons of God, without rebuke, in the midst of a crooked and perverse nation, among whom ye shine as lights in the world: Holding forth the word of life: that I may rejoice in the day of Christ, that I have not run in vain, neither labored in vain (Phil. 2:15–16 TAB).

The state of being single is a permanent state in life for some and a temporary state for others. Adam was created by God and experienced solitude in the garden before God created Eve. Singles, teenagers, and young adults experience a similar period of aloneness. The response of faith is to see singleness as a call to committed life.

Many singles experience the external influences of friends, family, associates, and their environment press them to choose the wrong mate. Because choices have consequences, the results of wrong choices leave many devastated. The results of desperate decisions reveal the necessity of praying through unto the breakthrough. The scripture declares, "the effectual fervent prayers of a righteous man availeth much" (James 5:16).

It is a necessity for single believers to fast, pray, study the Word, and remain divinely focused. They should not only attend sincere, anointed intercessory prayer groups, but consecrate and submit themselves unto the Lord with all fear and humility. They must learn to confess, believe the Word trusting that God is able to keep them during the hour of temptation.

Praying without ceasing, meditating upon God's word, and believing the scripture declares, "he that believeth shall not make haste," (Isa. 28:16). This is of utmost importance for the unmarried single. God changes the times and the seasons (Dan. 2:21). His timing is perfect, and at the right time, He will change your state of being from single to married. Continue in prayer and supplication before the Lord, He will bring the release of your mate in due season if you faint not.

Prayer Points

Confessions

Eph. 2:14: For He is our peace, who hath made both one, and hath broken down the middle wall of petition between us (Eph. 2:14).

Eph. 2:13: But now in Christ Jesus, ye who sometimes were far off are made nigh by the blood of Christ (Eph. 2:13).

Isaiah 34:16: Seek ye out of the book of the Lord, and read: no one of these shall fail, none shall want her mate: for my mouth it hath commanded, and his spirit it hath gathered them.

Jer. 1:12: Then said the Lord unto me, Thou hast well seen: for I will hasten my word to perform it.

Praise And Worship

1. Thank the Lord because your miracle has come.

2. Lord, help me be content with being single until my change comes.

3. Lord, help me stop dwelling on the state of singleness and think of unsaved friends and pray for them, (empowering them to resist the devil).

4. For deliverance for singles dealing with the spirits of loneliness, bitterness, self-pity, and impatience.

5. Pray that singles will use this time to grow in the Lord and be active servants.

6. Pray for singles to develop self-control and purity in the area of sexuality.

7. Pray that wrong or unequally yoked relationship would end.

8. Pray for a multiplication of godly men and women like the "loaves and fishes", (See Matthew 14 and 15 where Jesus fed thousands on a couple loaves and fishes).

9. Pray for God to groom Christian men to be the spiritual leader of a household.

10. Pray that the future marriages will be a ministry to the lost.

11. Pray that married people and ministers would become aware of the unique struggles that singles endure.

12. Pray for future godly spouses for singles.

13. Pray for people to commit to pray for singles daily.

Intercessory Prayer Points

Pray for the unmarried believer in each of the twenty-four hours - "Godly Mates" Is a: 34:16; "Destroying Strongholds/ Hindrances" Obadiah 1:3,4,17.

Midnight–1:00 am	An "Open Heaven" (Isa 64:1–65:1)
1:00 - 2:00 am	An Outpouring of the Spirit of Prayer (Zech 12:10)
2:00 - 3:00 am	Boldness for Witness
3:00 - 4:00 am	Reconciliation - Unity
4:00 - 5:00 am	Desire for single believers to be forgiven for sins that would hinder answer to prayers
5:00 - 6:00 am	The mind of Christ/mind to please God

6:00	-	7:00 am	Integrity and honest living in relationships and marriages
7:00	-	800 am	Salvation and reclaiming of singles/ unmarried/ unsaved backsliders (spirit of conviction)
8:00	-	9:00 am	Families and marriages; men; change in the conscious of the singles/unmarried regarding marriage; same sex marriages
9:00	-	10:00 am	Fresh anointing for Pastors and Spiritual Leaders; restore godly principles, standards, principles in marriages, families and relationships
10:00	-	11:00 am	Spiritual Hunger - more of the manifestation of His Word, in marriage relationships, etc.
11:00	-	Noon	Children - early salvation, special protection, and mind to walk and maintain the spirit of abstinence
Noon	-	1:00 pm	Singles will return unto God in spirit and truth - good works; transformed work places with Christian values, principles, etc.
1:00	-	2:00 pm	Spirit of worship - Thanksgiving to God
2:00	-	3:00 pm	Great Authority in the Word of God
3:00	-	4:00 pm	Singles - A desire for God and righteous living
4:00	-	5:00 pm	Filled and re-filled with the Holy Spirit
5:00	-	6:00 pm	Prosperity of living a God fearing, loving life
6:00	-	7:00 pm	Favor with God and man
7:00	-	8:00 pm	Spiritual Revival in the schools and colleges-public and private
8:00	-	9:00 pm	Humility - A broken and contrite spirit in following, obeying, and serving God

9:00	-	10:00 pm	Deliverance of captivities - drugs and alcohol - homosexual and lesbians and those in false religions and cults
10:00	-	11:00 pm	Civil Leaders would be turned by God towards righteousness, Godliness, and integrity
11:00	-	Midnight	The peace of Jerusalem (Ps 122:6–9)

The effectual fervent prayer of a righteous man availeth much (James 5:17)

Part Twenty-Three
ROMANCE/ INTIMATE RELATIONSHIP

Tell me where you're working–I love you so much–Tell me where you're tending your flocks where you let them rest at noontime. Why should I be the one left out, outside the orbit of your tender care?

If you can't find me, loveliest of all women, it's all right. Stay with your flocks. Lead your lambs to good pasture. Stay with your shepherd neighbors.

You remind me of Pharaoh's well- groomed and satiny mares. Pendant earrings line the elegance of your cheeks, strands of jewels illumine the curve of your throat. I'm making jewelry for you, gold and silver jewelry that will mark and accent your beauty.

When my King- Lover lay down besides me, my fragrance filled the room. His head resting between my breasts—- the head of my lover was a sachet of sweet myrrh. My beloved is a bouquet of wildflowers picked just for me from the fields of Engedi.

Oh, my dear friend! You're so beautiful! And your eyes so beautiful—- like doves!

And you, my dear lover- you're so handsome! And the bed we share is like a forest glen.

We enjoy a canopy of cedars enclosed by cypresses, fragrant and green (Song 1: 7–17 MSG).

Beauty Of Our Friendship

Friendship is a priceless gift
that cannot be bought or sold,
But its value is far greater
than a mountain made of gold.
For gold is cold and lifeless,
it can neither see nor hear . . .
And in the time of trouble
it is powerless to cheer . . .
It has no ears to listen
nor heart to understand,
It cannot bring you comfort
or reach out a helping hand.
So when you ask God for a gift
be thankful if He sends . . .
Not diamonds, pearls or riches . . .
but the love of real true friends.

ತ

(Author Unknown)

Friends And Lovers

My lovers and my friends stand aloof from my sore, and my kinsmen stand afar off (Ps. 38:11 KJV).

Lover and friend hast thou put far from me, and mine acquaintance into darkness (Ps. 88:18 KJV).

A friend loveth at all times (Prov. 17:17 KJV).

Behold, thou art fair, my love; behold, thou art fair; thou hast doves' eyes.

Behold, thou art fair, my beloved, yea, pleasant: also our bed is green.

The beams of our house are cedar, and our rafters of fir. I am the rose of Sharon, and the lily of the valleys.

As the lily among thorns, so is my love among the daughters.

As the apple tree among the trees of the wood, so is my beloved among the sons. I sat down under his shadow with great delight, and his fruit was sweet to my taste (Song 1:15–2:3 KJV).

A man that hath friends must show himself friendly: and there is a friend that sticketh closer than a brother (Prov. 18:24 KJV).

The Hebrew word chesed, means loving kindness, and describes a relationship bound together by love, loyalty, and commitment. Friendships that last are based on chesed–unconditional love, undying loyalty, and unending commitment.

In admiring the qualities and character he saw in Ruth, whose name means "friendship," Boaz praised her for her chesed (Ruth 3:10). Married couples must learn to build and develop a sincere meaningful relationship with each other. Life trials, tests, and challenges demand that couples develops stronger relationships with each other. They will need true friendship to sustain each other during the journey in life.

The scripture declares, "a friend loveth at all times." Married couples learn to draw closer unto God and each other during times of great testings and problems.

Sexuality: A Gift From The Creator

And God blessed them, and God said unto them, be fruitful and multiply, and replenish the earth, and subdue it; and have dominion over the fish of the sea, and over the fowl of the air; and over every living thing that moveth upon the earth (Gen. 1:28 KJV).

And now art thou cursed from the earth, which hath opened her mouth to receive thy brother's blood from thy hand (Gen 4: 11 KJV).

> And he said, I will certainly return unto thee according to the time of life; and, lo, Sarah thy wife shall have a son. And Sarah heard it in the tent door, which was behind him.
>
> Now Abraham and Sarah were old and well stricken in age; and it ceased to be with Sarah after the manner of women.
>
> Therefore Sarah laughed within herself, saying, After I am waxed old shall I have pleasure, my lord being old also (Gen. 18:10–12 KJV)?

> Let the husband render unto the wife due benevolence: and likewise also the wife unto the husband.
>
> The wife hath not power of her own body, but the husband: and likewise also the husband hath not power of his own body, but the wife (1 Cor. 7:3–4 KJV).

> (Continue yourself to your own wife) let your children be for you alone, and not the children of strangers with you.

Let your fountain (of human life) be blessed with the rewards of fidelity, and rejoice in the wife of your youth (Prov. 5:17–18 TAB).

The Creator, as a special gift allows a husband and wife to express oneness in intimate and exclusive love, designed sex. God gives sexual drives as the most natural high human bodies can experience. They are destructive only when uncontrolled or misused.

Many scriptures express the value for sex and celebrate it joyously. Any intimate sexual relationship outside of monogamous fidelity within the covenant of marriage is condemned as sexual immorality. Believers are expected to exercise self-control in overcoming improper sexual impulses, and not by asceticism, but by the power of the Holy Spirit.

There Are Certain Facts About Sex That Should Be Remembered:

> Sex is God-given (Gen. 2:18). Satan can offer nothing in the realm of sexuality except distortion and emptiness. The open discussion of sex is not wrong in itself, but it

is wrong when such discussions are outside the divinely assigned context.

Sex between a man and a woman is different than sex between animals (Gen. 2:19, 20). Human sexuality has a specialized purpose beyond procreation.

Sex is a total union, and thus both powerful and mysterious (Gen. 2:21–23). God made two out of one, and the two are not complete until they are reunited.

Sex is regulated and purposeful (Gen. 2:24–25). God Himself sets the boundary (Matt. 19:4–6). Anything short of the total and exclusive commitment between husband and wife is frustrating and destructive.

God approves the relationship in which husband and wife meet their physical needs in sexual intercourse (Prov. 5:15, 18, 19). Both husband and wife have sexual needs that are to be met in marriage (1 Cor. 7:13). Each is to meet the needs of the other and not his own.

The Purposes For Sexual Intimacy Are:

- Knowledge (Gen. 4:1)
- Unity (Gen. 2:24)
- Comfort (Gen. 24:67)
- Procreation (Gen. 28)
- Relaxation and play (Song 2:8–17; 4:1–16), and
- A defense against temptation (1 Cor. 7:2–5)

A husband is commanded to find satisfaction (Prov. 5:19) and joy with his wife, and to concern himself with meeting her unique needs (Deut. 24:5; 1 Pet. 3:7). A wife is responsible for availability, preparations, planning, and sensibility to meet his unique masculine needs (Gen. 24:67).

The Joy Of Romance

Thou will show me the path of life: in thy presence is fullness of joy; at thy right hand there are pleasures for evermore (Ps. 16:11 KJV).

Be glad in the Lord, and rejoice, ye righteous; and shout for joy, all ye that are upright in heart (Ps. 32:11 KJV).

And whatsoever mine eyes desired I kept not from them, I withheld not my heart from any joy; for my heart rejoiced in all my labour: and this was my portion of all my labour (Eccl. 2:10 KJV).

For he shall not much remember the days of his life: because God answereth him in the joy of his heart (Eccl. 5:20 KJV).

Now the God of hope fill you with all joy and peace in believing, that ye may abound in hope, through the power of the Holy Ghost (Rom. 15:13 KJV).

The spirit of joy is the reward of walking in faith. The scripture declares that the joy of the Lord is our strength. He gives us living water and we thirst no more (Neh. 8:10).

Joy flows in our heart from God as a result of faith and obedience unto God. The abundance of joy in our life, romance, and relationship is in direct proportion to the intimacy and steadfastness of our walk with the Lord. Sin in a believer's life can rob them of the spirit of joy (Ps. 15:8, 12). True joy is evident regardless of circumstances.

Romantic joy causes many who are not spirit-filled to become unbalanced and carried away with temporal pleasures.

However, spirit-filled believers have learned to experience joy and romance, to live and maintain a balanced walk with God, knowing that He has gives us all things richly to enjoy (1 Tim. 6:17).

The purpose of joy is to provide blessings for the believer. Joy enables us to enjoy all that God has given–health, family, friends, opportunities, salvation, and romance. In experiencing joy, it is shared with each other, and the body of Christ (Rom. 12:15).

Sexual Intimacy

Therefore a man shall leave his father and his mother and shall become united and cleave to his wife, and they shall become one flesh

And the man and his wife were both naked and were not embarrassed or ashamed in each other's presence (Gen. 2: 24–25 TAB).

And Adam knew Eve his wife, and she conceived, and bare Cain, and said, I have gotten a man form the Lord (Gen 4:1 KJV).

So they are no longer two, but one flesh. What therefore God has joined together, let not man put asunder (separate) (Matt. 19: 5–7 TAB).

Drink water out of your own cistern (of a pure marriage relationship), and fresh running water out of your own well.

Should your offspring be dispersed abroad as water brooks in the streets?

(Confine yourself to your own wife) let your children be for you alone, and not the children of strangers with you.

Let your fountain (of human life) be blessed (with the rewards of fidelity), and rejoice with the wife of your youth.

Let her be as the loving hind and pleasant doe (tender, gentle, attractive)—let her bosom satisfy you at all times, and always be transported with delight in her love.

Why should you, my son, be infatuated with a loose woman, embrace the bosom of an outsider, and go astray (Prov 5:15–20 AMP).

Although man and woman are extremely different physically, emotionally, and spiritually, they are designed by God to compliment each other. The scriptures emphasize the importance of becoming one flesh, which includes all aspects of life (Matt 19:5).

Becoming one flesh has significance only as it is acknowledged scripturally or according to God's principles. Thus intercourse, from this perspective, includes the exchange of thoughts and feelings. The act of marriage is the highest form of communication of love for one another and consummated with the ultimate expression of intimacy. It provides a language that can express love without words. Indeed, there are no words to express all that is experienced. Faith in God is the bond of the marriage covenant; sexual intimacy is the Holy Ghost's seal.

The quality of the celebration of sexual intimacy depends on the quality of the total marriage relationship. There can be little fulfillment in the realm of physical intimacy if there is little closeness in the overall union. God designed male and female to fit together, and instilled within each a desire for the other. No problems are exclusively sexual in nature. Difficulties in sexual intimacy are nearly always a symptom of problems in other areas of the relationship.

The attitude of the wife about herself, her husband, and about lovemaking will determine her response in physical intimacy. If expectations are unmet, or if negative emotions of jealousy, rejection, or bitterness exist, physical intimacy is hampered. Sexual union is not to be used as a weapon or a reward, but is nonetheless a rightful need and expectation of each married partner (1 Cor. 7:3–5).

Abstinence – Passion Held By Principle

> Blessed is the man that endureth temptation: for when he is tried, he shall receive the crown of life, which the Lord hath promised to them that love him.
>
> Let no man say when he is tempted, I am tempted of God: for God cannot be tempted with evil, neither tempteth he any man:
> But every man is tempted, when he is drawn away of his own lust, and enticed.
>
> Then when lust hath conceived, it bringeth forth sin: and sin, when it is finished, bringeth forth death.

Do not err, my beloved brethren (James 1: 12–16 KJV).

Dearly beloved, I beseech you as strangers and pilgrims abstain from fleshly lusts, which war against the soul (1 Peter 2:11 KJV).

Nevertheless, to avoid fornication, let every man have his own wife, and let every woman have her own husband (1 Cor. 7:2 KJV).

For this is the will of God, that you should be consecrated (separated and set apart for pure and holy living); that you should abstain and shrink from all sexual vice.

That each one of you should know how to possess (control), his own body in consecration (purity, separated from things profane) and honor

Not (to be used) in the passion of lust like the heathen; who are ignorant of the true God and have no knowledge of His will (1 Thess. 4:3–5 TAB).

Abstain from evil (shrink from it aloof from it) in whatever form or whatever kind it may be (1 Thess 5:22 TAB).

Today's world is an atmosphere filled with sexual implications in every aspect of life, from birth to adulthood. The style of clothing, to include fashions for babies, focuses on physical exposure to, including halter-tops, miniskirts, and revealing clothes for children. Everywhere you visit, the choice of clothing, music, place of fellowship, and recreation is more carnal oriented than heavenly.

The choice of music has influenced children and adults to the extent that the spirit of holiness and fear of the Lord have departed from many. Music sometimes reveals the talents, skills, and trained abilities of the singers and musicians more than the glory of God. It is a necessity for leaders and parents to take time and teach their children the difference between the anointing of God and talent.

Passion has been defined as "compelling emotion: lust; strong sexual desire; strong amorous feeling" (Random House Webster's College Dictionary). In viewing the definition of passion, Christian singles and all in the Body of Christ must distinguish the difference between "passion held by principle" and satanically incited lust. There has to be a sincere desire by every Christian to be kept by the Word and power of God. Standing on the principles of the Word of God is a keeper and controller for all Christians.

Every believer must learn to "flee fornication, youthful lusts, adultery, and all unprofitable works of the flesh" (1 Cor. 6:18; 2 Tim. 2:22; 2 Cor. 10:14). The lust of the eyes, the lust of the flesh, and pride of life have caused many to err from the faith and pierce themselves with many sorrows (1 John 2: 16 KJV).

Learning to abstain from lust can only happen through a sincere desire to be kept by His word remain in fellowship with Him, and fellow believers (1 Pet. 2:11).

Joseph's life was a perfect example of a young man determined to be kept by God. He positioned himself under the keeping power of God when he stated; his master had committed all that he had unto his hands; and had kept back nothing from him but his wife. Joseph loved God greatly, walked in His favor, and refused to sin against God and His master (Gen 39:9).

> And he left all that he had in Joseph's hand and he knew not ought he had, save the bread which he did eat. And Joseph was a godly person, and well favored.
>
> And it came to pass after these things, that his master's wife cast her eyes upon Joseph; and she said, Lie with me.
>
> But he refused, and said unto his master's wife, Behold, my master knoweth not what is with me in the house, and he hath committed all that he hath to my hand.
>
> There is none greater in this house than I: neither hath he kept back any thing from me but thee, because thou art his wife: how then can I do this great wickedness, and sin against God (Gen. 39:6–9 KJV)?

His master's wife spoke to Joseph day- by- day, but Joseph resisted the devil and he fled from him. He operated in the divine mindset, "abstinence held by principle." He was a young man who loved God, and his master, and walked in the character and integrity of God.

He fled from youthful lusts and maintained the abstinence principle.

He is a perfect example to many in the body of Christ, of living abstinence held by principle and walking in the character of God providing a witness that this lifestyle can be lived. Standing for righteousness, holiness, fear of the Lord, and resisting the devil empowered him to flee from youthful lust. This did not come without a price in his walk with God. The character of Christ within was worth the sacrifice and price he had to pay. He knew that holiness becometh His house- and the love he had for God, exceeded any temptation satan could send his way. He was a young man in whom the spirit and character of God dwelled.

Joseph no doubt considered the authority of Christ over human passion, then set his heart on his love for God and his master. Chastity means abstinence from sexual activity outside of marriage. For the Christian, there is one rule and one rule only. It is to abstain from sexual activity prior to marriage and total faithfulness within marriage (1 Cor. 7:1–9).

There are many Christians who are determined to be kept by the Word and power of God; and have learned to walk humbly, and softly before God with all prayer and supplication, confessing and meditating on His Word. This means learning the discipline of divine consecration, loneliness, uncertainty, hope, trust, and unconditional commitment to Christ. It is a divine commitment requiring that we walk in purity; overcoming unbridled compassion through the Word of God and the blood of Jesus.

Learning to set and keep our affections on things above enables every Christian to maintain our commitment unto God and His Word. The mindset is very important as we learn to "let this mind be in us which was also in Christ Jesus" (Phil 2:5). We learn to cast down imaginations, and every high thing that exalts itself against the knowledge of God, and bring every thought into the obedience of Christ (2 Cor 10:5). Every sexual desire that enters our mind is not healthy, and is a lie from satan. God does not give desires that cannot be fulfilled according to His standards of holiness.

Sexual union within marriage is natural, healthy, and pleasurable, not only for the moment, but for the duration of a couple's life together. Sexual intimacy is natural in the sense the original designer created. When abstinence is no longer protected and esteemed, there is dullness, monotony, and sheer boredom. By trying to grab fulfillment everywhere, you find it nowhere.

> Abstinence before marriage consists of walking in fellowship with God and each other in spirit and truth. Passion must be held by principle. The principle is love, not merely erotic, sentimental, or sexual feeling. There

is no other way to control passion and no other route to purity and joy. Choosing to avoid the sin of sexual immorality is God's ideal. If you have already given away your virginity, the message of the gospel proclaims new birth, a new beginning, and a new creator
(2 Cor. 5:17 TAB).

I'm Me—you're You

I cannot change the way I am,
And I really never try,
God made me different and unique,
I never ask him why.
If I appear peculiar,
There's nothing I can do,
You must accept me as I am,
As I accept you.
God made a casting of each life,
Then threw the old away,
Each child is different form the rest,
Unlike as night and day.
So often we will criticize,
The things that others do,
Do you know, they do not think,
The same as me and you?
So God in all his wisdom,
Who knows us all by name,
He didn't want us to be bored,
That's why we're not the same.
"Accept one another, then, just as
Christ accepted you, in order
To bring praise to God."
Romans 15:7 (NIV)

❧

Author Unknown

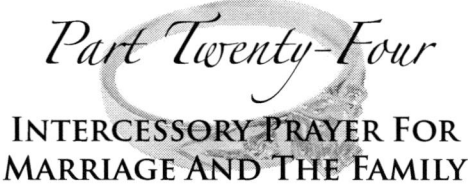

Part Twenty-Four

Intercessory Prayer For Marriage And The Family

Neither pray I for these alone; but for them also which shall believes on me through their word;

That they all may be one; as thou, Father, art in me, and I in thee, that they also may be one in us, that the world may believe that thou hast sent me.

And the glory which thou gavest me I have given them; that they may be one, even as we are one.

I in them, and thou in me, that they may be made perfect in one; and that the world may know that thou hast sent me, and hast loved them, as thou hast loved me.

Father, I will that they also whom thou hast given me, be with me where I am; that they may, behold my glory which thou hast given me: for thou lovedst me before the foundation of the world.

O righteous, Father, the world hath not known these: but I have known thee, but I have known these, and thee have known that thou hast sent me.

And I have declared unto them thy name, and will declare it: that the love wherewith thou hast loved me may be in them, and I in them (John 17: 20–26 KJV).

Be careful for nothing; but in everything by prayer and supplication with thanksgiving let your requests be made known unto God (Phil. 4:6 KJV).

If my people, who are called by My name, shall humble themselves, pray, seek, crave, and require of necessity My Face and turn from their wicked ways, then will I hear from heaven, forgive their sin, and heal their land.

Now My eyes will be open and My ears attentive to prayer offered in this place (2 Chronicles 7:14–15 KJV).

About Prayer For You

The Lord always hears our prayers,
But He does not always say, "Yes!"
Sometimes He says, "Wait"
Sometimes He says, "No"
For He has something better for us.
God's delays are not denials,
He has heard your prayer;
He knows all about your trials,
Knows your every care.
God's delays are not denials,
Help is on the way,
He is watching o'er life's dials,
Bringing forth that day.
God's delays are not denials,
You will find Him true,
Working through the darkest trials,
What is best for you.
☙
Author Unknown

The Trouble Tree

Sometimes It's How We Choose To See Things!

The carpenter that I hired to help me restore an old farmhouse had just finished a rough first day on the job. A flat tire made him lose an hour of work, his electric saw quit and now his ancient pickup truck refused to start. While I drove him home, he sat in stony silence. On arriving, he invited me to meet his family.

As we walk toward the front door he paused briefly at a small tree touching the tips of the branches with both hands. After opening the door, he underwent an amazing transformation, his tan face was wreathed in smiles and he hugged his two small children and gave his wife a kiss.

Afterward, he walked me to my car. We passed the tree and my curiosity got the better of me. I asked him about what I had seen him do earlier. "Oh, that's my trouble tree," he replied "I know I can't help having troubles on the job, but one thing for sure, troubles don't belong in the house with my wife and the children. So I just hang them up on the tree every night when I come home. Then in the morning, I'd pick them up again.

"Funny thing is," he smiled, "when I come out in the morning to pick them up, there aren't nearly as many as I remember hanging up the night before."

ॐ

Author Unknown

The Prayer Chair

A man's daughter had asked the local minister to come and pray with her father. When the minister arrived, he found the man lying in bed with his head propped up on two pillows. An empty chair sat beside it. The minister assumed the old fellow had been informed of his visit. "I guess you were expecting me," he said. "No, I wasn't; who are you?" "I'm the new minister at your church," he replied. " When I saw the empty chair, I figured you knew I was coming to visit.

"Oh yeah, the chair," said the bedridden man. "Would you mind closing the door?" Puzzled, the minister closed the door.

"I have never told anyone close, not even my daughter," said the old man." "But all my life I have never known how to pray. At church, I used to hear the Pastor talk about prayer, but it went right over my head."

The old man continued," "I abandoned any attempt at prayer until one day, about four years ago, my best friend said to me, "Prayer is just a simple matter of having a conversation with Jesus. Here's what I suggest. Sit down in a chair, place a chair in front of you, and in FAITH, see Jesus sitting in the chair. It's not weird or anything because He promised, 'I'll be with you always.' Then just speak to him, and listen, in the same way you're doing with me right now."

The father continued, "So I tried it. I've liked it so much that I'd do a couple of hours every day. I'm careful enough. If my daughter saw me talking to an empty chair, she either would have a nervous breakdown or send me off to the funny farm.

The minister was deeply moved by the story and encouraged the old man to continue on the journey. They anointed him with oil and prayed with him. Then he left.

Two nights later, the daughter called to tell the minister that her father had passed away that afternoon. "Did he die in peace?" he asked.

"Yes. When I was leaving for the store, he called me over to his bedside, told me that he loved me, and kissed me on the cheek. When I returned an hour later, he was dead," she continued, "but there was something strange about his death. Apparently, just before Dad died, he leaned over and rested his head on the chair next to his bed. What do you make of that?"

The minister, wiping a tear from his eye, said, "I wish we could all go like that."

(Author Unknown)

Intercessory Prayer For Marriage And The Family Family Intercessors

And he spake a parable unto them to this end, that men ought always to pray, and not to faint. Saying, There was in a city a judge, which feareth not God, neither regarded man: And there was a widow in that city; and she came unto him, saying Avenge me of mine adversary.

And he would not for a while: but afterward he said within himself, Though I fear not God, nor regard man; Yet because this widow troubleth me, I will avenge her, lest by her continual coming she weary me. And the Lord said, Hear what the unjust judge saith.

And shall not God avenge his own elect, which cry day and night unto him, though he bear long with them? I tell you that he will avenge them speedily. Nevertheless when the Son of Man cometh, shall he find faith on the earth (Lk 18: 1–8 KJV).

If my people, who are called by My name, shall humble themselves, pray, seek crave, and inquire of necessity My face and turn from their wicked ways, then will I hear from heaven, forgive their sin, and heal their land (2 Chr. 7: 14 KJV).

Prayer is the God- given opportunity to become intimately acquainted with Him. As a conversation with God, prayer enables the believer to build a personal relationship with the Lord. Prayer is an expression of a believer's dependence on God and, at the same time, an affirmation of God's promise to the redeemed for spiritual power.

While many believers desire to spend time with God in prayer, few actually do. Spiritual discipline is necessary to make prayer a priority in our lives. God, however, has made prayer a priority- directing His children to pray often, and always. Therefore, prayer should become a priority for us.

Families are very important in laying the foundation of prayer in the lives of their children. Prayerlessness has caused a great impact on the family, to include confused values, unnecessary sufferings, hasty decisions and impulsiveness in the lives of many. Lack of character and the necessity of living a God- fearing and Christian life on earth, develops in many lives because of deviation from the principles and guidelines of the scriptures.

There is a global call and necessity for every family, adult and child to return to prayer and supplication. The scriptures speak repeatedly of the importance of prayer. Paul says to pray about everything (Phil 4:6). Families and believers should make all their requests known unto God. In addition, believers are admonished to pray regularly and frequently. David went as far as to promise the Lord, "Evening and morning and noon I will pray" (Ps. 55: 17).

Jesus prayed for extended periods of time, especially when making important decisions (Luke 6: 12).

Prayer should occupy a place in the heart and the family; it needs to be a place in the home. Families should plan a special time and place of prayer as a part of their daily schedule (Luke 18:1).

Families must learn to focus on the necessity and priority of prayer in the family. Developing and growing in prayer through sharing their commitment to pray for each other, encourage, support the family during times of life's challenges, trials and testing should be the unity of every family.

Prevailing in prayer brought great deliverance to the widow in the city. The Greek word "nikao" means, "to subdue, conquer, overcome, prevail, get the victory." Webster defines "prevail" as "to gain ascendance through strength or superiority; triumph; to be or become effective." "The effectual fervent prayers of a righteous man availeth much' (James 5:16).

One of the greatest problems twenty- first century Christianity is experiencing is prayerlessness. Families and believers must learn the necessity of praying without ceasing. The scripture declares, "men ought always to pray, and not to faint" (Luke 18:1). Many of the things we call prayer mean prayerlessness to God. Sincerely praying with all prayers and supplication takes commitment and dedication unto God.

There is a necessity for every family to lay, develop and maintain an altar of prayer for building the foundation of prayer needed in the home. The altar of prayer is needed in every family and home. If a family does not have an altar, the manifestation of prayerlessness affects the entire family. It has been said that a family that "prays together stay together". A prayerless family will always disperse and experience defeat and failures.

The scripture declares, "pour out thy fury upon the heathen that know thee not; and upon the families that call not on His name" (Jer. 10: 25 KJV).

They are all hot as an oven, and have devoured their judges; all their kings are fallen: there is none among them that calleth unto me (Hos. 7: 7). This is the lamentation of God about prayerlessness. It was not as if they were not praying at all, but as far as God was concerned, their prayers did not go past the ceiling. If you do not wage war against and overcome prayerlessness, it can destroy your spiritual walk with God.

Family Intercessors
God Seeks Intercessors

And he saw that there was no man, and wondered that there was no intercessor: (no one to intervene on behalf of truth and right) (Isa. 59: 16 TAB).

Yet have not gone up into the gaps neither made up the hedge for the house of Israel to stand in the battle in the day of the Lord (Ezek. 13: 5 KJV).

And I sought for a man among them, that should make up the hedge, and stand in the gap before me for the land, that I should not destroy it; but I found none (Ezek. 22:30 KJV).

The world's statistical report states that there are 254 million people in this world. With such an astronomical number, the necessity and call to prayer is a great demand among our families.

Abraham walked close and was faithful unto God. He was found faithful unto God. He refused to hide from Abraham that which He did. What a beautiful walk with a God.

He further stated that Abraham would become a great and mighty nation, and all the nations of the earth would be blessed in him; and that he knew him, that he would command his children and household after him, that they would keep the way of the Lord, to do justice and judgment, that the Lord may bring upon Abraham that which he hath spoken of him.

And the Lord said, because the cry of Sodom and Gomorrah is great, and because their sin is very grievous, I will go down now, and see whether they have done altogether according to the cry of it, which is come unto me; and if not, I will know.

And Abraham drew near and said, Wilt thou also destroy the righteous with the wicked? Peradventure there be fifty righteous within the city, wilt thou also destroy ad spare the place for the fifty righteous that are therein? That be far from thee to do after this manner to slay the righteous with the wicked; and that the righteous should be as the wicked, that be far from thee: shall not the Judge of all earth do right.

Abraham spoke and said, behold now I have taken upon me to speak unto the Lord, which am but dust and ashes." He started with "Peradventure there be fifty righteous within the city, and went to ten, stating he would not destroy the city for ten's sake.

Abraham was the intercessor in his day, interceding unto God on behalf of his family. The ministry of intercession is much needed in families and the world today. God is still calling for intercessors who loves Him, His people, and are willing to dedicate and consecrate themselves to the ministry of prayer and supplications, and to flow in God's love and grace.

He has given us the precious gift of the Holy spirit in our hearts crying Abba, Father (Gal. 4:6).

Praying with all prayers and supplications for the needs of our families, husbands, children, marriages and love ones enables families to enlarge their hearts, and unite on one accord and intercede for saving the unsaved, unchurched, unsatisfied and uncommitted. Also, for those who are saved to grow up into the fullness of maturity in Christ Jesus. This is the fulfillment of the ministry of intercession on the earth.

Pray one for another that the power of God's love or agape love operates and flows through each other in united prayer for the family. When families experience the overflow of God's love, power and anointing; it releases the healing, deliverance and power of God in that family, setting the captives free.

Prevailing in prayer with all supplication is to be made for all believers. Families should feel compelled and fervently provoked to pray "with all prayer and supplication praying during all seasons, watching thereunto with perseverance and supplication for each other and the Body of Christ." It is the time for prayer, with all supplications for the needs of our families and singles in the Body of Christ.

Families should rise up, denounce the spirit of prayerlessness and receive the spirit of prayerfulness in the name Jesus. There is a universal call for families all over the world to give themselves to pray without ceasing, with all love and faith, proclaiming the Word of God. "The effectual fervent prayer of a righteous man availeth much" (James 5: 16).

Families should not only pray for each other, but singles, married couples and families to strive sincerely to follow and obey Him in all things.

Restoring The Spirit Of Prayer And Intercession
Intercession In The Family
The Power Of United Family Intercession

> If my people who are called by my name, shall humble themselves, and pray, and seek my face, and turn from their wicked ways; then will I hear from heaven, and will forgive their sin, and will heal their land
> (2 Chr. 7: 14 KJV).

> With all pray and supplication praying at all seasons in the spirit and watching thereunto in all perseverance and supplication for all the saints (Eph 6: 18 KJV).

> I have set watchmen upon thy walls, O Jerusalem; they shall never hold their peace day nor night; ye that are the Lord's remembrances, take ye no rest and give him no rest
> (Isa. 62: 6–7).

Every family has forerunners who were the first to experience salvation, acknowledge Jesus as Savior and Lord, submit to the foundational teaching of Christ, leadership and grow up into the maturity of Christ Jesus.

God is calling intercessors unto Him who are willing through a life of consecration and dedication to launch forth and maintain the ministry of prayer and supplication in the family. They are determined to overcome satan by the blood of the Lamb, by the words of their testimony, and love not their lives unto death (Rev. 12:11).

Many are requesting like David, that the walls of their hearts would be enlarged, enabling them to pray without ceasing for not only their family, but to intercede day and night for the entire Body of Christ.

Families should learn a lesson from David's ministry. During the early reign of his ministry, he carried the Ark wrong, which resulted in the death of Uzzah and the Ark ending up in the house of Obededom's. The blessings of God flowed greatly on Obededom's and his entire family during it's lodging in his house.

Prayer changes things and people. Families' striving to survive without prayer and supplication weakens the opportunities for victory and success in the family. Every life and home needs an altar of prayer and supplications. The scripture declares that Christ is able to save them to the uttermost who come unto God by Him, seeing He ever liveth to make intercession for them (Heb 7: 25).

He bore the sins of many, and made intercession for the transgressors (Isa. 53:12).

Families in the name of Jesus, call upon Him and He will show you great and wonderous things. Rise up and fight the good fight of faith. Forget those things which are behind and press forward to those things which are before. Stand in the gap for your family members. Destroy the works of the devil, confess the Word of God, which declares, "and this is the victory that overcometh the world even our faith.

Part Twenty-Five
Marriage And Romance

If you do not know (where your lover is), O you fairest among women, run along, follow the tracks of the flock, and (amuse yourself by) pasturing your kids beside the shepherds tents.

O my love (he said as he saw her), you remind me of my (favorite) mare in the chariot spans of Pharaoh.

Your cheeks are comely with ornaments, your neck with strings of jewels (Song 1:8–10 TAB).

Like an apple tree among the trees of the wood, so is my beloved (Shepherd) among the sons (cried the girl). Under his shadow I delighted to sit, and his fruit was sweet to my taste.

He brought me to the banqueting house, and his banner over me was love (for love waved as a protecting and comforting banner over my head when I was near him).

Sustain me with raisins, refresh me with apples, for I am sick with love (Song 2:3–5 TAB).

Romance And Passion

Let him kiss me with the kisses of his mouth! (she cries. Then, realizing that Solomon has arrived and has heard her speech, she turns to him and adds) For your love is better than wine!

(And she continues) The odor of your ointments is

fragrant; your name is like perfume poured out. Therefore do the maidens love you.

Draw me! We will run after you! The king brings me into his apartments! We will be glad and rejoice in you! We will recall (when we were favored with) your love, more fragrant than wine. The upright (are not offended at your choice, but sincerely) love you.

Behold, thou are fair, my love; behold, thou art fair, thou hast doves' eyes within thy locks: thy hair, is as a flock of goats, that appear from Mount Gilead.

Thy teeth are like a flock of sheep that are even shorn which came up from the washing; whereof every one bears twins, and none is barren among them. Thy lips are like a thread of scarlet, and thy speech is comely: thy temples are like a piece of a pomegranate within thy locks.

Thy neck is like the tower of David built for an armory, whereon there hang a thousand bucklers, all shields of mighty men.

Thy two breasts are like two young roes that are twins, which feed among the lilies (Song 4:1–5 KJV).

Until the dark break, and the shadows flee away. I will get me to the mountain of myrrh, and to the hill of frankincense.

Thou art all fair, my love; there is no spot in thee.

In the Song of Solomon, his lyrical pen shares the testimony of love, romance, and passion two people experienced for each other. His Shulamite lover was loved passionately. Every fiber of her being echoed with responsive, adoring, and affection for her lover.

Romance offers the lover an opportunity to focus on responsibilities rather than privileges. Rather than dwelling upon selfish needs and what others should do, the romantic lover is ever conscious of what he or she can do to show love for the other person.

Among the most beautiful joys and pleasures married couples

experience is when they through the day-to-day challenges and encumbrances of life, spend quality time with each other, enjoying their God given gift. Married couples must learn to acknowledge His gift and thank Him for His love and divine covering. Often in learning to accept life's trials, tests and challenges; couples allows prayerlessness to cause them to neglect and become insensitive to each other's needs. However, the power of love is the determining factor that keeps the romance lively, blissful, and full of happiness.

Romance has to be kept blissful in a marriage to keep the flow of continuous love, passion, and intimacy. When agape love meets Eros, the passion, pleasure, enjoyment, and excitement flows from heart to heart.

In the Song of Solomon, he memorialized his deep love for the Shulamite woman, and was led to write a series of songs. It was evident that romance was very present in their relationship. Romance is kept blissful and alive in marriage as the couple learns to continue in prayer and supplication, and learn to release and cast their day-to-day cares upon the Lord. All couples should learn and take time to minister unto each other; share, and enjoy the beautiful times of love, passion, and romance with each other.

Taking Time For Romance

Let the husband render unto the wife due benevolence: and likewise also the wife unto the husband.

The wife hath not power of her own body, but the husband: and likewise also the husband hath not power of his own body, but the wife.

Defraud ye not one the other, except it be with consent for a time, that ye may give yourselves to fasting and prayer; and come together again, that Satan tempt you not for your incontinency (1 Cor. 7: 3–5 KJV).

Live joyfully with the wife whom you love all the days of your vain life, which He has given you under the sun– all the days of futility. For that is your portion in this life and in your work at which you toil under the sun (Ecc. 9:9 TAB).

Love, romance, and passion–flowing from the heart–should be vibrant, powerful, blissful, and a constant flow lasting all day long. Holding hands, a tender kiss, or a simple "I love you" should permeate the room with love.

Married couples should learn to manage their time effectively and always take time to minister to each other, letting each other know they are precious, valuable, adorable, and greatly loved.

Women are challenged daily with many roles and responsibilities. However, in learning to plan your daily schedule, set aside quiet time to spend with the Lord and minister unto your husbands. Learn to enjoy all that God has given you richly to enjoy. Focusing on daily priorities and necessities is important, however, reserving meaningful time for romance is needful and special for you, your mate and family. Your happiness flows in the entire home. They experience your love and lack of love. Your example and rays of hope what God can do in and through the marriage and relationship.

Taking time for romance does not necessarily mean expensive romantic getaways and spending money not included in your budget. People, places, things, and events do not bind romance and love. They are in the heart. That which is in the heart is, and can only be bound by the restrictor. Learn to take time and spend quality moments with each other, sharing the good things God has given us richly to enjoy.

Part Twenty-Six
SPIRITUAL COMPATIBILITY

Do not be unequally yoked with unbelievers [do not make mismated alliances with them or come under a different yoke with them, inconsistent with your faith). For what partnership have right living and right standing with God with iniquity and lawlessness? Or how can light have fellowship with darkness?

What harmony can there be between Christ and Belial (the devil)? Or what has a believer in common with an unbeliever?

What agreement (can there be between) a temple of God and idols? For we are the temple of the living God; even as God said, I will dwell in and with and among them and will walk in and with and among them, and I will be their God, and they shall be My people (2 Cor. 6: 14–16 TAB).

The Compatibility Challenge

Do not be unequally yoked with unbelievers (do not make mismated alliances with them or come under a different yoke with them, inconsistent with your faith). For what partnership have right living and right standing with God with iniquity and lawlessness? Or how can light have fellowship with darkness?

What harmony can there be between Christ and Belial (the devil)? Or what has a believer in common with an unbeliever?

What agreement (can there be between) has the temple of God and idols? For we are the temple of the living God: even as God said, I will dwell in and with and among

them and will walk in and with and among them, and I
will be their God, and they shall be my people
(2 Cor. 6:14–16 TAB).

Today, countless Christian singles are seeking the perfect mate, or their soul mate as it is referred to in the twenty first century. Many singles are obviously in the wrong place, at the wrong time, and doing the wrong things. They have left the scriptural principles of God's purpose for their life and have willfully planned their own life purpose and destiny.

The scriptures explicitly focus our mindset in the area of spiritual compatibility, keeping us in check that this is the first principle in choosing your mate. Compatibility in choosing your soul mate challenges the mindset of many and causes others to totally miss the mark during the selection process.

In search for the "perfect match" or "soul mate," God alone chooses the times and the seasons. It is of utmost importance that we learn how to wait upon Him.

Looking for relationships without Jesus being the center of our lives is like trying to drive an automobile without an engine.

Being unequally yoked to an unbeliever means our spiritual fellowship is out of sync (darkness vs. light) with His divine will. It means we are not experiencing the true joy of worshipping Him in spirit and truth. We were created for the glory of Christ and His Kingdom. Our identity is in Christ. We are adopted, chosen, and complete in Christ. The adversary, satan, the spirit of darkness is a deceiver, father of lies, whose purpose is to undo the work of God (Mark 4:15). The description of satanic character and work of darkness, totally opposes the work of God, and urges people to renounce Him (Gen 3:4, 5). The portrait of the adversary reflects the character of deception, lies, evil, hatred and all works of evil.

Can two walk together except they be agreed (Amos 3:3)? Many Christians have purposely "joined" themselves to an unbeliever, compromising their walk and the principles of the Word of God. They do this with the premise that their walk with God and knowledge of His Word would deliver their mismated alliance. However, all believers walking in the wisdom of the Word know, and understand that spiritual deliverance is a process. It is progressive and takes time.

Marrying an unbeliever, according to the scripture, is a mismatched *joining*. Your choice of deliverance is *"Jesus Is The Way,"* and theirs "leave my demons alone." Right living and right standing with God is your way, iniquity and lawlessness theirs.

> But ye shall destroy their altars, break their images, and cut down their groves.
>
> For thou shalt worship no other god: for the Lord, whose name is Jealous, is a jealous God.
>
> Lest thou make a covenant with the inhabitants of the land, and they go a-whoring after their gods, and do sacrifice unto their gods, and one call thee, and thou eat of his sacrifice;
>
> And thou take of their daughters unto thy sons, and their daughters go a-whoring after their gods, and make thy sons go a-whoring after their gods.
>
> Thou shalt make thee no molten gods
> (Ex. 34:13–17 KJV).

The scripture clearly describes the impact of selecting unbelievers as mates. This spiritual incompatibility not only causes many to forfeit their right standing with God, but compromises the principles of His word. The sharing of faith, principles, values, and even our conversation is different. We are instructed to destroy their altars, break their images, and cut down their groves. We should not allow them to destroy our altars and incite us to compromise our Christian principles. We are called to be the light of the world and a light unto unbelievers, that the salvation of Christ maybe extended to the end of the earth (Isa. 49:6). We are instructed to have no fellowship with the unfruitful works of darkness, but rather to reprove them (Eph. 5:11).

Singleness Of Heart

> The light of the body is the eye: if therefore thine eye be single, thy whole body shall be full of light (Matt. 6:22 KJV).
>
> The light of the body is the eye: therefore when thine eye is single, thy whole body it also is full of light: but when thine eye is evil, thy body is full of darkness (Luke. 11:34 KJV).

And they, continuing daily with one accord in the temple, and breaking bread from house to house, did eat their meat with gladness and singleness of heart (Acts 2:46 KJV).

Keep thy heart with all diligence; for out of it and above all are the issues of life (Prov. 4:23 KJV).

Apply thine heart unto instruction and thine ears to the words of knowledge (Prov. 23:12 KJV).

Servants, obey in all things your masters according to the flesh; not with the flesh; not with eyeservice, as menpleasers; but in singleness of heart fearing God (Col. 3:22 KJV).

My son, give me thine heart and let thine eyes observe in my ways (Prov. 23:26 KJV).

Servant, be obedient to them that are your masters according to the flesh, with fear and trembling, in singleness of your heart, as unto Christ (Eph. 6:5 KJV).

The scripture declares, "the heart is deceitful above all things, and desperately wicked; who can know it" (Jer. 17:9)? Christian singles must learn to keep and maintain their mindset on things above, and not on worldly things. Learning to have the mind of Christ (Phil. 2:5), letting that mind be in you which was also in Christ Jesus, enables you to keep the right mindset concerning all things.

Christian singles who have learned how to develop and maintain the right mindset (through Christ His Word) realizes that they are never alone. Therefore, loneliness does not impel them into disillusionment, illusion, and feelings of grandeur. They have learned that God will keep us in perfect peace as our mind is stayed on Him (Isa. 26:3). Love is said to be blind, and would blind the hearts and minds of all who are lead by the vanity of their mind, and the deceitfulness of riches. It is great confidence and assurance to know our Heavenly Father is a keeper, and preserver of all who desire to be kept during the hour of temptation.

Hearing From God

> The Lord God hath opened mine ear and I was not rebellious, neither turned away back (Isa. 50:5 KJV).

> And thine ears shall hear a word behind thee, saying, This is the way, walk ye in it, when ye turn to the right hand, and when ye turn to the left (Isa. 30: 21 KJV).

> Rise up, ye women that are at ease; hear my voice, ye careless daughters, give ear unto my speech (Isa. 32:9 KJV).

The scripture declares not to put faith in every spirit, but to prove (test) the spirits whether they proceed from God, because many false prophets are gone out into the world (1 John 4:1).

We serve a God who has never made a mistake. He neither sleeps nor slumbers (Psalms 121:4). In learning to follow God, we learn to seek and hear His voice. The voice of God is His Word, and because His voice is His Word, "It shall not return unto Him void, but it shall accomplish that which He pleases, and shall prosper in the thing whereunto He sends it" (Isa. 55:11).

One of the greatest benefits in following our Heavenly Father, is knowing that He careth for us, came to do us good, and have our best interest at heart. He reassured us in His Word when He declared, "my sheep hear my voice, and I know them, and they follow Me (John 10:27).

Not discerning the voice of God during the mate selection process has deceived many. The reason many fail to discern the voice of God is because their feelings, emotions, and ways are hindering them from hearing, receiving, and believing His Word. The scripture declares, let no man say when he is tempted, he is tempted of God, for God cannot be tempted with evil, neither tempteth he any man (James 1:13–14). Feelings, emotions and unbridled passions will draw away, entice, and bait evil desires for all who have not learned to keep their flesh under subjection to His word (James 1:15–16).

Interestingly enough, we do not see the total picture as He does. He sees the beginning and ending of all things. He is the Alpha and Omega (Rev. 1:8).

Missing the mark through failure to discern the voice of God has created much unnecessary suffering in the lives of many believers. I believe Smith Wigglesworth stated it beautifully when he said, "I am not moved by what I see, what I hear, or what I feel, but only by the Word of God.

> Blessed is the man that walketh not in the counsel of the ungodly, nor standeth in the way of sinners, nor sitteth in the seat of the scornful. But his delight is in the law of the Lord, and in His law doth he meditate day and night. And he shall be like a tree planted by the rivers of water, that bringeth forth his fruit in his season; his leaf also shall not wither; and whatsoever he doeth shall prosper (Psalm 1:1–3 KJV).

Staying in the scripture was Jesus way of withstanding satan's temptations. The Word of God is a mirror to the soul (James 1:22–25); it is a lamp unto the feet for guidance (Psalm 119:105); it is a cleansing agent, a two-edged sword, laying bare the heart (Heb. 4:12); and it is food for the spirit. Believers must know that satan departed from Jesus for a season. When the devil ended (the complete cycle of) the temptation, he (temporarily) left Him (that is stood off from Him) until another opportune and favorable time (Luke 4:13). Jesus went back full of the power of the [Holy] Spirit. We need the power and Word of God to live victoriously in this life (Luke 4:14).

Walking In Agreement With God

> What agreement (can there be between) a temple of God and idols? For we are the temple of the living God: even as God said, I will dwell in, and with, and among them and will walk in and with and among them, and I will be their God; and they shall be My people (II Cor. 6:16 TAB).

Christian singles are challenged daily to seek God's will and ask His wisdom in choosing the right mate. The scripture teaches that walking in agreement with His will is the result of walking in agreement with the Word, and letting this mind be in you, which was also in Christ Jesus (Phil. 2:5).

Walking in agreement with God is developed through daily prayer, study of the scriptures, continuous fellowship with fellow believers, obeying His Word, and abiding in His presence. The scriptures renew our thinking according to His Word, empowering us to deal with circumstances that befall us in daily life. Worldly ideas, attitudes, wrong thinking, and prejudices are replaced by thoughts that conform to God's Word and ways. Conforming to God's ways takes time, and there are no shortcuts.

Christian singles who have continuous fellowship with the Lord through prayer and His Word learn to renew their mind daily through the scriptures. They make scripturally informed decisions. Walking in knowledge of His will enables us to walk in, and remain in right standing with Him because we learn to seek His will daily in prayer and study of the scripture.

Jesus provided the perfect example during His earthly ministry. He spoke and walked in complete unity with the will of the Father. He spoke explicitly in John 10:30, declaring He and His Father are one.

Marrying Outside Your Faith

When the Lord your God brings you into the land which you are entering to possess, and has plucked away many nations before you, the Hittites, the Girgashites, the Amorites, the Canaanites, the Perizzites, the Hivites, and the Jebusites, seven nations greater and mightier than you;

And when the Lord your God gives them over to you and you smite them, then you must utterly destroy them. You shall make no covenant with them, or show mercy to them.

You shall not make marriages with them; your daughter you shall not give to his son nor shall you take his daughter for your son,

For they will turn away your sons from following Me, that they may serve other gods; so will the anger of the Lord be kindled against you and He will destroy you quickly.

> But thus shall you deal with them: you shall break down their altars and dash in pieces their pillars and hew down their Asherim (symbols of the goddess Asherah) and burn their graven images with fire.
>
> For you are a holy and set-apart people to the Lord your God; the Lord your God has chosen you to be a special people to Himself out of all the peoples on the face of the earth (Deut 7: 1–6 TAB).

The scriptural definition of marriage is a union of two people who become one (Three-In- One Concise Bible Reference Companion). It is further defined it as- wedlock;

the institution by which men and women are joined together and form a family, (Matt. 6:6). The choice of partners becomes very important, since each will identify with the other in the union. Acknowledging Jesus as Savior and Lord, commitment to live according to the principles and guidelines of His Word is the foundation and cornerstone of our lives. Thus, the destiny of our life has been formed and will determine the fulfillment of that vision.

The scripture warns against marriage outside of your faith because of the propensity to result in dangerous compromise, and tragic abandonment of our commitment to Him.

Historically, interfaith marriages frequently led to the worship of other gods. The wise King Solomon ruled everything but his own heart wisely. His seven hundred wives and three hundred concubines not only continued to worship their false gods, but also led him to worship their pagan deities.

What leads many Christians to marry outside their faith? It is apparent that the faith of your spouse and their expression of faith must be respected, as each person simultaneously tries to hold on to their own faith. Additionally, if children are born to such a union, parents must agree upon how to nurture their children spiritually. Believers are cautioned against marrying outside of their faith (1 Cor. 7:39; 2 Cor. 6:14). Such marriages are problematic and are prone to fail when both spouses are strong in their respective faiths.

In times past, the tendency to intermarry was not based upon love, romance, or any other intention, other then to improve a family's economic and social position in life. The prophet Malachi spoke strongly against Hebrew men divorcing their Hebrew wives to marry "daughters of a foreign god" (Mal. 2:11–16).

However, we are living under a new and better covenant. We have the Holy Spirit abiding within us. It reveals the motives and intents of our heart; and the wisdom, knowledge, and hidden revelations of the gospel of Jesus Christ. It also empowers and constrains us from fulfilling the lust of the eyes, pride of life, and the lust of the flesh. We are strengthened with all might within our inner most being, empowering us to say "no" and mean it. Before His empowerment, we would have compromised to the desires of our flesh.

The danger of interfaith marriage extends beyond a dilution of faith and a straying from pure worship of the one true and living God. It includes loss of language, thought, understanding, and expression at the most basic cultural level, including access to scripture. Thus, in marrying outside of the faith, God's people destroy their own identity and taint the favored status they enjoy as the people of God.

Part Twenty-Seven

Christ Centered Marriages
"Families Who Prays Together, Stay Together"

I have manifested thy name unto the men which thou gavest me out of the world: thine they were, and thou gavest them me; and they have kept thy word.

Now they have known that all things whatsoever thou hast given me are of thee.

For I have given unto them the words which thou gavest me; and they have received them, and have known surely that I came out from thee, and they have believed that thou didst send me.

I pray for them: I pray not for the world, but for them, which thou hast given me; for they are thine.

And all mine are thine, and thine are mine; and I am glorified in them.

And now I am no more in the world, but these are in the world, and I come to thee. Holy Father, keep through thine own name those whom thou hast given me, that they may be one, as we are.

While I was with them in the world, I kept them in thy name: those that thou gavest me I have kept, and none of them is lost, but the son off perdition: that the scripture might be fulfilled.

And now come I to thee; and these things I speak in the world, that they might have my joy fulfilled in themselves.

I have given them thy word; and the world hath hated

them, because they are not of the world, even as I am not
of the world.

I pray not that thou shouldest take them out of the world,
but that thou shouldest keep them from the evil.

They are not of the world, even as I am not of the world.

Sanctify them through thy truth: thy word is truth.

As thou hast sent me into the world, even so have I also
sent them into the world.

And for their sakes I sanctify myself, that they also might
be sanctified through the truth (John 17:6–19 KJV).

F-A-M-I-L-Y

I ran into a stranger as he passed by.
"Oh, excuse me please," was my reply.
He said, "Please excuse me too;
I wasn't even watching for you."
We were very polite, this stranger and I.
We went on our way and we said goodbye.

But at home a different story is told,
how we treat our loved ones, young and old.
Later that day, cooking the evening meal,
my daughter stood beside me very still.
When I turned, I nearly knocked her down.
"Move out of the way," I said with a frown.

She walked away, her little heart broken.
I didn't realize how harshly I'd spoken.
While I lay awake in bed,
God's still small voice came to me and said,
"While dealing with a stranger . . .
common courtesy you use,

but the children you love,
you seem to abuse.
"Look on the kitchen floor;
you'll find some flowers there by the door.

"Those are the flowers she brought for you.
She picked them herself, pink, yellow and blue.
She stood quietly not to spoil the surprise,
and you never saw the tears in her eyes."

By this time, I felt very small
and now my tears began to fall.

I quietly went and knelt by her bed;
"Wake up, little girl, wake up," I said.

"Are these the flowers you picked for me?"
She smiled, "I found 'em, out by the tree.
I picked 'em because they're pretty like you.

"I knew you'd like 'em, especially the blue."
I said, "Daughter, I'm sorry for the way I acted today;
I shouldn't have yelled at you that way."

She said, "Oh, Mom, that's okay.
I love you anyway."
I said, "Daughter, I love you too,
and I do like the flowers,
especially the blue."

Are you aware that: If we die to morrow, the company that we are working for could easily replace us in a matter of days. But the family we leave behind will feel the loss for the rest of their lives. And come to think of it, we pour ourselves more into work than to our family–an unwise investment indeed. So what is moral to the story? Do you know what the word "FAMILY" stands for?

FAMILY = (F)ather (A)nd (M)other, (I) (L)ove (Y)ou

༒

Author Unknown

Family: Christ Centered Marriages

And if it seems evil unto you to serve the Lord, choose for yourselves this day whom you will serve, whether the gods which your fathers served on the other side of the River, or the gods of the Amorites in whose land you dwell; but as for me and my house, we will serve the Lord (Josh. 24:15 KJV).

And you shall love the Lord your God with all your (mind and) heart and with your entire being and with all your might.

And these words which I am commanding you this day shall be [first] in your [own] minds and hearts; and [then]

You shall whet and sharpen them so as to make them penetrate, and teach and impress them diligently upon the [minds and] hearts of your children, and shall talk of them when you sit in your house and when you walk by the way, and when you lie down and when you rise up (Deut. 6:5–7 TAB).

A family has been defined as a household of individuals living together. God designed marriage before there was any creative activity. It is to be a picture of His own relationship with His people, to pattern the relationship between Christ and His church.

God's divine plan for the family is that the husband is assigned the primary responsibility for Christ like, servant leadership in the home (Eph. 5:23–29). The wife is then expected to respond in honoring and affirming her husband's leadership (Eph. 5:21,22,33; 1 Pet. 3:1–4), bringing a much needed balance between leadership and servant-hood. Married couples are to have a partnership that glorifies God.

Millions of husbands and wives have forgotten their God ordained roles and responsibilities, and are not walking in line with His principles and guidelines. In order for divine order, love, unity, and peace to flow in a home, it must first "begin with the head of the household." Headship does not merely prescribe who does what, but is a basis for moving forward the goals of a family in an orderly manner. The husband is not Christ, however, he should encourage his wife and children to give allegiance to Christ and depend on Him.

In a fallen world, there is no such thing as a perfect family. Children have many needs: physical needs (food, shelter, clothing); emotion needs (love, acceptance, affirmation); intellectual needs (the opportunity to learn daily living skills and to develop intellectually); and spiritual needs (guidance in how to know God personally and to mature in that relationship). However, God's divine plan and order for the family is that parents will teach their children in the admonition of the Lord.

Married couples accepting the responsibility of parenthood must understand that it involves a process of making disciples of their children. Parents are to teach obedience, and not just bring children under parental authority in order to bring them to salvation and spiritual discipline (Heb. 12:11). While punishment may sometimes be a part of discipline, much more is involved in moving a child from parent-controlled behavior to self-controlled. Independent decision-making is ultimately a God controlled lifestyle in which the child learns to make wise, God-honoring decisions on its own (Heb. 12:10–11).

The Christ Centered Family structure is a very viable unit. Man, with all his wisdom, knowledge, and understanding, can never create a unit like the family. The ultimate survival of the family is dependent upon man yielding, surrendering, obeying, and following God's divine order for the family.

Married couples following God's plan for their lives can rise up through faith in God's Word. They can destroy generational curses that resulted from sin and disobedience, and release generational blessings through love, obedience, faith, and fulfilling His will on earth.

Family Worship: Sharing Praise And Worship

These are the singers heads of the father's houses of the Levites, dwelling in the temple chambers, free from other service because they were on duty day and night (1 Chr. 9:33).

Behold, Bless (affectionately and gratefully praise) the Lord, all the servants of the Lord (singers) who by night stand in the house of the Lord (1 Chr. 9:33).

Lift up your hands in holiness and to the sanctuary and bless the Lord (affectionately and gratefully praise Him)!

The Lord bless you out of Zion, even He who made heaven and earth (Ps. 134:1–3 TAB).

Families have the responsibilities to teach godly principles from one generation to another. The family's spiritual heritage is crucial in God's plan. Generation to generation shall praise thy works to one another, and shall declare His mighty acts (Ps. 145:4). The very essence of transmitting redemptive history is the sharing of the story of redemption from one generation to the next. He is accessible to those who seek him. He fulfills our desires, delivers, and preserves us.

The home provides a vital, living example of true Christianity. Children must be taught to talk to God about everything, from major decisions in their lives to simply finding a school to attend. Faith must become a part of everyday life. Families must establish special times of family prayer and Bible study, and infuse faith into the routine of family life. A family can do this by gathering to praise and worship and engaging in discussions about the Lord and the scripture. A spiritual heritage builds a wall of security and protection around the home.

It is a beautiful time of sharing, responsibility, and privilege for married couples to provide an atmosphere of worship for their loved ones (Prov. 31:18).

The privilege of passing on this kind of spiritual heritage goes beyond the walls of the immediate family circle. The repercussions of a truly Christian home can be widespread and persist long after the initial influence. We remain faithful to God because He remains faithful to us (Ps. 89:1).

Family devotions do not have to be long and drawn out–just a simple Bible reading or a brief prayer. Reading scripture and praying are important enough for married couples to keep trying to instill them as a family habit, even if interruptions, failures, and minor disasters occasionally disrupts (Deut. 6:7).

It's vitally important for Christian families to spend time together in prayer and Bible reading. It is a priceless experience to have parents share spiritual truths from the scriptures, and to hear parents ask for God's blessing and protection for each person in the family. Finding time, seeking His wisdom and guidance in decision making, and being patient and persistent, are all common challenges associated with family devotions. Families should strive to be consistent. This will help the children to develop a love for scripture and a habitual reliance on the power of prayer. Every family heritage of faithfulness must begin with someone. Let the beginning be with your marriage.

We as Christians have learned that our emotions and self-pity are not the solutions to the problem. The greatest comfort we as Christians have is knowing that the Comforter abides with us forever (John 14:16). He turns our hopelessness, frustrations, anxiety, and confession of "nobody loves me" around.

He is gracious and knows our deepest desires. He strengthens us to get up and move on. We renounce, destroy the works of the enemy; and refuse to wait for other people to pity us, but learn to get up and go forward in the name of Jesus.

The greatest asset we as Christians have in our lives is our personal walk and relationship with our heavenly Father. We have learned to cast all of our cares upon Him and make all our requests known unto Him, for "He careth for us" (1 Pet. 5:7). When we are obedient to His Word and are willing to do whatever it takes to be made whole, He will send Jesus in the form of a person, a scripture, or a new thought in our mind. Learning to act upon what His Word instructs us to do is the solution to all our problems.

The scriptures declare "there is nothing too hard for God" (Jer. 32:17). When Christian families grab hold unto this revelation in faith, regardless of the problem or whatever the circumstance, we experience the reality of "this is the victory that overcometh the world, even our faith" (1 John 5:4).

Family Problem Solving

Lean on, trust in, and be confident in the Lord with all your heart and mind and do not rely on your own insight or understanding.

In all your ways know, recognize, and acknowledge Him, and He will direct and make straight and plain your paths (Prov. 3:5–6 KJV).

The steps of a good man are ordered by the Lord: and he delighteth in his way (Ps. 37:23 KJV).

A man's mind plans his way, but the Lord directs his steps and makes them sure (Prov. 16:9 KJV).

Crisis and trials attack every family. However, the good news is that the Lord desires to be the "repairer of the breach" for families experiencing severe problems, providing solutions to what appear to be unsolvable problems.

The first step in solving any problem is admitting there is a problem, whether it is physical, emotional, or spiritual. In the scripture, Jesus asked the man who had been lying by the pool of Bethesda for thirty-eight years a very important question. "Do you want to be made well (John 5:1–15)? In other words, "Do you care enough about your problem to do something about it–even if it requires on your part, some action, effort, sacrifice, or suffering?"

Family: Living And Sharing The Faith Principle

Look at the proud: his soul is not straight or right within him, but the (rigidly) just and the (uncompromisingly) righteous man shall live by faith and in his faithfulness

For therein is the righteousness of God revealed from faith to faith; as it written, The just shall live by faith (Rom 1: 17 KJV).

But that no man is justified by the law in the sight of God' it is evident: for, the just shall live by faith (Gal 3: 11 KJV).

For whatsoever is born of God overcometh the world; and this is the victory that overcometh the world, even our faith (1 John 5:4 KJV).

Then touched he their eyes, saying According to your faith be it unto you (Matt. 9:29 KJV).

The righteousness of God is revealed from faith-to-faith, as it is written, "the just shall live by faith (Hab. 2:4). God's covenant with Abram (later changed to Abraham) came to him in a vision, saying, "do not be afraid, Abram, I am your shield, your exceedingly great reward" (Gen. 15:1–3). He was concerned that he was childless, and the heir of his house was Eliezer of Damascus. However, God wanted Abram to know that he was not going to be his heir, Eliezer was not going to inherit his earthly substance, but his own son would be his heir (Isaac inherited all that he had; he gave gifts unto his other children born after Sarah's death- (Gen. 25:5–6).

Abraham and his wife were up in years. They realized that they had no children to leave their earthly substance unto. The word spoken unto him by God was a revelation that took his level of faith to the next level, placing on it the seal of justice, causing him to increase from faith to faith (Rom. 1:17).

The confirmation of the covenant God made to Abraham was divided into five parts:

- God reminded Abraham of His faithfulness in the past (v. 7).
- God gave a sign to confirm His promise (vv. 8–12).
- God specified the provision of the covenant (vv. 13–16).
- God ratified the covenant by a divine appearance (v. 17).
- God concluded the covenant with an unconditional promise (v. 18).

Abram was ninety-nine years old when the Lord appeared unto him, changed his name to Abraham, and made His covenant with him. It confirmed that He would greatly increase him (Gen.12: 2) exceedingly, make him a father of many nations, and bless he and his wife Sarai (changed her name to Sarah) with a son. The son's name was Isaac, who was born at the set time the next year (Gen. 17:1–21).

Abraham lived the life of faith, and provided an example of faith for his son and the generation of believers today. He staggered not at the promises of God through unbelief; was strong in faith, giving glory unto God; and called those things, which be not as though they were (Rom. 4:17,20).

Faith in God empowers us to "call those things which be not as though they were," walk in faith, wait upon the manifestation of God's word, and live the life of faith by the Word of God through His power (Rom. 4:17).

Part Twenty-Eight
Marriage Relationship and Finance

Will a man rob or defraud God? Yet you rob and defraud Me. But you say, In what way do we rob or defraud you? (You have withheld your) tithes and offerings

Ye are cursed with the curse, for you are robbing Me, even the whole nation.

Bring ye all the tithes into the storehouse, that there may be meat in mine house, and prove me now herewith, saith the Lord of hosts, if I will not open you the windows of heaven, and pour you out a blessing that there shall not be room enough to receive it (Mal. 3:8–10 KJV).

But thou shalt remember the Lord thy God: for it is He that giveth thee power to get wealth, that He may establish His covenant which He sware unto thy fathers, as it is this day (Deut. 8:18 KJV).

And I will rebuke the devourer for your sakes, and he shall not destroy the fruits of your ground: neither shall your vine cast her fruit before the time in the field, saith the Lord of hosts.

And all nations shall call you blessed: for ye shall be a delightsome land, saith the Lord of hosts (Mal. 3:11–12 KJV).

Charge them that are rich in this world, that they be not highminded, nor trust in uncertain riches, but in the living God, who giveth us richly all things to enjoy (1 Tim. 6:17 KJV).

Marriage Relationship And Finance

Can two walk together, except they be agreed
(Amos 3:3 KJV)?

For the love of money is the root of all evil: which while some coveteted after, they have erred from the faith and pierced themselves through with many sorrows
(1 Tim. 6:10 KJV).

Bring ye all the tithes into the storehouse, that there may be meat in mine house, and prove me now herewith,, saith the Lord of hosts, if I will not open you the windows of heaven, and pour you out a blessing, that there shall not be room enough to receive it.

And I will rebuke the devourer for your sakes, and he shall not destroy the fruits of your ground; neither shall your vine cast her fruit before the time in the field, saith the Lord of hosts (Mal. 3:10–11 KJV).

Marriage relationship and finances have tremendously affected millions of families today. Severe financial problems and poor management skills have created insurmountable problems in many relationships in the body of Christ. Financial misunderstandings have created distressful and painful struggles within many marriages. Regardless of the type of battle, financial problems have a tendency to escalate and create the spirit of division, discord, and dissension in the marriage.

The most important thing for any married couple is learning to openly and honestly communicate, and develop a sound scriptural based financial understanding before the marriage. Both partners enter the marriage from different financial backgrounds. Indeed, their level of financial growth and maturity should be based on the scriptures and faith in the Word of God.

Married couples must maintain open communication during the marriage. Communication has been defined as the exchange of ideas and information by talk, gestures, or writing (Random House Webster's College Dictionary). It is an active process that is present in all meaningful relationships. Communication is not only talking, but also listening and understanding. Though individuals have different communication styles, spiritually mature, married believers should seek continually to improve their communication with each other.

Words are powerful. The spoken word can provide encouragement or discouragement. The scripture leads believers to speak, confess the Word, and "call those things which be not as though they were" (Rom. 4:11). The book of Proverbs discusses the importance of listening with understanding to others who speak (Prov. 11:12, 18:2, 13:29, 20). In marriage relationships, there are concerns that must be addressed. Communication must be conducted to maintain the relationship.

Words alone cannot fully express meaning. Body language, facial expression, tone of voice, and other means of non-verbal communication are essential for effectiveness. Studies in communication patterns have concluded that two-thirds of the intent of a message is communicated non-verbally, while only one-third of the message is communicated through words.

The scripture emphases the significance of communication, and outlines instructions concerning verbal behavior (Eph. 4:25–32).

Married couples are to encourage to:

- Speak the truth in love
- Control angry words (v.26)
- Speak words of encouragement and healing
- Avoid unkind or bitter speech (v. 29)
- Speak words of forgiveness (v. 32)

Married couples who are determined to follow God's plan for their finances realize that learning to effectively communicate with each other is the key to applying divine principles for covenant living. God honors His Word. Married couples striving to communicate, walk, believe, and live in line with the Word of God have learned that "His Word shall not return unto Him void", but shall accomplish that which He please, and shall prosper in the thing whereto He send it (Isa. 55:11).

Misguided Financial Principles / Wise Financial Management

> Keep out of debt and owe no man anything, except to love one another; for he who loves his neighbor (who practices loving others) has fulfilled the law (relating to one's fellowmen), meeting all its requirements (Rom. 13:8 TAB).

> Will a man rob God? Yet ye have robbed me. But ye say, wherein have we robbed thee? In tithes and offerings.

> Ye are cursed with a curse: for ye have robbed me, even this whole nation.

> Bring ye all the tithes into the storehouse, that there may be meat in mine house, and prove me now herewith, saith the Lord of hosts, if I will not open you the windows of heaven, and pour you out a blessing that there shall not be room enough to receive it (Mal. 3:8–10 TAB).

There are millions of Christian marriage relationships that have been destroyed because of financial problems. Financial problems causes more married couples to separate and divorce than any other problem.

The scripture declares that the love of money is the root of all evil, not money itself. Misunderstandings in the area of finances cause many married couples to abandon the faith, forget their covenant of finance, and walk in doubt and unbelief. Faith cometh by hearing, and hearing the Word of God (Rom. 10:17). The scripture has not changed in reference to financial conditions and circumstances. Faith in God Word turns hopeless circumstances around.

Developing and maintaining a close walk with our Heavenly Father dismisses all unscriptural, and erroneous financial teachings. The scripture corrects us from the error of our thinking and ways. We learn to let that mind be in us which was also in Christ Jesus (Phil. 2:5).

There was a married couple in the Bible named Ananias and Sapphira who apparently had an agreeable marriage. They cooperated with each other, even in an evil thing. They made a fatal mistake in judgment. They mixed greed with generosity. The members of the church in

Jerusalem sold their property and presented the proceeds as a gift to the apostles. Such selfishness warranted admiration, and their gift of money was then used to help the poor.

Selfishness and deceit entered into the hearts of this couple. They sold their plot of ground, but submitted only a portion of the profits. The couple then lied about the full price received for their land, and kept part of the money for themselves. With perceptive insight, Peter challenged Ananias about his duplicity and sin against God. Ananias, caught in his own deliberate lie, fell down and died instantly. Several hours later, Sapphira came to Peter, unaware of her husband's deceit, also lied, and immediately fell down and died. She was buried next to her husband.

Misguided values, wrong thinking, and financial principles causes many Christians to suffer unnecessarily. Christian couples are blessed to have Christ and the Word of God as the head of their lives, providing divine instructions and guidance concerning all financial matters. The scripture declares in all thy ways acknowledge Him and He shall direct thy paths (Prov. 3:6).

Financial Priorities In A Marriage

But seek (aim at and strive after) first of all His and His righteousness (His way of doing and being right) and then all these things taken together will be given you besides (Matt. 6:33 TAB).

Keep out of debt and owe no man anything, except to love one another; for he who loves his neighbor (who practices loving others) has fulfilled the law (relating to one's fellowmen), meeting all its requirements (Rom. 13:8 TAB).

He who tills his land shall be satisfied with bread, but he who follows worthless pursuits is lacking in sense and is without understanding (Prov. 12:11 TAB).

Better is the (uncompromisingly) righteous have the abundance (of possessions) of many who are wrong and wicked (Ps. 37:16 KJV).

Couples must learn to openly and sincerely communicate all financial issues and concerns before marriage effectively. Developing sincere and viable communication with each other is a sustaining factor for the success of their marriage.

The scriptures declare He has given us all things richly to enjoy (1 Tim. 6:17). In giving us all things richly to enjoy, couples must learn to make sound financial choices concerning where, how, and wise ways to effectively manage their finances. To set priorities is to determine what is important for the home and how finances are to be apportioned– that is, who and what will take precedence over all financial payments.

Good financial planning is a part of wise stewardship. To be truly wise stewards, married couples must believe assuredly that the money being managed is someone else's money–God's money. Having this perspective gives a person the freedom to use finances as a tool to accomplish God's purposes, recognizing that no one comes into this world with possessions, and no one will leave with anything (Eccl. 5:15).

God has given every married couple the power to get wealth (Deut. 8:18). In empowering us to get wealth, it's the wisdom we use in managing our finance that determines our success or failure–to include paying tithes or failing to give Him His tenth. The day will come when He will ask for an account of how we managed the resources He gave us (Luke 19:11–26). Married couples who manage financial resources wisely are a blessing to each other, the family, and the kingdom of God (Prov. 31:28).

It Is Wise For Married Couples To Remember:

The earth and all its fullness is the Lord's (Ps. 24:1). Every resource, even finance, is His and we are simply stewards of His resources.

- Avoid an overly consumptive lifestyle. The Bible teaches moderation in all things (1 Cor. 9:25).
- Avoid debt (Prov. 22:7; Rom. 13:8).
- Maintain a savings program (Prov. 12:11).
- Set long-term goals (Prov. 13:22).
- There are many Christians experiencing financial conflicts in

their marriages and relationships today. It's a source of strength, encouragement, and support to stand upon the Word of God knowing that "there is nothing too hard for God" (Jer. 32:17). We do not need to spend a lot of time feeling frustrated, hopeless, powerless, or resentful, "faith in God's Word turns hopeless circumstances around." We learn to prevail in prayer, knowing that "the effectual fervent prayers of a righteous man availeth much" (James 5:17).

Finance And Marriage

> For the love of money is the root of all evil: which while some coveted after, they have erred from the faith, and pierced themselves through with many sorrows (1 Tim. 6:10 KJV).

> Will a man rob God? Yet ye have robbed me. But ye say, wherein have we robbed thee? In tithes and offerings.

> Ye are cursed with a curse: for ye have robbed me, even this whole nation.

> Bring ye all the tithes into the storehouse, that there may be meat in mine house, and prove me now herewith, saith the Lord of hosts, if I will not open you the windows of heaven, and pour you out a blessing that there shall not be room enough to receive it (Mal. 3:8–10 KJV).

The scripture declares, "money answereth all things" (Eccl. 10:19). Money is a defense (Eccl. 7:12). Every couple should develop a sound financial understanding before marriage, and learn to communicate their financial goals and vision for the marriage. Many marriage relationships are not working harmoniously and on one accord as a result of financial problems.

Many husbands and wives are married but maintain separate accounts. One pays three bills and the other pays two bills, and the savings remain empty. The impact of the lack of money in a marriage is devastating. It causes much pain and sorrow, and consequently ends in divorce for a lot of couples. Managing money wisely not only demonstrates that the couple "is not walking and living under the curse of the law, but have been redeemed from the curse of poverty" (Gal. 3:13).

> "The thief cometh not, but for to steal and to kill, and to destroy: I am come that they might have life, and that they might have it more abundantly" (John 10:10).

Financial mismanagement, pressures, and the stress of household pressures creates the spirits of strife, division, and dissension in many marriages. It also escalates the circumstances to broken relationships and in some cases eventually divorce. Learning to communicate openly and honestly about financial concerns prior to marriage empowers the couple to develop a financial understanding, equipping them to destroy the works of the devil in their relationship and home. The blessings of obedience (Deut 28:1–14) positions married couples to experience financial prosperity and success in their marriage. Equally, the curses of disobedience position couples to experience financial defeat and failure in their marriage and home (Deut. 28:15–64).

The scripture declares "and this is the victory that overcometh the world, even our faith" (1 John 5:4). God's original plan for His man, Adam, was that he be a wealthy man and never have to experience the challenge of poverty. However, Adam sold out to the devil, and the devil became the god of this world (2 Cor. 4:4). Believers have learned to trust and follow God, who has all power in heaven and on earth, exceeding all the works of the devil. In learning to experience life more abundantly, we must learn to abide in Him, let His Word abide in us, and work together with Him in all things.

❧

> But my God shall supply all your need according to His riches in glory by Christ Jesus (Phil. 4:19 KJV).

❧

The scripture teaches us that "our soul wait thou only upon God, for our expectation is from Him." As we look unto Him, the author and finisher of our faith, He shall supply all our needs according to His riches and glory. God is the greatest provider there is. He is a bountiful provider. The silver and gold are the Lords, the earth, and the fullness thereof.

The greatest hindrances to receiving financial increase in our marriage are strife, offenses, failure to pay tithes and offerings, and being impatient. Deception and a lack of knowledge are also great hindrances in receiving from God.

Knowledge is power, and where the Word of the king is, there is power (Ecc. 8:4). It is glorious and wonderful to behold couples tapping into the unsearchable riches of God, learning and experiencing the faithfulness of God in every aspect of their lives. They believe the scripture which declares, "He is faithful that has promised, and is not a man that He should lie" (Heb. 10:23; Num. 23:19).

Believers must learn to walk in and apply the Word of God in all things. The scripture declares, "according to your faith, be it unto you" (Matt. 9:29). We must choose to believe the scriptures, learn to stand and act upon His word in all aspects of our life. His Word is totally ineffective, invaluable, and of no effect if we choose not to believe and apply it in our daily lives.

Part Twenty-Nine
RECEIVING GOD'S BEST

And their father Israel said unto them; If it must be so now, do this; take of the best fruits in the land in your vessels, and carry down the man a present, a little balm, and a little honey, spices, and myrrh, nuts, and almonds (Gen. 43:11 KJV).

The land of Egypt is before thee; in the best of the land make thy father and brethren to dwell, in the land of Goshem let them dwell; and if thou knowest any men of activity among them, make them rulers over my cattle (Gen. 47:6 KJV).

And Joseph placed his father and his brethren, and give them a possession in the land of Egypt in the best of the land, in the Rameses, as Pharaoh and commanded (Gen. 47: 11 KJV).

Look even out the best and meetest of your master's sons and set him on his father's throne, and fight for your masters' house (2 Kings 10:3 KJV).

Out of all your gifts ye shall offer every heave offering of the Lord, of all the best thereof; even the hallowed part thereof of it (Num 18: 29 KJV).

This is what the Lord commands the daughters of Zelophehad! Let them marry whom they think best; only they shall marry within the family of their tribe (Num. 36:6 KJV).

But earnestly desire and zealously cultivate the greatest and best gifts and graces (the higher gifts and the choicest graces). And yet I will show you a still more excellent way (one that is better by far and the highest of them all–love) (1 Cor. 12:31 KJV).

Receiving God's Best
Renouncing Satan's Counterfeit

Take of the best fruits in the land (Gen. 43:11 KJV).
Of the Lord, of all the best thereof (Num. 18:29 KJV).
Them marry to whom they think best (Num. 36:6 KJV).
What seemeth you best I will do (2 Sam. 18:4 KJV)?

Recently the world witnessed the marriage of a celebrity to her childhood friend–only to hear of an annulment within the next twenty-four hours. The publicity of this marriage left an impact on millions of young people whose thoughts, mindsets, and opinions were perhaps already distorted by the world's principles and values on marriage and sexuality.

Christians are the most blessed people on this earth. Blessed, because our foundation for life and marriage is based upon God's purpose and plan. The original purpose for marriage was, and is intended to be our road map and guidelines for living. We are taught and instructed in His Word to follow, pray, and seek God's guidance before making major decisions in our lives. The fear and reverence of God is the beginning of wisdom. Therefore we don't look for life's meaning through media hype's, fantasies, and worldly lifestyles. We learn to base all our decisions upon His Word.

Show me thy ways, O Lord, teach me thy paths
(Ps. 25:4 KJV).

Lead me in thy truth, and teach me: for thou art the God of my salvation, on thee do I wait all the day (Ps. 25:4–5 KJV).

Trust in the Lord with all thine heart: and lean not unto thine own understanding

In all thy ways acknowledge him, and he shall direct thy paths (Prov. 3:5–6 KJV)

Be not wise in thine own eyes, fear the Lord and depart from evil (Prov. 3: 7 KJV).

"Teach me, O Lord, the way of you statutes, and I will keep it to the end.

Give me, understanding, that I may keep your law, yea, I shall observe it with my whole heart.

Make me to go paths of thy commandment; for therein do I delight"

Include my heart unto thy testimonies and not to covetousness.

Turn away mine eyes from beholding vanity: and quicken thou me in thy way (Ps. 119: 33–37 KJV).

Marriage is honorable and the bed undefiled. The obvious example of disrespect for the sanctity of marriage not only provides a poor example for confused unbelieving singles, but ridicules the precious gift God has given unto man.

Although dating relationships are not described in the scriptures, it is subject to God's principles pertaining to relationships. The dating game truly leads to hurt, sorrow, confusion, embarrassment, and disappointment. The guidelines in God's Word are the foundation for peace, joy, and happiness in our walk with him, marriage and daily living. God is wisdom, knowledge, and understanding, and "wants the best for you, even more than you want it for yourself." (Gen. 2:18). Truly waking up the next morning and deciding you married satan's counterfeit is not God's perfect will for His sons and daughters. Many are praying, abiding in Him, letting His Word abide in them, and are continuously praising and worshipping Him for release of heaven's best. The scripture declares in all thy ways acknowledge Him, and He shall direct your paths (Prov. 3:5–6). Developing and maintaining a lifestyle of Christian living, praying and diligently studying His Word positions us to wait on, and receive Heaven's best for our lives. Our marriage vows states "until death do us part," meaning it is for a lifetime.

Waiting For Heaven's Best

The word wait has been defined as to delay; stay in anticipation of (The Three-In-One Concise Bible Reference Companion). During his waiting process, Job–after being stripped of all his worldly wealth, his children, his men and maid servants–"positioned himself in faith before his God," and stated, "All of my appointed days will I wait till my change come" (Job 14:14). He realized the he didn't understand what had befallen him. No one else understood what had befallen him causing him to wait until God brought about the change he desired in his life. Therefore, the attitude he displayed in waiting upon God's deliverance was very important. Was he going to wait in anger and bitterness? Was he going to complain, murmur or whine during the entire test? Was he going to lengthen or shorten his test by remaining humble in godly expectancy? Or was he going to wait in prayer, fasting and dwelling in faith in God's presence? He could have done as his wife instructed him, " Job, does thou still retain thine integrity, curse God and die (Job 2:9).

During the waiting process singles must learn that God does not violate the principles of His Word to accommodate desperation and panic. He leads, guides, and directs us according to His Word. For those who are waiting for Heaven's mate, God's preparation and processing are always best.

The scripture states a wife has unique needs that are best met by her own husband:

- Spiritual leadership, including family worship of prayer and Bible study (1 Pet. 3:7).
- Personal affirmation (Eph. 5:25).
- Tender loving care, including touching, courteous and loving words (Prov. 5:19).
- Intimate, sensitive, and understanding communication (Song 2:16).
- Integrity worthy of respect and transparency so that nothing is hidden (Gen. 2:15).
- Provision and sustenance as well as protection (Gen. 2:15).
- Commitment of loyal devotion (Ecc. 9:9).

For single women desiring a husband, the scripture declares a man has unique needs that are best met by his wife:

- A husband needs to have the respect of his wife (Eph. 5:3). He needs her sincere admiration.
- A husband needs appreciation. To appreciate means to recognize worth, to hold in high regard, or to respect (Eph. 5:3). A wife needs to express gratitude for her husband's life, faithfulness, work, provision, and care.
- A husband needs affirmation. A wife should speak kind words (Prov. 31:26) and assure her husband of her love and fidelity (Prov. 31:11,12).
- A husband needs sexual fulfillment and sensitivity on the part of his wife to this need (1 Cor. 7:3–5).
- A husband needs a home to which he can go for comfort and peace (Gen. 24:67).
- A husband needs to find his wife attractive and be proud of her (Prov. 31:28,29). He needs to share mutual fellowship and fun with her.

Husbands and wives should be considered a precious gift from God, and be treated with sensitivity, tenderness, and love. To meet each other's needs requires time, as well as listening, touching, doing kind deeds, and creativity in the act of love (Ecc. 4:9–12). One of the best revelations for singles desiring Heaven's best is that the Word of God is the same yesterday, today, and forever. It never changes. The needs of man and woman remain the same. We must surrender our will unto God, and obey His statues to receive Heaven's Best.

Many singles and those desiring Christ centered marriages today have missed the fundamental teachings on marriage and the family. Misguided, worldly, and confused values have influenced the mindset of many delaying their growth and maturity in understanding sound Christian principles. These works of the flesh have provoked many to miss Heaven's best and settle for satan's less in their lives. Christian values are based on Biblical principles, which essentially is the fruit of the spirit.

The spirit of truth, integrity, and singleness of heart are qualities of character. Several distinct features mark the Biblical model of integrity:

- Innocent actions (Gen. 20:5).
- A clear conscience (Acts 24:16).
- Fear of God, truthfulness, and opposition to covetousness (Ex. 18:21).
- Blameless and uprightness (Job 2:3; Ps. 25:21).
- Righteousness (Ps. 7:8).
- Freedom from that which is shameful, crafty, or deceitful (2 Cor. 4:2).
- Refusal to serve idols (Ps. 24:3–5).
- Disassociation with evil doers (Ps. 26:4).
- Honorable behavior (2 Cor. 8:21).
- Integrity of heart guides a person into right and rewarding situations (Prov. 11:3).
- Integrity is more acceptable to the Lord than sacrifice (Prov. 21:3).
- A person's integrity silences critics (1 Pet. 2:13–17).

In essence, integrity provides a mindset toward righteousness and an abiding intent to fulfill the will of God.

Singles are learning to wait patiently and humbly upon God in prayer and supplications, fasting, and abiding in His presence. Singles are learning to surrender their will unto the Lord, the inward workings of the Holy Spirit and bring forth much fruit of the Spirit, and character of Christ.

Time management- to include abiding in His presence is invaluable in our Christian walk and desire to draw closer to Him in Spirit and truth. Jesus said in the Word "seek ye first the kingdom of God, and His righteousness; and all these things shall be added unto you." Set your affections on things above, and not on things on the earth (Col. 3:2).

Time management is not just keeping busy, but includes finding God's focus for your life. Seeking Him for direction, and moving forth to accomplish God's ordained goals for your life requires sacrifice, sincerity and a desire to please Him. First, acknowledge that you have time–the same amount He has given unto everyone. Then, with His help, determine how to use your time (Prov. 3:5, 6). Many are distracted, unfocused, and are totally sidetracked in allowing others to decide their priorities (Rom. 12:2). When we desire to fulfill God's destiny in our lives, we learn to "lay down or set aside our agenda," and follow His agenda for our lives.

The scriptural principles in reference to "idleness", refers to those who are lazy, slothful, sluggard and has a slack hand. It outlines clarity and purpose concerning labor and work (Luke. 10:7). Given the admonition that we are to work six days and rest one (Ex. 34:21), we conclude that the Bible, refers to a balanced living. However, today's singles who are distracted through many concerns and life issues causing them to lose focus in fulfilling their destiny and purpose. . .

Singles sincerely desiring to receive Heaven's mate should ask themselves three main questions. The first question is, do I truly desire to marry Heaven's mate? Second, am I prepared to receive and minister unto Heaven's mate? Third, am I willing to share this mate once released unto me, with the Kingdom of God allowing he or she to fulfill God's divine purpose in their life? If you answered, yes to all three questions, "your best is yet to come." Humbly submit and open your heart for entrance into Heaven's mate preparation process.

In the process of preparing and waiting for Heaven's mate, seek to draw closer unto the Lord. Avoid the spirit of idleness, the spiritual state of lukewarmness, distractions, and discouragements experienced by many who have lost focused in fulfilling their destiny and purpose. Desire earnestly the best gift and allow Him to begin and complete his work within you.

God's Timing Is Perfect

"But time and chance happeneth to them all"
(Ecc. 9:11 KJV).

Be careful for nothing, but in every thing by prayer and supplication with thanksgiving let your requests be made known to God,

And the peace of God, which passes all understanding shall keep your hearts and minds through Christ Jesus"
(Phil. 4:6–7 KJV).

The enemy has blinded the hearts and minds of many believers during the "waiting and preparation process." In a world of over six billion people, many believe that there are no Christian men available in the world. They are looking through a glass darkly. They are not looking through the eyes of the spirit, but the flesh. They are refusing to believe the scriptures, which declare, "according to your faith, be it unto you" (Matt. 9:29); and "there is nothing too hard for God" (Jer. 32:17). "Delight yourself in the Lord, and He shall give thee the desires of thine heart" (Psa. 37:4).

Singles who are waiting on the Lord in patient expectation will discover a peace, security, refreshing and renewal in fellowship with Him. By waiting humbly on the Lord, and praising Him for answered prayer, the psalmist was not disappointed. The Lord responded to his cry for help and gave him stability and a "new song," which became his testimony to others. The Lord gave him a spirit of stability.

Waiting on the Lord is essential for our Christian's growth and development. It is this form of spiritual discipline, resulting from obedience and faith, that produces abundant blessings in our lives.

Growing in the wisdom, knowledge, and understanding of our Lord produces an increase in the fruit of patience in our lives. This helps believers to mature in Christ and walk in the will of God for our lives. Waiting patiently upon God, hearing, and obeying His voice enables us to avoid errors in judgment during the mate selection process. We know we are led by Him and learn to follow His promptings. An attitude of commitment and holiness positions us to receive God's releases and breakthroughs. Learning to develop spiritual discipline is manifested in Bible study, prayer, fellowship, fasting, service, witnessing, and submission to spiritual leadership, training, and development.

Waiting on God through spiritual discipline is essential to receive deliverance from the power of sin. Without learning to patiently wait upon Him, believers cannot develop a steadfast walk with Christ. Growing in faith and receiving our heavenly rewards, awaits those who love Him, and are committed and dedicated to pursuing and fulfilling His purpose and destiny in our lives.

Consequently, confess and proclaim, "I am not only prepared for Heaven's mate, but am ready to join hand and hand to pursue and fulfill God's purpose and destiny for our lives.

Part Thirty
Heaven's Mate Exit

That will be the day when seven women will gang up on one man, saying, we will take care of ourselves, get our own food and clothes.

Just give us a child. Make us pregnant so we'll have something to live for.

And that's when God's Branch will sprout green, and lush. The produce of the country will give Israel's survivors something to be proud of again. Oh, they'll hold their heads high! Everyone left behind in Zion, Jerusalem, will be reclassified as holy"–alive and therefore precious God will give Zion's women a good bath. He'll scrub the bloodstained city of its violence and brutality; purge the place with a firestone of judgment.

Then God will bring back the ancient pillar of cloud by day and the pillar of fire by night and mark Mount Zion and everyone in it with His glorious presence, his immense, protective presence, shade from the burning sun and shelter from the driving rain (Isa. 4:1–6 MSG).

Heaven's Mate Exit

Seek out of the book of the Lord and read: not one of these (details of prophecy) shall fail, none shall want and lack her mate (in fulfillment). For the mouth (of the Lord) has commanded, and His spirit has gathered them (Isa. 34:16 TAB).

For I know the thoughts and plans that I have for you,

> says the Lord, thoughts and plans for welfare and peace
> and not for evil, to give you hope in your final outcome
> (Jer. 29:11 TAB).

> I (the Lord) will instruct you and teach you in the way
> you should go; I will counsel you with my eye upon you
> (Ps. 32:8 TAB).

Beloved Singles, God wants you to marry Heaven's Mate, even more than you want it for yourself. He knows the thoughts that He has toward you, thoughts of peace, and not of evil, to give you an expected end (Jer. 29:11). If you have read this book and sincerely desires His chosen mate- Heaven's Mate is yours.

This book is designed to walk you through the process of making a prosperous and successful journey from single life to marriage. The book emphasizes the necessity of first seeking the kingdom of God, and His righteousness, and letting all these things be added unto you (Matt 6:33).

God has chosen the right mate for you. He knows the name of the mate He has chosen, where he is, what he is doing and when He will bring the two of you together. Many forget the scripture, which declares He is the Alpha and Omega, the beginning and the ending. He knows all things (Rev. 22:13).

Destiny has to meet purpose to fulfill His plans for your life and marriage. He knew you before you were conceived in your mother's womb (Jer. 1:5), and His thoughts and plans toward you are to give you an expected end. Heaven's Mate is an expected end for all who will follow, trust, obey and wait on Him to fulfill His purpose and plans in their lives. Heaven's Mate is the fulfillment of the scripture "but seek ye first the kingdom of God, and His righteousness; and all these things shall be added unto you (Matt. 6:33).

"Your best is yet to come" as you sincerely submit your life and destiny unto Him, and trust Him to watch over His Word to perform it.

To God be the glory, henceforth now and forever more. Amen

Heaven's Mate Faith Declaration

THE BENEFITS OF WAITING AND SERVING THE LORD

Bless (affectionately, gratefully praise) the Lord, O my soul; and all that is [deepest] within me, bless His holy name!

Bless (affectionately, gratefully praise) the Lord, O my soul, and forget not [one of] all His benefits-

Who forgives [every one of] all your iniquities, Who heals [each one of] all your diseases,

Who redeems your life from the pit and corruption, Who beautifies, dignifies, and crowns you with loving-kindness and tender mercy;

Who satisfies your mouth [your necessity and desire at your personal age and situation] with good so that your youth, renewed, is like the eagle's [strong, overcoming, soaring]!

The Lord executes righteousness and justice [not for me only, but] for all who are oppressed.

He made known His ways [of righteousness and justice] to Moses, His acts to the children of Israel.

The Lord is merciful and gracious, slow to anger and plenteous in mercy and loving-kindness.

He will not always chide or be contending, neither will He keep His anger forever or hold a grudge.

He has not dealt with us after our sins nor rewarded us according to our iniquities.

For as the heavens are high above the earth, so great are His mercy and loving-kindness toward those who reverently and worshipfully fear Him.

As far as the east is from the west, so far has He removed our transgressions from us.

As a father loves and pities his children, so the Lord loves and pities those who fear Him [with reverence, worship, and awe].

For He knows our frame, He [earnestly] remembers and imprints [on His heart] that we are dust.

As for man, his days are as grass; as a flower of the field, so he flourishes.

For the wind passes over it and it is gone, and its place shall know it no more.

But the mercy and loving-kindness of the Lord are from everlasting to everlasting upon those who reverently and worshipfully fear Him, and His righteousness is to children's children—

To such as keep His covenant [hearing, receiving, loving, and obeying it] and to those who [earnestly] remember His commandments to do them [imprinting them on their hearts].

The Lord has established His throne in the heavens, and His kingdom rules over all.

Bless (affectionately, gratefully praise) the Lord, you His angels, you mighty ones who do His commandments, hearkening to the voice of His word.

Bless (affectionately, gratefully praise) the Lord, all you His hosts, you His ministers who do His pleasure.

Bless the Lord, all His works in all places of His dominion; bless (affectionately, gratefully praise) the Lord, O my soul!
(Ps. 103: 1–22 TAB)

Appendix 1:
Biblical Translations

TAB	The Amplified Bible Grand Rapids: Zondervan (1965)
CEV	Contemporary English Version New York: American Bible Society (1995)
GWT	God's Word Translation Grand Rapids: World Publishing, Inc. (1995)
KJV	King James Version
LB	Living Bible Wheaton, IL: Tyndale House Publishers (1979)
Msg	The Message Colorado Springs: Navpress (1993)
NAB	New American Bible Chicago: Catholic Press (1970)
NASB	New American Standard Bible Anaheim, CA: Foundation Press (1973)
NCV	New Century Version Dallas: Word Bibles (1991)
NIV	New International Version Colorado Springs: International Bible Society (1978, 1984)
NJB	New Jerusalem Bible Garden City, NY: Doubleday (1985)

NLT	New Living Translation Wheaton, IL: Tyndale House Publishers (1996)
NRSV	New Revised Standard Version Grand Rapids: Zondervan (1990)
Ph	New Testament in Modern English by J. B. Phillips New York: Macmillan (1958)
TEV	Today's English Version New York: American Bible Society (1992) (Also called Good News Translation)

Appendix 2:
Resources

RESOURCES FOR GIVE ME HEAVEN'S MATE AT YOUR BOOKSTORE OR HTTP://WWW.GIVEMEHEAVENSMATE.COM/

1. *Give Me Heaven's Mate Prayer Journal.* Singles and Married Partners Prayer Journal reflecting the necessity of daily prayer and supplication in our walk with God and relationship with each other.

2. *Give Me Heaven's Mate Marriage Diary.* Inspirational Scriptural daily journey through the process of waiting on your mate.

3. *Give Me Heaven's Mate Marriage Quotes; Marriage Favorite Quotes;* (wisdom for singles and marriage couples and encouragement to comfort and warm their hearts and soul.

4. *Give Me Heaven's Mate Devotional.* A marriage devotional for women believing God to enjoy a healthy, balanced and happy life through fellowship with Christ.

5. *Give Me Heaven's Mate Singles Workbook.* A Workbook for walking singles through the journey of singleness to marriage through sound scriptural principles and guidelines.

6. *Give Me Heaven's Mate Married Couples Workbook.* (A Workbook for providing scriptural principles for establishing and maintaining a healthy, happy marriage in the twenty first century.

7. *Give Me Heaven's Mate Marriage And Family Workbook.* A Workbook providing divine principles and guidelines for families believing God for Godly mates/ spouses for their children in the twenty first century.

8. *Give Me Heaven's Mate Teens Straight Talk Workbook.* (A Workbook providing Straight Talk scriptural principles, walking Teens through

the journey of waiting for the mate God has chosen and enjoying their youth.)

9. *Give Me Heaven's Mate Children Workbook.* (A Children's Fun Inspirational Marriage and Family workbook explaining God's purpose and plan for the family.)

10. Give Me heaven's Mate Living Life Together In Marriage. Principles and guidelines to assist in keeping the family focused on God's purpose and plan for marriage.

11. *Give Me Heaven's Mate Family Prayer Journal.* (The companion prayer journal teaching families the principles of praying without ceasing, specifically for godly mates and healthy marriages within the family).

12. *Give Me Heaven's Mate Inspirational Calendar.* (A twelve month inspirational life's purpose, destiny, and monthly focus on walking in and applying divine marriage principles to enjoy your walk with God, marriage, family and ministry.

13. *Give Me Heaven's Mate Marriage Preparation Journal.* (An inspirational journal with scriptural principles to encourage, establish and strengthen the walk and lives of singles and believers waiting upon their mate.)

14. *Give Me Heaven's Mate marriage Proverbs.* (A mini-book of marriage proverbs and quotes to enlighten and reflect on the joy of marriage and life.)

15. *Give Me Heaven's Marriage Reflections Journal.* (This marriage reflections journal provides inspirational scriptures on the purpose of marriage, and his divine destiny to bring balanced, healthy relationships into the union of marriage.

FOR SINGLES, MARRIED COUPLES AND FAMILY MINISTRY

Email joan@givemeheavensmate.com for a free subscription to Give Me Heaven's Mate Newsletter, a weekly email newsletter for singles and others waiting on God for their mate.

For information on the many different Give Me Heaven's Mate Conferences, Seminars, and Retreats, contact Give Me Heaven's Mate, P.O. Box 1134, Clinton, MD 20735. Telephone: 1-(888)-877-1805

FREE RESOURCES

Email joan@givemeheavensmate.com for a free subscription to the monthly *Give Me Heaven's Mate* Newsletter.

Let us know which of these free items you would like by emailing joan@givemeheavensmate.com

GMHM Intercessory Prayer Ministry

GMHM Singles Ministry

GMHM Married Couples Ministry

GMHM Family Ministry

GMHM Teens Ministry

GMHM Children Ministry

GMHM Covenant Partners

Information on GMHM Marriage Retreat

Information on Conferences/ Seminars/ Workshops

Information on GMHM Family Partners

Appendix 3:
"None Shall Want Their Mate" Biblical Translations

Search the book of the Lord and see all that he will do; not one detail will he miss; not one kite will be there without a mate, for the Lord has said it, and his Spirit will make it all come true (Isa. 34:16 TLB).

Seek from the book of the Lord, and read: Not one of these will be missing; None will lack its mate. For His mouth has commanded, and His Spirit has gathered them (Isa. 34:16 NASU).

Dirshuw mee'al- ceeper Yahweh uwqraa'uw 'Achat meeheenaah lo' ne'daaraah 'ishaah rᵃ'uwtaah lo' paaqaaduw Kiy- piy huw' tsiwaah Wᵃruwchow huw' qibtsaan <END HEBREW> (Copyright (c) 1994 by Biblesoft.). (Isa 34:16 Interlinear Transliterated Bible)

Search in the LORD's book of living creatures and read what it says. Not one of these creatures will be missing, and not one will be without its mate. The LORD has commanded it to be so; he himself will bring them together (Isa. 34:16 TEV)

Inquirid en el libro de Jehová, y leed si faltó alguno de ellos; ninguno faltó con su compañera; porque su boca mandó, y los reunion su mismo Espíritu. (from RVR 1960 © 1960 Sociedades Biblicas en América Latina.) (Isa 34:16 SBAL).

Seek and read from the book of the Lord: Not one of these shall be missing; none shall be without her mate. For the mouth of the LORD has commanded, and his Spirit has gathered them (Isa. 34:16 RSV).

Search the book of the Lord, and see what he will do. He will not miss a single detail. Not one of these birds and animals will be missing, and none will lack a mate, for the Lord has promised this. His Spirit will make it all come true (Isa. 34:16 NLT).

Seek from the book of the Lord, and read: Not one of these will be missing; None will lack its mate. For His mouth has commanded, and His Spirit has gathered them (Isa. 34:16 NAS).

Seek Ye out of the book of Jehovah, and read: no one of these shall be missing, none shall want her mate; for my mouth, it hath commanded, and his Spirit, it hath gathered them (Isa. 34:16 ASV).

Search from the book of the Lord, and read: Not one of these shall fail; not one shall lack her mate. For My mouth has commanded it, and His Spirit has gathered them (Isa. 34:16 NKJV).

Seek ye out of the book of the Lord, and read: no one of these shall fail, none shall want her mate: for my mouth it hath commanded, and his spirit it hath gathered them (Isa. 34:16 KJV).

Look in the scroll of the Lord and read: None of these will be missing, not one will lack her mate. For it is his mouth that has given the order, and his Spirit will gather them together (Isa. 34:16 NIV).

Seek out of the book of the Lord and read: not one of these [details of prophecy] shall fail, none shall want and lack her mate [in fulfillment]. For the mouth [of the Lord] has commanded, and His Spirit has gathered them (Isa. 34:16 AMP).

Seek and read from the book of the Lord: Not one of these shall be missing; none shall be without its mate. For the mouth of the Lord has commanded, and his spirit has gathered them (Isa. 34:16 NRS).

Dear Reader,

In this book I present to you God's purpose and plan for marriage, with scriptural principles to assist you in focusing your life on fulfilling His purpose for your marriage. In the twenty-first century, millions of Christian singles, married couples, divorcees, widows, widowers, children, and families are missing God's purpose for marriage and the family, and are compromising their Christian morals and values to receive Satan's counterfeit. He has not changed His Word and purpose to accommodate our desires, but still requires that we would pray, study His Word, and wait upon Him to bring His Word to pass. He watcheth over His Word to perform it, and is the same today, yesterday, and forever. Why compromise your Christian morals for that which is not God's best for you and your family? Why subject your family to generational curses that can be passed from generation to generation, when you have not taken time to pray, seek and wait upon the revelations from God for the answer to your situation? He has given us all things richly to enjoy–including marriage and His abundance of generational blessings - to pass from generation to generation. Choose to seek and wait on God to bring the right mate in your life, and pass the blessings of God from generation to generation in your family.

> Beloved,
> Joanne Williams
> The Author

Singles comprise the most disheartened segment in the church and world today. Visit any church, prayer group, supportive or singles ministry. Adding to the ever-increasing factor of disillusioned, never married singles in the Christian environment and world is the rise in the statistics of Christian divorcees, with numbers now exceeding those of the secular world. The new suddenly singles from failed marriages are eclipsing the number of men and women in the church (particularly women), who are waiting . . . for the *Perfect Mate! Positioned! Prepared,* and have never found a spouse. With the world's statistics of men to women, single people are speaking, acting and making desperate decisions. Desperation has caused many to abandon their Christianity, forget God's principles and values, and revert to worldly wisdom to choose and select their mate. The Spirit of desperation, prayerlessness, misguided values, and cyber surfs creativity have caused many to forget that God has not changed His original plan and purpose for marriage and the family. In "*Give Me Heaven's Mate,* the spirit of wisdom, knowledge and revelation of His word unveils many applicable truths for today's generation. This book takes you on a marriage preparation journey from a personal encounter with Jesus, to developing and maintaining a relationship with Him, your prayer life, and character development. The process of preparation, seeking, waiting, revealing, meeting and receiving your mate, requires submitting unto Him, His purpose, and plan. Choosing the mate God has chosen, the waiting process, involves the process of loving, growing together, supporting each other and enjoying your marriage, life and ministry together.

Dr. Joanne Williams
Pastor/ Teacher/ Counselor/ Author
Jubilee Christian Center
Clinton, MD

Contact author Joanne Williams
or order more copies of this book at

TATE PUBLISHING, LLC

127 East Trade Center Terrace
Mustang, Oklahoma 73064

(888) 361 - 9473

Tate Publishing, LLC

www.tatepublishing.com